LAID BARE

"I read *Laid Bare* straight through with stunned fascination. John Gilmore is such a terrific writer, and this book is so surprising. The opening chapter is really a masterpiece all by itself, it recreates an entire era, and brings Joplin to life at a moment when things could have gone any number of ways for her. You're left imagining yourself in the same boat, faced with all the existential choices everyone has to make, which can lead anywhere, not 'inevitably' to fame and/or self-destruction.

"Gilmore deals with mythically familiar subjects, but not to turn them inside out. Instead, he boils off the myth and shows you how things really were, and what things felt like to the people living what later became a myth. Most books that try to do this take the later myth as something almost ordained by fate—which is only true *ex post facto*—so that the other parts of a celebrated person's life are simply rendered as obstacles and setbacks to the ultimate goal; the people they knew 'on the way up' become extraneous minor characters, etc. That approach only reinforces the unfortunately widespread belief that celebrities are the only people who have real lives. Gilmore shows what a pile of shit that ultimate goal really is, and that the people who get there are completely warped by the process of getting there and that they don't change into wonderful beings just because ten million people know who they are. They just have a big arena in which to be assholes.

"I think, ultimately, Gilmore's work is as much opposed to gossip as it is to mythmaking, because both are different faces of celebrity-worship, an epidemic mental illness in our society. When you find someone who isn't infected with it to one degree or another, you realize, as somebody once said, that sanity is the most profound moral option of our time."

Gary Indiana

Laid Bare

A Memoir of Wrecked Lives
and the Hollywood Death Trip

John Gilmore

LOS ANGELES

Cover Design: Jeff Lyons

I have obliged those few who asked that their names be changed to protect their privacy. My sincere thanks go to Jan Tumlir, Melissa Hoffs
and Ron Stringer for their dedicated involvement and fine-tooth editing, to Virginia Jacks for her thorough proofreading, to my friend Tony
Mostrom and to Nick Bougas for valuable input, to my publisher Stuart
Swezey how had the guts to take this on, and to Jean-Claude Carrière
of Paris who first gave me the idea to write this "naked" book.

John Gilmore

Amok Books are available to bookstores through our primary distributor:
SCB Distributors, 15608 South New Century Drive, Los Angeles, CA
90248. Phone: (310) 532-9400. Fax: (310) 532-7001.

UK Distributors: Turnaround Distribution, Unit 3 Olympia Trading
Estate, Coburg Road, Wood Green, London N22 6TZ.
Phone: 0181 829 3000. FAX: 0181 881 5088.

Non-bookstore Distribution: Last Gasp Distribution,
777 Florida Street, San Francisco, California 94140.
Phone: (415) 824-6636. FAX: (415) 824-1836.

To view the complete Amok Books catalog, please go to the Amok
Books website at www.amokbooks.com. For personal orders, please
contact Book Clearinghouse, 46 Purdy Street, Harrison, New York
10528. Phone: (800) 431-1579. Fax: (914) 835-0398.

For my daughter,
URSULA MAURA GILMORE

Hollywood Blvd., 1964

"The bottom line fascination we hold for Hollywood is not the gold, not even the magic, but the suspense of tragedy—the waiting for those absurdly beautiful people to fall off their tightropes and wreck their lives."

Thomas Thompson

"If there is still one hellish, truly accursed thing in our time, it is our artistic dallying with forms, instead of being like victims burnt at the stake, signaling through the flames."

Antonin Artaud

Contents

Taking a Piece of Her Heart

WHO COULD LOVE JANIS JOPLIN? Kris Kristofferson said he'd tried, but the money and the fame had shot her up too fast . . .

Was she loved by the bisexual friends or lesbians she'd see when the mood struck her? Was she loved by her mother and father? Her sister? What about Michael J. Pollard—the stubby actor who played my younger brother on a New York television show, and who cried so much when Janis died? Or the square she was engaged to marry? Country Joe McDonald? Myself? In the rapid-fire Hollywood hustle, could I have loved Janis, and left my wife and child for a nose-first skid into rock and roll's hallelujah? Did the creeps and losers on the East Coast streets, or the ones she'd find in San Francisco or L.A., care about her?

Dennis Hopper supposedly told a pal he'd have liked to see her body laid out after she was dead. He said, "I want to stand there naked myself and look at her naked corpse, and not touch her, man, but let her spirit come into me . . ." Warren Beatty said she was too messy for him personally. She was "too loud," he said. She drank too much, and "didn't have good manners."

The Grateful Dead's Jerry Garcia said, "I'm tired of caring about

1

her . . . She was a hard case chick doing what she was doing as hard as she could do it. She did what she did and that was it. She died at the best possible time to go, and if you know any people who get past that point, they go into a decline and it's all over . . . but going up, it's like a skyrocket, and Janis was a skyrocket chick."

Jack Nicholson told me he wanted to get it on with Janis but that she'd probably laugh at him because of the cornball dope and biker movies he'd made. "She'd think them hilarious," he said. He was in my office at Robert Levy's Pebble Productions in Hollywood, staring at a poster-size photo of Janis with one breast exposed. She'd signed it with love and kisses. Unlike Warren Beatty, Jack wanted to know the details of the relationship I'd had with Janis. He said he'd go home, put on "Take A Piece Of My Heart" and trip the rest of the day.

I was trying to get Jack a job writing scripts. He was on the slide-side, seeking some stability with a career in shreds. "Man, I'm broke and I'm sinking," he told me. "I feel like every step I'm taking, I'm going to fall into a fucking hole." I wasn't broke then, but I'd been as broke as Jack when I'd first met Janis six years earlier in San Francisco. Back then, nobody knew or cared who she was—a lump-faced kid with sores on her skin, frumpy like someone working a hot-dog stand. She was "floatin'." There was "no such thing as God," she said, because if there was, he'd set her straight with a stash of dope "that'd make the devil's hair stand on end." That was all she wanted, all she cared about.

Between staying stoned and singing blues or folk for tips, she said the only other thing she wanted was to get laid three times a day. "I don't mean by the same guy," she told me. She had a whole pack of friends, and sometimes she balled some of them, she said, although I didn't always believe she was balling "friends." One would-be musician said he never saw her before the night he took her to his room over a bar across from City Lights book shop. "She fucks like a truck," he said. "She wants to get on top and jam up and down. She practically busted my rib cage."

She once arranged to use the screened-in porch of a black girl named Chip. "Just to pull a few bucks ballin' for bread," she told Chip, grinning. Later she confessed she couldn't get anyone interested in balling her and paying for it, so she didn't have any money for dope.

Floating. None of us had any money.

One day Janis wanted to borrow carfare to go downtown to a coin shop on Market Street out toward the Bay Bridge. She'd found an old penny in her tip cup at the coffeehouse where she'd been singing. She showed me the penny and I said, "So what?" She said that Chip was a silversmith, and that she'd looked it up in a coin book at the library and said it was worth twenty or thirty bucks.

"On that," she said, "I can stay stoned for a couple of weeks!" She told me this while we were having coffee in the bagel shop on that triangle of Vallejo Street and Grant in the North Beach section, a hangout for artists, poets and drifters, and a handful of Beatniks who still hadn't sold out—a small island with little cash flow.

When a movie script deal about L.A.'s famous Black Dahlia murder case fell through, I'd moved Cecilia, the Hungarian dancer I'd been living with, and our six month-old baby, out of Hollywood and up North where I'd landed a part-time proofreading job with a Bay Area paper. I remained in touch with actor Tom Neal, who was co-producing and planning to star as the aging detective on the unsolved murder. "Any day now," he'd say, "we're going to land the financing to get this cocksucker on a roll."

I was writing a couple of cheap paperbacks for an L.A. publisher who, like Tom, hadn't been able to pay me what was owed. I was almost broke after paying the tab in the bagel shop, and only had a dime to give Janis for carfare. She told me later she'd spent the dime on a Tootsie Roll and walked to the coin shop since nobody would give her a ride hitchhiking.

It was a long way, and when she got to the coin shop they told her the penny was worth only a couple dollars because it wasn't in mint condition. Janis saw this as a deliberate attack. The "fates" were bringing her down, she said, for "kicking over the holy ideas" she'd been saddled with back in Port Arthur, and for going around saying there wasn't any God.

She was still mad that night when I saw her at the coffeehouse. Her pasty-faced lethargy was gone and she was snapping, her gestures whip-like and erratic. She kept talking about being screwed out of the money for the penny. "Mint! Mint!" she kept saying. "What the fuck's *mint*?"

I was with my friend Dick Warren, a painter I knew from New York who'd fallen down a flight of stairs in the Woolworth Building and was trying for disability. Luckily, he'd brought along a cigar tube of pills. I urged him to let Janis have what she wanted. He'd also brought a pint of Old Crow which we passed back and forth, Janis gulping it to chase the pills. Since she knew Dick had money she went into a patter—her usual spiel when fishing for compliments or dope or sympathy. She liked people to feel sorry for her, and she worked the act like a nervous juggler or a one-armed paperhanger. She was good. She could look almost tragic, crushed, dead on the top. But beneath the patter her feelings ran wild; they were trapped inside her, jarring out against her nerves.

Janis, who'd be *numero uno* Queen of Rock in a short time, had bad skin and "not a pot to piss in," as she put it, and a look that flip-flopped between plain crazy and open-eyed unconsciousness. I believed it was the pills because I'd seen that look before. I told her about a girl I knew in New York who did bennies by the bagful. Her heart became enlarged to the point of putting pressure on her other organs, and this caused some kind of epilepsy-like fits for which she had to be hospitalized.

"The story doesn't mean anything," Janis said. "It was obviously the chick and not the dope."

We got into a conversation about altering one's perceptions. I'd talked to Aldous Huxley the year before at the Hollywood Franklin Hotel just after his hillside home burned down. I'd see him in the hotel coffee shop across the street from the Hollywood Tower where I lived, in Dick Powell's old second-level penthouse. Huxley drove a late-model four-door, leaning close to the wheel and squinting through the windshield. There was a round metal ashtray with a rubber suction cup stuck to the dashboard in which he had water and a yellow flower picked from the burned property. He very politely told me that due to the experience of losing everything in that devastating fire, his doors of perception had not only been opened but "torn off the hinges."

Janis said she didn't care about her personal perceptions, only about staying high, because when she wasn't high it was like "falling on your ass without any pants on." Like the rug that was yanked from under Huxley, who died shortly after the fire.

Staying stoned kept Janis on her feet, but she had to be careful, she said. She drank, too, though not as much as she would later when she could afford "sugared booze," as she called it—part Jack Daniels, part Southern Comfort (which she called "sugar")—"Presto! Fire water!" Drinking the cheap stuff in the coffeehouse, she'd let out a high-pitched yell like nails going down a blackboard or someone stepping on a cat's tail. Everybody cringed except the dishwasher, a skinny guy with a soggy apron dragging down on his shoe tops and soapy steam over his glasses. He'd come out to see what she was yelling about.

"You are one cool chick," he'd say. He liked her so much he'd bring cheap bottles of wine to share with her in the rear. She said the booze leveled out the speed. "It keeps me from racing too high," she said, "like keeping a tab on the score." She'd pop speed to get over the nose dive from booze, keeping a "tab" on the speed with a little grass or some hash if she could get her hands on any.

I remember Janis one night, very late, in the far dark corner with the dishwasher after drinking a bottle of Night Train, tilting to one side like she was slowly falling over. He had his left hand crossed under his right arm and his fingers bunched and pushing between her legs while he held a cigarette in his right hand.

The weather had been rotten. "Cold," I wrote in a letter, "drizzly gray and foggy, and the sun never shines." Janis was hanging around another coffeehouse on Grant near Green Street, one of the few Beat-bohemian joints still going—a bleary place that smelled of mold and iodine, and ammonia used in the mop water. It was a storefront, but the glass on Grant was sashed over with layers of sacks and cloth. The woodwork was old San Francisco gingerbread painted to match the yellowing walls, cluttered with beatnik paintings, mostly abstractions that looked like wilting flowers or chunks of decomposing meat, the rickety chairs and tables around the floor, and the steam pipes that kept the air too hot and gassy from the mop water fumes. They burned incense to kill the smell, and people sat around sweating in the baggy clothes they wore against the cold outside.

The first night I heard Janis sing was after I'd been sitting about an hour in that coffeehouse with Dick Warren. She came in with a shaggy guy in sneakers with the toes cut out. I'd see this guy with Janis again, and I'd meet him again after he'd wound up with a group called Jefferson Airplane.

Janis had some metal rings and an identification bracelet on her wrist, and she kept raising her arm and shaking the sleeve higher, jingling the bracelets. Dick pointed her out right away. "Now *she* belts a song," he said. "She's really good." He said she'd get around to singing when a few more customers showed up. "She likes a lot of people listening to her."

A poet was reading from scraps of papers he'd scribbled on, but nobody was paying attention. With his sunken cheeks he reminded me of the poet Maxwell Bodenheim in Greenwich Village. When I thought about Bodenheim I always pictured him lying on the floor in that crummy room where he'd been murdered along with his young wife, who had been stabbed with a hunting knife. She was on the bed, with a coat thrown over her body. Neither were wearing shoes. Bodenheim had holes in his socks and a single gunshot in his chest.

I was glad when the skinny poet walked away and Janis and the shaggy guy took his place.

She had a banjo and was doing something with the capo while the guy strummed an old Gibson guitar. Janis finally got on a stool next to him, propped a foot on the rungs and started to sing.

The place quieted down and most everyone was listening. She closed her eyes, still holding the banjo but not playing it, and sang a blues number I'd heard in New Orleans the year before, while snooping around for a movie I was writing for director Curtis Harrington.

A makeshift spotlight rigged high on the coffeehouse wall opposite the piano was shining down behind Janis. She wasn't directly in the light—more a silhouette against the thick blue smoke floating in the air.

Dick had been right: she was good. She sang low, slurring almost as though choking back cries, underplaying words in a trembling way that carried the threat of something bottled up and moving inside her like a riptide. She coddled syllables with her mouth, did things to the words with her throat and tongue that gave them new meanings, that made you feel them more intensely, although there was a sense, too, that she wasn't even sure what she was doing. Her voice would crack a little—a sharp tone pushing through a soft word. It was odd, like she'd been struck with a pain, but she kept right on singing without slowing down, just pushing the words together.

Once finished, the clapping seemed to slacken her and she grinned, nodding to the crowd. She sang a couple more songs: easy ones, folk stuff. She was a gal that went out the gate full-tilt, and for the rest, she just played along. When she went back to the table in the rear, Dick said I should talk to her and maybe hook her up with Herb Cohen in L.A., who ran a couple coffeehouses like the Unicorn and Cosmo Alley where Ginsberg and Ferlinghetti read their stuff to jazz. My first wife, Gina, had worked both places for Herb and I knew him pretty well. I said it wasn't a bad idea. Janis had a way of getting it across.

I liked the song and told her so. Janis asked if I knew what it was.

I said I'd heard it before, in New Orleans, and thought it was Muddy Waters. "Some of it was Muddy Waters," she agreed. "I kind of improvise what I can't remember."

She laughed and suggested trading places with me, meaning she'd prefer New Orleans to where she was. I said I didn't live in New Orleans but I'd take a rain check on getting back down there. "Or," I said, joking around, "we could go together—make it in three days." She said she didn't want to wait that long, and if I had fast wheels we could do it in a day and a night as long as we hit Port Arthur on the way. "I haven't got a car," I said. "Not even a slow one."

"So there goes Basin Street," she said, still smiling. "We're both stuck in fuckin' Frisco . . ." Later I'd hear her throwing out little lines like that to see if people picked up on them, if she could get some banter going. She liked that, and the higher she got on speed the more she liked it. She said it could be like music—like blues and jazz, and you just went up and kept "tearing it off, and then another one . . ."

Racing down to Louisiana hadn't been a serious proposal, though it could've been. We probably would've hit the road if I'd had a car and wasn't with the Hungarian and our baby daughter.

I told Janis about Herb Cohen, and she said, "Sure, why not? An L.A. gig's as good as anywhere if they're paying for it." I said she'd have to negotiate. She asked if I thought the L.A. guy would pay her expenses to come down and check it out. I said it wasn't likely. She gave a fake smile, rolling her eyes, and said, "Well, that's show biz for you."

You wouldn't have thought by her manner that she was as talented as she was. Her sallow, bumpy skin turned red at times like there was something wrong with her health or her blood was going bad.

I saw her a few days later when a cold wind was blowing through the streets and the coffeehouse door was open—no customers in the room, but the steam pipes were hissing and the heat was going out the open door.

Janis was in the corner on a low stool near the piano, next to a window that was curtained off. Tight rolls of burlap and dirty napkins were wadded around the edges of the window. Some empty beer bottles sat on the piano keys, and Janis was leaning back over the stool, sucking in her stomach to fasten the buttons on her pants. The trouser legs were baggy like work pants, but so tight at the waist and seat the seams were busting. She was barefoot, and besides the pants, she wore only

7

a brassiere, a faded, orange-pink pushup thing with a wide, big band around the ribs like something an old lady would wear. When she saw me standing in the doorway she made a funny, self-conscious face, not about being caught in that particular brassiere, but about being caught wearing one in general. When I nodded, she said, "I'm only wearing this thing 'cause my tits are cold."

She'd been sitting on a folded army blanket and couldn't find one shoe, but quickly pulled on a large knit sweater that had baggy sleeves full of snags and so many loose threads it looked like fringe hanging down. She put on a jacket, a small man's Italian cut with slanted pockets she had trouble getting her hands into. "You got a cigarette?" she asked. I gave her one and she said, "Just crashing on short notice, you know." I nodded. "Got kicked out of the place I was staying at," she explained. She took a few drags and asked if I had any dope. When I told her I didn't, she got nervous and exasperated. "Fuck no," she cursed. "Nobody's got any dope." Which wasn't too far from the truth, but she got into a funk about people holding out on her—how they couldn't help her or wouldn't help her. She didn't even want *much* dope, she said, but they were keeping it to themselves and wouldn't share it. The fucking world was rotten, she said. It wasn't that she was shooting shit like a lot of people, so she couldn't see what they were being so selfish about.

Looking me squarely in the face, she said, "I'm not going to kiss their ass, man. You know what I mean?" I said I did, although I didn't. All she wanted was some decent dope.

Late at night when she seemed to be the most awake, her eyes big and shining, she'd look spooked-out: a moon-faced teenager on a paranoid trip. It was the pills she was dropping. But earlier in the day when her eyes were like slits in putty, she looked older than her twenty years, and stared around defensively. A couple of times she was so bulked up in two or three sweaters she looked barrel-chested, walking around barefoot in the cold—her feet red under swollen ankles. She was a ragamuffin, someone that you're afraid to look at too hard because she'll probably ask for spare change. She'd be called a street person today; back then, a vagrant, a drifter. Too young to be booked as a derelict, although she was almost busted a couple of times while panhandling Broadway, and did get arrested for shoplifting.

A small percentage of what the coffeehouse took in was paid to Janis on the nights she sang, plus a little from the tip cup, a coffee can near the singer or whoever was reading poetry or playing a guitar. The tourists still came to see the beatniks; like penitents they willfully exposed themselves to the scorn like the hiss of a snake, of the hangers-on. Or the crowd was there to listen to songs and hear the poets, and they would drop money in the can. That was where Janis later found the penny. She'd told me, "I remember my daddy saying a penny that's dated before the first World War is going to be worth something."

After the awful "gypping" she'd experienced because the penny hadn't been mint, she'd pocketed the two bucks they'd paid and bought a half-pint to dump in her java that night. She'd wanted pills, and said she was afraid of drinking and "not having something" in her system to stay "smoothed out." She worried about booze because it had killed Hank Williams' bladder and bowels, she said, and she'd been told he didn't feel pain when a cigarette went out in the spit on his lip. I said it was true about his bladder because I'd drank with Williams in a parking lot and he'd pissed his pants without knowing it. Janis said at one point during her life in Port Arthur, she thought of Hank Williams as an angel that came down through the roof and slept in her bed.

Dick told her I'd been an actor and hung around with James Dean in New York, and that I'd had motorcycles, and that Dean and I had partied with some oddball chicks.

Janis said she'd worn a ring on a piece of string around her neck that was supposed to carry a memory of Dean. She'd read the magazine stories about his "talking back from the grave" and wanted to know: Was he or wasn't he dead? From what she could gather, his growing up in an Indiana hick town had to be as suffocating as her own childhood in Port Arthur. It turned a person into "a *lusus naturae*," she said, wiggling her eyebrows up and down. "It means you're a freak of nature." Then she said, "Isn't that what we are?" I recall laughing and her mentioning the words were French. I said it sounded Latin to me, and she replied, "Well, it probably is. I can't tell a Frenchman from a greaseball except the wop's supposed to have the bigger dick of the two."

She made people mad and seemed to do it on purpose. Then she'd feel bad and want their sympathy. One night I saw her hit a guy with her fist. I thought they were kidding around, but they weren't, and she was about to hit him again when someone grabbed her arm. That didn't stop her. She threw a punch with her other hand and got him in the stomach. Another time she almost got into a fight with a mean-looking bastard even I wouldn't have tangled with. She knew him, and was laughing, when he said something she didn't like—that she was a "goofball on legs," something about her brain being bopped out of sync—and then she said something about knocking his teeth out.

He only grinned, showing slabs of teeth like a dog daring her to try it. She said, "Lucky nobody gives a shit what a stupid person thinks." Then her manner and tone changed; she became hushed and confidential. "Last time I saw you," she said, "you said you'd be holdin' the next time you're in and you'd get me straight. I mean, didn't you say that? Don't you fuckin' lie and say you haven't scored, man, because I know you have. Okay, man?"

I can still remember her—nodding her head, mad, and her upper body bobbing like she had a hinge at the waist, and that wide, open-mouthed, plain-faced smile that wasn't joyful, but belligerent. "She looks for trouble so damned easy," Dick Warren said, "she's going to get herself killed one way or another." Not only because she was so ready to pick a fight, but because she did it alone, fogged-out, a nowhere-to-crash-half-the-time loner pushing, pushing. Her mouth drew up at the corners, showing more lower teeth than upper ones. She was a tough-talking chick, ready to slug it out, but then suddenly grinning and being a pal—and this in turn gave way to something neither sexy nor vulnerable, but sad: a kind of child you had no idea what to do with.

She'd sit and twist her hair. Once she said she thought she had lice and needed "a fuckin' monkey" to pick the bugs off her scalp and keep her groomed. I'd seen her comb her hair up high on her head, or pull it back and sort of tie it there, leaving a halo of stray hairs that looked like wires sticking out of her head when lit from behind. Sometimes she'd plaster it down with a strong-smelling pomade that flattened her hair out wet and shiny, and stiff as a dead bird. Once she wore a pink bow on a curved comb as big as something out of the *Little Rascals* movies. She confused people.

I remember Janis sitting in a coffee joint talking about Cowboy Copas and Patsy Montana and how she always wanted to be like Patsy Montana. "I've never told nobody that," she said. Singers like Joe Turner, Leadbelly, Big Mama Thornton and Bessie Smith she felt connected to on the outside, but "on the inside," she said, "my ass is as white as Patsy Montana and Doris Day's ass!"

10

I said, "Prove it," just joking, and she gathered her shirt in one hand and pulled it up on one side of her chest, showing a bare white breast. She laughed and got red in the face, and I felt a little shaky.

It was like she had a mental list of the things Dick told her, some true and some not; for instance that I knew Josh White, the great blues man, when in fact it was White's girlfriend, a Greenwich Village waitress I knew. She was an actress I'd stayed with, a couple of weeks off Sheridan Square, when she'd been studying with Lee Strasberg. I'd told Dick she didn't give a shit who thought she was a whore because of being White's mistress—she'd ride proud in the world sitting on Josh's shoulders, even though he was married at the time.

Dick told Janis I knew a lot of movie stars and that Tex Williams was a friend of my family. I'd been an artist, he'd said, been to Paris and even painted pictures for Herb Cohen's beatnik cafes.

When Janis told me she'd wanted to be a painter and live in a Paris garret, she was chewing on a big wedge of onion. It was one of the few times I saw her eating. Peeling away layers of the onion, she put sugar on it to keep from crying. As we talked she scratched and dug at her throat, her skin breaking out red where she'd rubbed it with wet, onion-juice-laden fingers.

Janis asked me about the time I'd seen Hank Williams at the Grand Ole Opry, and about drinking with him in an L.A. parking lot a few months before he died. At twenty-nine, he was just four years older than James Dean at the time of his death, but she didn't think it was such a "sorry picture"—neither Hank's early death nor Dean's. "Williams wrote what—a hundred and fifty songs?" she said. "Couldn't read or write music?" If she could do a tenth of what Hank did in the next forty years of her life, she said, she'd be blessing the day she was born instead of calling it a day "God didn't wanna get out of bed and said, 'Fuck it' . . ."

Blood transfusions by way of the blues, she said, were what she needed, and what she got, from Bessie Smith and Big Mamma, "So I get blacker the more blues I sing." She truly believed she'd been torn somewhere in her life between the Negro world and Patsy Montana's, and this "eclipse," as she called it, was going to keep her "hollowed out"—unable to "sit herself down" in either world. If she didn't do it, she said, "the thing'll backfire," and she had no intention of following Hank or James Dean to an early grave.

It didn't matter what she "willed" herself to do, because life was like bowling, she said. She liked to bowl but she wasn't any good at it. "The Man upstairs says this chick's an alley cat—an ugly chick that bowls in the gutter every time." What she was good at, she said, was getting high, and if it was possible for me to score by that afternoon she'd see that I got the best seat in the house when it came to the day of reckoning.

She wasn't good at scoring dope either, she claimed, and couldn't stay as stoned as she wanted. She said she had to please people or do what she didn't want to do in order to get high. There wasn't anything more important than being stoned, she said, except "lovin'," but even that was more rewarding if you were high. She was probably good at "lovin'," she claimed, but because she wasn't a glamour queen she didn't think she'd score so hot in that department, either. "People I want to ball," she said, "just don't seem to be on the same wavelength as me."

Janis wanted to know if James Dean was queer. I didn't believe he was, but that was a whole other can of peas. "It wouldn't bother me," she said. "I know queers that're okay, and it only makes a problem if you want to ball someone who doesn't want to ball you, or who's queer for someone of their own sex . . . If you ball your friends you don't get into hassles about people being hung up . . . It can be a guy or a chick in the sack," she said, rambling on, "and that's what makes you even more a freak."

After hanging around Grant and talking to Janis, I got the feeling she pushed the hard-ass speed act to cover something else. I didn't know clearly what it was. Dick said she was scared and mixed up and it was almost impossible to get a look at what she wanted to hide, like she wasn't in touch with it at all.

I recall seeing her only a couple of times in a dress, looking like a dance hall floozy or a short man dressed as a woman, and bungling attempts at "romance" by sleeping with anyone she thought desired her for whatever reason she'd dream up. Some, like the guy with the slab teeth or the one across the alley from City Lights, used her, she told Chip, "like you'd use a hole in the fence." She couldn't get close to coming with these guys she was balling because they'd finish quick and make excuses to get away.

She blamed herself—it was always her fault and never the other person's. Even with bad dope, it usually boiled down to being Janis's fault. Those she floated around with did not hesitate to let her take the fall. They seemed a scroungy, conked-out lot, some shooting heroin without worrying who knew, or when or where it came from. It reminded me of the New York days when Dennis Hopper was staying with me on 17th Street, and my never-present roommate Norman had his junkie friends stopping by to shoot up and nod out under the sink.

Despite what's been said or written about Janis shooting smack on Grant, she was not—at that time. Heroin wasn't easy to come by. In North Beach it cost more money to make a solid connection than most people were able to pay for the dope. But Janis was guilty by association.

Dick had been popping for more than a year, but he said Janis turned down an offer to try and was scared. Chip was shooting a little— skin shots at first—and Janis did some coke-sniffing, but couldn't stop throwing up. She said she'd make a rotten junkie and was afraid it'd ruin her will to sit on top of the "eclipse, because a fuckin' devil's at the bottom of the hole."

Plus, she was convinced she couldn't carry a tune and was "a musical failure." A lot of negative vibes were being launched along Grant, and I made notes about how "the girl from Texas" seemed pulled to the sorry side of things—like someone walking out of a Hank Williams song. She could sway into bad scenes as though it were a calling, more trusting of many people than she should have been.

One time, sharing booze, she was squirming on the seat and it would've been easy to sack her down, but I didn't. Again she put her hand up under the sweater, scratching at her tits. I thought she'd pull it up again, but she just said fleas were eating her alive.

Because of the beautiful Hungarian freedom fighter I was living with, the mother of my daughter, I'd temporarily given up the non-monogamous sex chase. I felt my days of juvenile glory before the movie cameras were behind me, and I was only trying to keep my head above the economic undertow. I rarely smoked dope, and I wasn't doing pills, and half the people I knew thought I was a square—some even thought I was a cop, undercover among the die-hard Beats—but that was okay. A benny now and then to keep me pounding at the typewriter all night was about the extent of the dope I did back then. Janis and I were at different ends about dope. I drank and I'd been hooked on sex—my fast fix for the past few years, which I'd temporarily kicked, and Janis wasn't the prize to pull me off my track of reformation. Plus I thought I'd get a dose of something—the least of which

13

was clap—if I got into her pants.

Partying with "the girl from Texas" was something around a distant corner, though always in the air, ever since that morning I caught her wearing the old lady's brassiere.

She was shooting speed not long before we went in separate directions, sticking the needle under her skin a little in Dick's kitchen. They'd fix in the breakfast nook, using a drugstore hypo to shoot it. But even then, Janis didn't tie off like Dick or the people I knew in New York. Janis said she'd pulled the rubber tube for him one night and he stuck the needle in, drew some blood up into the tube, then pushed the whole mix right in.

Chip was skin-popping smack by then, so it was around and always present. She was shooting it into the back of her hand, or on the inside of her calf above the ankles. If she shot it into her thigh or arm she'd be a junkie, she thought, and nobody wanted to be a junkie. She said, "It's something you kind of hit at by a weird default you don't even know you have . . ."

She'd told Dick she thought Janis was crazy because Janis said if she could be as black as Chip she'd give her soul to Satan. Chip said, "I told her if I had half the talent she did I'd be in New York instead of suicidin' with a bunch of freaks in San Francisco. She ought to wake up and make it happen the color she is, and stop dreaming there's a nigger underneath her lily-white hide." Chip also sang folk songs, but had given up because "being a Negro without a name," as she put it, she couldn't get a gig in Frisco or L.A., despite any rumors of racial acceptance. "Rhythm and blues—okay," she said, "but no intermixing of color on the stage . . ."

One night Chip, Janis, Dick, the Hungarian and our baby, and I met at a little Italian place on the corner near the park. Chip and Dick were high, but Janis was a real mess. She had some pills that looked old and crystallized, blank capsules with bands around them. She slopped food around like a spastic, had trouble finding her mouth with the fork, and swayed back and forth, waving her hands. Chip had talked to Dick about some contacts for Janis in L.A., maybe singing at the Troubadour or getting in with Lenny Bruce. We were going to make a plan, but Janis couldn't even manage a plate of spaghetti.

When we left she took the spumoni in a paper cup, then bought a quart of beer at the market by Columbus, across from the park. She took a few swigs standing on the sidewalk, then started puking in the bushes. Chip and Dick said enough's enough and walked the other way to the wharf, leaving Janis, who told me she was in pain. She kept vomiting after swallowing beer, and I said, "Stop drinking the damned beer!"

She handed me the bottle but there was puke on it. The Hungarian asked her if she wanted to bed down on our couch, but Janis only wanted to know if I had any uppers. "Even low-grade?" she pleaded. "I coulda sworn these fuckers were uppers, man, but I'm going down fast—something's all fucking wrong . . ." I said I didn't have any, but she didn't believe me. While my girlfriend and the baby horsed around on the grass, Janis sat on a bench and tried to eat the spumoni. It was late, I recall, and the baby was half-asleep. I asked Janis if she wanted to take a taxi with us back to our place. She'd stopped throwing up and said, "I'm going to be mad if I don't get something in my system to straighten me out." She asked me if I was sure I didn't have any dope, and again I said no. She nodded—as much as calling me a liar—and walked off, taking the beer but leaving the spumoni on the bench.

Maybe twice I saw her with a guy from Texas who didn't like me and whom I didn't like. We didn't even know each other, but according to Janis he figured she'd been making it with me the same time she'd been making it with him. She said they had a lot in common, like Port Arthur music and dope.

During those days I hadn't experienced a sense of "North Beach community," but more a kind of alienation, a fierceness in those around me. I'd managed to write a paperback that Gold Medal wanted, though they hadn't advanced me any money yet. The proofreading job had gone down the tubes a couple of months before and we were behind in the rent. Out of the blue, Lee Wallace, then heading Casting at 20th-Century Fox in Hollywood, came to my rescue. He had a part for me in a movie with Lauren Bacall and Carol Lynley, if I wanted it. We'd hit a couple of hard days when the freedom fighter and I went without grub and the baby had only pancake batter to eat, so there wasn't much decision-making. I borrowed a few bucks, and we were heading back to L.A., sneaking out at night to make the move.

Before I left, I saw Janis in a Chinatown drugstore. I remember the Seeburg Solotone record selector on the old soda fountain, and Janis on a stool in front of it with her head going back and forth to the music. She looked *pretty,* a lot of makeup on her eyes like a Paris whore, and a fishnet tee-shirt tucked into tight jeans. A long, braided, Indian sort of sash was around her waist with the end hanging to her knees.

She'd put her coins in the jukebox and asked if I'd lend her enough for some french fries. I got two orders of fries, which she ate with a mountain of salt and ketchup. A lot of things were happening in New York, she said, and people were hitting out for the Village folk scene. She wasn't sure what she was going to do and asked, "What're *you* doing?" It occurred to me that we were both sort of launching the idea of going to bed right then. I asked if she remembered showing me her breast, and she got very docile and said, "You want to look at it again?" I sort of laughed though she hadn't said anything funny, and told her I was going out of town. I shook her hand, which felt small and warm, and realized that my fidelity to the Hungarian was something Janis had no way of understanding. That earlier night in the restaurant and park, it was as though my baby had been nothing more than a duffel bag. It was, for Janis, like those invisible boundary lines just didn't exist.

I didn't tell her I was heading to Hollywood, but in case she made it to New York I gave her a couple of names to look up. I wrote the numbers on the back of a snapshot of Hank Williams taken in Fort Worth in '52. Janis looked at it, eating the fries, then stuck the picture up under her shirt against her bare stomach, saying her pockets were too tight. I left the change on the counter. She dropped one of the nickels in the slot to play the same song again, giving me a funny, almost sad smile as she rocked on the stool, singing silently with the lyrics while her smoky eyes seemed so separated from the rest of her face.

Looking Back at Hank Williams

HIS BLADDER WAS IN ROTTEN SHAPE, and he was stewed, though the two cowboys with him said Hank hardly ever boozed a performance. It was around spring of '52, and Williams was going bald. His face looked like a dead man's.

I never figured out if the picture of Hank I'd given Janis had been taken before or after I met Hank in the Riverside Rancho parking lot. He'd been pretty wobbly before he started sharing the Johnny Walker Red with me and Barry Bowron—son of L.A.'s then-mayor Fletcher Bowron—and another pal, Mike Parey, a Hell's Angels biker with a fat-bob Harley that had caught Hank's eye.

I'd wrecked my hotrod Ford in the Mojave desert months before, but with a couple of radio and acting bits, I was soon driving a '50 Mercury. Like Hank's song, I had "two-dollar bills to boot" and "the place just over the hill" was the Riverside Rancho.

"King of Western Swing" Spade Cooley had made it big there during the war, with Tex Williams singing in his band. Cooley moved to the Santa Monica Ballroom the year after V-J Day, and Tex (no relation to Hank) formed his own Western Caravan band at the Rancho. It wasn't long after they began broadcasting Spade's Jamborees from the ballroom that Cooley killed his own wife and went to prison.

"Smoke, Smoke, Smoke That Cigarette," Tex's big one, was known around the world. Tex was starring in movies and lived in Bel-Air off Sunset Boulevard. He was also friends with my father at the Hollywood Masonic Lodge, and often sang Bob Nolan's Sons of the Pioneers songs at shows and festivities. Once I walked with Tex across Hollywood Boulevard for cigarettes. We looked at the footprints outside Grauman's Chinese Theater, and a few people asked Tex for his autograph. We were talking about Gene Autry because Autry was considering me for a run in a new series. His Flying A Studios were opposite Hollywood High, where I was going to school. My girlfriend Sherry's father was Autry's head cameraman and friends with Jock Mahoney, the lead in the new project. I was being slated as Mahoney's kid sidekick—an orphan he'd rescued from a bunch of Apaches.

Autry was filming in Bakersfield, and Tex said another boy he knew, Hank Williams, was in Bakersfield "or maybe down in San Diego on the road." Hank was going to be in L.A. long enough to play a weekend at the Rancho for Tex, who invited Barry Bowron and myself to catch Hank's performance.

Tex later told me Hank's appearance had been a spur-of-the-moment decision. He said, "Hank was coming to town about a movie deal, and we got to chewing the fat about the Rancho, and I said I sure wish he'd come over and play a Saturday night, and Hank said that's what he had in mind if it suited me. I said it suited me fine."

Marty, the owner of the Rancho, worried about booking Hank for fear he'd fill the ballroom then fail to show, too drunk to make it. According to Dallas, Tex's wife and also a singer; Marty put a lot of faith in Tex's judgment. "Marty knew that if something went wrong," she said, "Tex would right it in a matter of minutes. If Hank had some kind of problem, Tex would back Hank up."

"Hank's a funny bird," Tex said that night at Grauman's Chinese. "He's got a truckload of troubles hitched to himself. Cut off like he is from Nashville, he's a salmon in the desert. The damn guy's running headlong at disaster, but nobody can figure it out." He said he loved Hank even though he was having a hard time making it to dates. But Tex knew he'd show at the Rancho. "It's a certain way we have of saying something and setting it between us."

Tex and Dallas convinced Marty of Hank's sincerity about staying sober long enough to do the show. Hank had been jailed for shooting

a revolver in a hotel, and I'd been told he hardly ate anymore and sometimes couldn't remember where he was or where he was going . "His
problems are getting the best of him," Tex said. "But I'll take his word
because on certain things he's as solid as gold. I hope this'll be one of
those occasions where he shines through."

Phones were jumping at the Rancho, Dallas told me later, and by
that afternoon they were taking reservations, "and the Rancho didn't
take reservations," she said. "We would just fill the place until the fireman
came around warning us to herd a bunch of the people back out into
the parking lot until the next show."

As soon as I learned about Hank's appearance, I called Barry
Bowron. We'd talked about forming a group called the Tumbleweed
Trio while we were students at the Marion Colbert School for
Individual Instruction. I passed on the news and drove to Mike Parey's
in Burbank. A little older than Barry or myself, Mike hung with a
rowdy bunch of Valley Hell's Angels. His father had been a drummer
for Spade Cooley, and Mike played the best non-professional boogie
piano I'd ever heard. Today, when I catch certain pieces of boogie, I
think of the suntanned girls at the Burbank pool, jitterbugging in their
bathing suits beside the Coke machine while Mike played the old
upright piano.

Barry and I were at the Rancho when Mike showed up in his
leather jacket with the skull on the back. He wasn't wearing Hell's
Angels' colors, so he looked just like any other cycle-hound. We met
in the Rancho's coffee shop, which occupied the west end of the brown
wooden building. The rest of the structure housed the dance floor and
the bar upstairs. A long, narrow platform along a side wall made up
the stage, backed by a big "Home on the Range" mural that was brown
as resin from all the smoke.

Other writers have described the Rancho as a "ballroom," but that
isn't accurate. A wooden honky-tonk down in a gully with a barn-like
dance floor and a bar in the hayloft is closer to fact. You turned off
Riverside Drive, which borders Griffith Park on the north of
Hollywood, and drove down into a wide dirt parking lot. (Most of this
lot, on the corner heading into Glendale, was occupied by a baseball
field and a swimming pool.) At the top of the slope and along the road
ran a railing of two-inch steel pipe fitted into concrete to keep cars from
crashing down into the parking lot.

Behind the frame building the ground leaned to the rim of the L.A.

River, a wide concrete storm drain designed to solve the city's flood problems, which it hadn't.

The Rancho's big sign sticking up from the roof on stilts, announced DANCING to the passing traffic. On nights when the fog crept low, the sign had a pale green look of peeled paint, but at other times it glowed brightly, all the reddish-pink lights blinking on and off. After a while, the bulbs started popping out and nobody replaced the dead ones.

We sat in a booth by the window, eating chili burgers and pushing the jukebox buttons—Hank's songs, Teresa Brewer, Tennessee Ernie Ford, Kay Starr, Les Paul and Mary Ford's "How High the Moon," Hank Snow, or Frankie Laine's "Mule Train," while headlights from cars coming off Riverside angled up and down the driveway like searchlights. People were pouring in to see Hank, even though he'd just been on the Kate Smith Show. Neither Barry nor Mike had ever seen him perform.

Almost three years earlier I'd taken a Greyhound bus to Memphis to see my grandfather, Claude "Mac" McFerran, a railroad locomotive engineer for the Illinois Central. Nothing was as important to my grandfather as an Illinois Central locomotive—not his own son, home, wife or daughters (one was my mother), all of whom fled Mac's indifference to find lives of their own away from the South. His claim to fame was having ridden with the legendary Casey Jones shortly before the engineer's fatal accident. Mac retired after fifty-six years of operating steam and diesel engines from New Orleans to Sioux City. He played guitar and wanted to be a singer like Jimmie Rodgers, the "singing brakeman," and while Mac strummed along with the radio or phonograph, and knew performers from his tent-show hopping in the late 1920s and '30s, he couldn't "break away from the road long enough to learn a decent song." Country-and-Western star Red Sovine once rode with Mac in an engine and said it inspired him to write one of his songs. He understood Mac's love of trains, as did singer Red Foley, whom Mac had met in Chicago, and while Mac admired these men, he never understood their admiration of him. Wherever Foley appeared, Mac had an open door to the best seats in the house, and in Nashville that meant the Ryman Auditorium, the home of the Grand Old Opry at that time.

After getting into Memphis, Mac and I hightailed it to Nashville to visit the Opry. He gave me a blank Illinois Central notebook to doodle in, and I started making notes about the railroad stops and what we ate: eggs sunny-side up and roundhouse pork chops; black-eyed peas and T-bone steak in another place that looked like the picture on the Log Cabin Syrup bottle. I wrote about the taxi we took to downtown Nashville and the badge on the driver's cap that had a small electric lightbulb in it.

He drove us around back of the Ryman, which seemed like an old foreign hospital in a movie, or a dingy church with its arch-shaped windows. Some of these appeared to be boarded over, but the waiting crowd was lined down the alley and around the block. There was a mystery about the old wood doors of the Ryman, the concrete steps and the stream of feet up and down, and the security guard Mac talked to—a Ku Klux Klansman from Jackson, a hundred or so miles west along the rails.

We went backstage through a rear door to one side—an area overhung with rows of backdrops and huge curtains on pulleys and ropes, crowded with performers, hot and busy as a movie set. In a few minutes Red Foley was shaking Mac's hand. When Foley shook mine, he also held my arm and shook that as well. I think of *Chattanooga Shoeshine Boy* and the line about popping a shine rag when I remember Foley's teeth—a "Pepsodent Smile" carried all the way through. Little Jimmy Dickens and Minnie Pearl were behind us as Foley told a man in a straw hat and sleeve garters to seat us up front. The man said they were all filled up, and Foley, still smiling, said, "Well, scoot them on over, hoss!"

I remember hallways and doors, drapes and platforms, and seeing Kitty Wells and Hank Williams laughing with a fat man by a water cooler. Jam Up and Honey, a pair of white comics in black face, were laughing with Hank, and Jam Up spotted my grandfather and came over to say hello. Kitty Wells had a scarf or long silk handkerchief she kept wiping her neck with as she and Hank talked to the fat man. I heard Hank's voice above the other sounds—a high, sharp pitch. "That's the fellow everyone's here to see," the man in the straw hat said as he led us down onto the floor of the auditorium. He said to someone else, "Foley says to seat them up front," and the other person asked some people to "squeeze to the right" on the church pew. Mac and I were on the end seats just right of center.

The only people who ever wanted to know what other performers I'd heard that night at the Ryman were my uncle—shooting coyote in the Mojave Desert—and Janis Joplin, years later in San Francisco, and before I was halfway through telling her the story, she had dropped a wad of burning hash into her lap and almost set her crotch on fire.

Tense excitement shot through the crowd when Hank finally approached the WSM microphone. They began applauding and whistling, stomping and shouting even before he opened his mouth. He twiddled the tuning pegs of his guitar uncomfortably as Foley joked about Hank's being "hankering lean as a stovepipe" and needing to be "stuffed full of possum." Even though he was standing right up to the microphone, Hank's voice didn't sound as clear as it had backstage. I could hear him snatching his breath as he twisted his face to the side with a sort of sheepish look that had nothing to do with Foley's joke. Some private game Hank had going with the audience—laughter exploding sporadically to show they knew what he meant, whatever it was. His angular fingers clutched the guitar as though he expected it to break away from him any moment, and that strained look—each minute he stood there without music seemed to bring him more pain. When Foley said, "Now, Hank, you're going to give us a song," the shouting and stomping broke out again and Foley backed away, giving the audience a little salute. They kept cheering as Hank maneuvered his guitar, then tipped his head to the microphone, still looking back to one side of the band.

He said, "Okay, boys, we're all here to make some music so we might as well get her going . . ." Putting his mouth close to the microphone and leaning forward, he said to the crowded auditorium, "This here song's about a purr fella with a rough row to hoe, so we're gonna see where we go with this." There was a loud ping as his finger flicked a string, and then his right foot went thump-thump-thump on the boards of the stage, and on the fourth thump the fiddle slashed in as sudden and loud as a gun.

Hank's voice broke out above the band as though letting loose something he'd carried all knotted and bunched and struggling to get out. It was leaping free as the fiddle bow sawed and Hank cried out, mouth to the microphone, his breath a scratching noise rarely heard on records.

It's been written that Hank dipped his knees as he sang, but he also swung them from side to side in a slow-motion Charleston, half-bent and almost crouching over the guitar, face breaking out in sweat. He kept his upper body stiff like the bones were somehow fused, and turning his head he had to turn his shoulders, too. His eyes were almost angry—he didn't love anybody in that crowd. The skin hardly moved on his rigid face, except to wrinkle at the edges like a stiff decal smudged off under water.

Desperate is the way I'd describe Hank's singing, like a man cornered by something. He'd look through people as if seeking some secret exit through which to make a mad dash.

Years later, I didn't find that frantic look at the Rancho. Numb with booze, he looked as though he'd been stuffed by a taxidermist and wound up with some electric gadget that spewed out the song. I'd stood at the foot of the stage, and could only trust Tex Williams' opinion that Hank felt comfortable in the honky-tonk—on a long, loose rein, somehow. It was the space around him: when his music ricocheted through an enormous area, his personal space seemed to shrink in.

A couple of times at the Opry he had looked furtively at his wristwatch as though late for an appointment, but the crowd was yelling for "Lovesick Blues." Before he finished what he was singing, he nodded to the band—no break in the music, and they jumped right into "Lovesick Blues." A few times Hank's body jackknifed backwards and forwards as he sang, and the tendons stuck up in his neck and the backs of his hands.

His performance stunned me. It would take years to sort out the impact. The experience had a life of its own, more than Hank's songs or the band or the wild crowd.

They went crazy during "Lovesick Blues." A middle-aged woman to the right of us fell forward out of the pew onto her knees, gasping and clutching her face. Girls were screaming, men beat on the benches, determined, swept up. It made me uneasy. I'd experience nothing close to it until years later when I'd see Judy Garland—or watch Janis going all the way at the Monterey Pop Festival.

Hank's piercing glare never slackened. He didn't smile or flirt or cajole—his looks weren't even friendly. He'd squeeze his eyes shut on certain cracks or jumps in his voice, that foot thumping like a rabbit's though he had the look of a howling dog.

We were pooling resources in the Rancho cafe, Barry and my Hell's Angels pal, Mike, waiting to see Hank charge the batteries once again. Mike had gone out to check when the show would be starting, while Barry and I listened to the music beating through the east wall of the building. It wasn't Hank's Drifting Cowboys, more like the swing beat of the Caravan. Mike quickly reappeared at the window and knocked on the glass, saying something I couldn't quite hear about "Hank Williams" and pointing to the parking lot. He hurried into the cafe, shouting, "Williams is pissing in the lot behind my bike!"

Barry and I followed him out to his Harley, which stood against the embankment between a big Packard and a panel truck. The Packard's left rear door was open, and two men were standing between the car and Mike's bike—one tall and lean like a rake handle, wearing a white suit with black music notes all over it like splotches of paint in the near-dark. The Packard faced the slope, and another man was reaching into the back seat. The taller one was Hank. He wasn't pissing right then, but he didn't have his hat on and the lights reflected off his balding scalp. He was leaning with one arm on a high-rise grip of Mike's angel wing handlebars and holding a paper sack the size of a milk bottle. When he saw the three of us approaching, he bent into the car and came out with his hat.

Mike was the first to reach him, and he nodded to Hank, saying something I couldn't hear. Hank said, "I sure do thank you for saying that." Then he smiled and said, "You don't think I hurt your motor-*sackle* none?" Shaking his head almost apologetically, Mike told Hank he could ride the bike if he felt like it. Nobody could hurt a Harley Davidson, he said.

Hank said, "I was looking at this here doohickey, a-gettin' a fix on its purpose, and I see there's one of these what you call suicide gears—"

"—shifters," Mike said. "You're right. It's called a suicide clutch because you got to let go with one hand to shift while you're squeezing with the other. No brake, no gas."

"Sounds like a fella's got his job cut out," Hank said, winking to the other cowboy standing beside the car.

"You get used to it like anything else," Mike said. "I'm serious, if you want to ride it, just take it out." Mike said he'd be honored, but Hank waved his hand, shaking his head a little.

"I'm just killin' time on solid ground," Hank said, "partakin' 'til they're ready for us inside . . ." He said the last time he was on a motor*sackle* it had tried to get out from under him. "Just like a lot of gals I know," he said, and Mike laughed. Hank said, "You bein' one of these Harley fellas, you know that notion of goin' over the side of the road." He reached up his hand and made a fish-tailing motion. "Creepin' away from the road," he said.

"Going to the high side," Mike said. "A bike'll do that on a winding road or a curve in the highway."

"You're right about that highway," Hank said. "I don't recollect the particular road, but seems to me there was some pitch in it like an old road, sunken down in the middle, and the hind end of the motorsackle was a slidin' uphill of it."

"Going to the high side," Mike said again.

"That's just what she did," Hank continued. He moved the top of the sack away from the mouth of the bottle and drank from it, then looked at me and asked Mike, "This here your brother? You California fellas just all this naturally good-lookin'?" Hank switched hands with the paper sack and reached out to shake my hand. He said, "I'm called Hank."

I remember his handshake as if it were yesterday. A lot of people have joked around, saying, "Let me shake the hand that shook Hank Williams'," but it was really a funny feeling. His hand felt like bones, long and sinewy, and hard as though made of something other than skin. And icy, as if he didn't have any blood in his veins. I was reminded of touching my dead grandmother, the first dead person I ever touched. I was in the slumber chamber with my mom, seeing my grandmother laid out, and we talked about how her skin felt, and what the undertakers had done to get her looking as good as she did, and what they'd done to Jean Harlow with some kind of rubber tube or siphon device.

After shaking my hand, Hank stepped back like he was about to fall, then leaned towards Mike's bike, grabbing the seat to balance himself. "You don't mind if I sit on your saddle?" he asked Mike. Hiking a leg up and over, he eased onto the bike, his knees jutting out to the sides like a wishbone. Mike monkeyed with the headlight and ignition, saying he'd kick it over if Hank wanted to rev it a little, which seemed like a good idea. In a second the ignition was on. Mike turned down the pedal on the kick starter, then pushed down hard with his boot and the engine fired up. Hank laughed, nodding, but looked scared, and his teeth were very yellow. Mike twisted the grip a couple of times, stirring up some backfires, then killed it because Hank seemed too nervous and the other cowboy looked about ready to shut it off himself. "Bet she'll rip," Hank said. "Is she fast?"

Mike grinned. "Drives the cops nuts . . . But like I said, on the open road it can get a little spooky."

"Like knocking some gal up," Hank said. He glanced at the cowboy and said something, and the cowboy said he didn't know for sure if Hank had done it, and Hank said, "Oh, like shit it wasn't!" He'd handed the sack to Mike, and was straddling the bike with both hands on the grips. "This boy's right," he said. "This goin' to the high side's the way of puttin' it that makes it understandable." He said to Mike, "Talkin' about headin' for trouble . . ."

He gestured to pass the bottle along, and I took a gulp. It was Johnny Walker Red and I gasped. When Hank tipped it back, he seemed to just pour it down into himself as if swallowing water. Then he got off the bike, tilted closer to the car fender and said the cowboy was "Roy Rogers—here to make a motion picture movie about the pitiful side of life."

The cowboy said, "I'm not Roy Rogers, but if the law comes through here they're gonna be doin' some Roy Rodger'n with us lickerin' up juveniles."

Hank feigned a shocked look. "Are y'all juveniles?" he asked. We shook our heads, and Hank said, "Better finish what we're doin' before the law does get here." Then he asked, "What time *do* they get here?"

"The bewitchin' hour," the cowboy said, shaking his head. Hank offered the sack to Mike, who said no thanks and passed the bottle back to me. I drank as Hank watched me with a curious smile. He said I had a "yearnin' look" and looked like I was goin' through life sideways . . . like seein' what he's maybe leavin' behind . . ." Barry wanted to take some pictures and Hank said he didn't mind, so Barry snapped off some shots with his new flashbulb attachment. I handed the bottle back to Hank, who shook it and said it felt like "half a pint," and then drank it straight down. There was a trickling sound, and I thought the liquor was leaking out of the sack. But it was Hank pissing in his pants as he drank. The urine trickled through his trouser leg to form a puddle around his double-eagle boots. Hank apparently didn't notice it, though he straightened up from the fender. When he saw the puddle at his feet, he said, "Well, sonova*bitch!*" and spat down at the ground. The cowboy brought a small suitcase from the car and said something to Hank about changing his pants. Then Hank started to laugh. It was a hee-hawing sound like a donkey, and he rubbed his forehead hard with the fingers of both hands. He looked like a zombie.

Two other men had come out of the Rancho, one I recognized from the Caravan band. They looked at Hank disgustedly and at us, and one said they were set up inside. The Roy Rogers one said, "He doesn't do this as a rule, you understand . . ."

"It ain't their fault," Hank said. "Go on in and I'm comin' in." The men turned back to the Rancho as Hank climbed into the Packard to change his pants. "Now I 'spose I'm ready," he said, and as he climbed out and came forward he put his hand on my shoulder. We walked to the side of the Rancho with his hand placed there as though on a stick or a rudder. When we got to the door, he said, "You boys come in with us and enjoy the show." Then he said something like, "Any man that's been sharin' don't need a breach in companions . . ." He turned his head to Mike, who was right behind us. Hank's neck looked skinny, the collar sticking away from his skin when he moved his head. Caught between the dark of the parking lot and the bright lights of the ballroom, He looked very tall and wide, like a cut-out figure or a flat cowboy suit with wide padded shoulders hung out on a stiff clothes hanger. He said to Mike, "Some time, son, we're gonna take one of those rides."

"I'll ride you up the grapevine," Mike said eagerly. "A person can have a swell time heading up the mountains. Hell, it'll haul ass to Vegas quicker'n a car."

Hank asked the cowboy, "We been to Nevada?" but before he was answered, he said to Mike, "It's dark here as I reckon it gets there . . . They all run into one another, even for a natural-born traveling man I'd be all busted up come down on the side of night."

We followed Hank and the cowboy through the side door into a sort of atrium and past a stone wishing well and fireplace. Straight ahead through the big doors was the dance floor, the ballroom and the stairs to the second-floor bar.

Up on the Rancho's small stage, Hank and the Drifting Cowboys punched right into the music. It was the first time I'd heard "I'll Never Get Out of This World Alive," and Hank sang it twice. Where he sang, "No matter how I struggle and strive," on the last part of "strive," his upper teeth and lower lip pulled the word out. The last sound to it, the "v-e," sort of caught and hung vibrating even while he'd gone on with "I'll never get out of this world alive."

Less than eight months later he'd be dead, keeled over in the back seat of his Cadillac convertible on the way to a big show in Canton. The driver kept going in the middle of the night, thinking maybe Hank was dead but unsure of what to do if he was, and knowing he'd get yelled at if he tried to wake him and he *wasn't* dead.

The cream of Nashville's music had the best seats at Hank's funeral, including those who'd fired him from the Grand Old Opry not long after I'd seen him there. More than ten thousand people pressed at their backs to get a glimpse of Hank in the coffin. He didn't look too bad. World-renowned music-maker Roy Acuff came out on stage unsteady from a little too much "nippin'" in the back. Hank's coffin was in the orchestra pit, and when the service was finished, Acuff said to a friend, "If Hank could see us now, he'd say 'I told you so. I said I could draw a bigger crowd dead than all of you alive.'"

Hank had been dead about three years when I ran into Tex Williams eating pancakes in the Mayflower Coffee Shop on Hollywood Boulevard. I'd seen him a couple of times at Republic Studios when I'd been on movie interviews, but he'd never had time to talk about Hank. Tex asked me to join him in the Mayflower, and after some talk about my father and the Hollywood Masonic Lodge, I brought up Hank's aborted movie career. He had signed a contract to make pictures, then just turned his back on it. Slim Whitman once told me, "Oh, Hank forgot about it. He couldn't remember he'd done it, because he wasn't sober when he'd signed for all that money."

Hank's movie stardom was tossed out before it began. Tex said, "It could've taken place, by god—not like John Wayne or Tex Ritter, but he could've done better than Bob Wills, who wanted to be a movie star more than anything. Like Gene Autry did. Bob thinks of himself that way, and he's told me as much. Hank never said a thing about movies, because he didn't care about 'em."

Tex pointed to a sign on the coffee-shop wall, the Optimist's Creed: "As you ramble on through life brother/whatever be your goal/keep your eye upon the doughnut/and not upon the hole." For Hank, "Life was the hole," Tex said. "He lived in life's hole and never got out. Even though he had fame by the tail and could've pulled himself through like you'd use a rope to get out of any hole, he couldn't hold it. He took fame down in the hole with him." Tex said that Hank had liked him, that they'd appreciated one another. "But we never did have a close affiliation outside of music. I don't know if anybody did or could have, because Hank was all alone. He had a streak like one of those characters chasing a carrot that's hung on a stick attached to his head. Spade Cooley was no different, except for his ability to trick people, and he was crazy to be top man on the hill so he never got stuck in a hole. Spade was chasing carrots front *and* hind end, and that divides a person." Hank didn't want to settle for a good-sized hunk of the dough-nut, as Tex had done. "Hank was a divided fellow," Tex said, "and lacked Spade's sense of trickery. Couldn't play both ends." Spade want-ed the whole doughnut, Tex told me, while Hank saw only the hole. It was Hank's outstanding talent as an artist that kept him alive as long as he lasted. "There was nothing," Tex said, "to be improved upon. The boy's life burned up fast."

Tex looked at me across the table and, almost mysteriously, said, "Hank's existence was misery and sadness. He lives on in people's insides, a real disturbance in other people's souls . . ."

CONFESSIONS OF AN L.A. SON

"I'VE HAD MY COCK SUCKED BY FIVE of the big names in Hollywood," James Dean said to me one night on the set of *Rebel Without a Cause*. "I think it's pretty funny. I wanted more than anything to just get some little part, something to do, and they'd invite me for fancy dinners overlooking the blue Pacific, and we'd have a few drinks, and how long could it go on? That's what I wanted to know. The answer was it could go on until there was nothing left, until they had what they wanted and there was nothing left . . ."

"So I decided," he said, with a Brando-like droop of his head, "they'd had all they were going to get except this—" he suddenly thrust his hand with the middle finger straight as a bolt. "Now," he said, "I've got them by the fucking balls."

Natalie Wood, also starring in *Rebel Without a Cause*, later told me the important thing was to make as much money as possible and never turn anything down that offered maximum exposure. "To avoid getting into trouble like Jimmy's doing," she said, "you have to control how you live, and you can't rock the boat. I like to think I've been a success in Hollywood and control the way I live." But Natalie's questionable early death would seem to suggest that she did not work the plan to perfection.

Jimmy had once reached down and put his hand under the front of Natalie's skirt. She jerked up because he pinched her bare thigh and said, "Damnit! I asked you not to pinch me like that."

I first met Natalie almost three years before *Rebel* was filmed. Jimmy had already left Hollywood for New York, sick of the "revolving meat rack," as he called it, where "every time you turn your head, someone's going for your prick."

Film director Irving Rapper, who'd made some classic American movies such as *Now Voyager, Born Bad*, and *The Corn is Green*, interviewed me for a film he was doing at Columbia. I was still in Hollywood High, almost six feet tall and "an outstanding juvenile," Rapper told my agent, Wynn Rocoamora. Rapper had other projects he said he wanted to discuss and suggested a "lunch interview" in Beverly Hills. Carol Burnett, who edited the Hollywood High newspaper, told me I was "really lucky" to have someone as important as Rapper taking an interest in me. She suggested I "bend over backwards" to get into his good graces, and I told Carol I'd do that but that I was a little worried about having to bend over frontwards.

The director called to cancel the meeting due to a story conference, but asked if I could have dinner at his house in Malibu. When I told Carol, she said, "If you don't go—*I'll go!*"

I eagerly accepted the director's invitation, and we dined on the terrace "overlooking the blue Pacific," as Jimmy later described it. A black servant in a white waistcoat served drinks and food on silver platters. Shortly, the servant left, and while Rapper smoked a foul-smelling cigar and talked on the telephone, I sat drinking cognac.

Finished temporarily with the phone, Rapper sat across from me so close our knees were almost touching. He stared intently and said, "People must fall in love with you all the time . . . What do you do about it?" I said I didn't know about people falling in love with me. He wanted to know if the idea of *men* falling in love with me made me uncomfortable, and I said it did. "Do you suppose it is possible for a man to fall in love with you immediately?" he asked. I said I didn't know. "If a man did fall in love with you, what would you do about it?" he continued, drinking quickly, sloppily, his eyes blurry. His mouth was thick and stained brown from the cigar. "What if *I* was in love with you?" he asked. I tried pushing the subject in another direction by talking about my girlfriend Sherry, whose father was Gene Autry's cameraman,

31

but Irving had fallen from the chair and on to the floor in front of the couch, his hands on my legs. I recall my first thought was to shove him away, until I noticed a glass table to one side and imagined him cracking his head. I got up and excused myself as he grew pale and worried. I was welcome to stay the night, he said, regaining his dignity despite the amount he'd drunk. The sheets were silk, and I could bathe in a marble tub with honey added to the water "for the skin . . ."

Saying no thanks to the bath and bed caused problems about my part in the picture. Rapper said I was too tall and outstanding-looking for the juvenile role. He was thinking of cutting it from the script unless someone convinced him to keep it in.

He later told my agent I should look more seriously into seeing Irving Rapper when I'd "matured somewhat more." He said my understanding of "Hollywood etiquette" was "detrimentally amiss."

My second manager was Natalie Wood's agent, Henry Willson, though she fared better with him than I did. He was handling Tab Hunter, Robert Wagner, Rock Hudson, Race Gentry, Rory Calhoun and several handfuls that he used as birdseed for the bigwig homosexual producers and casting agents, who were in the majority in that occupation.

While he was finishing *Rebel Without a Cause*, Jimmy and I compared names—a kind of joke we made up; hotshots who had put the make on us. Apart from Irving Rapper, we'd known one other producer in common, a guy who bounced around Hollywood and Palm Springs and Bel-Air. He did mostly television, and became associated with Ida Lupino and Howard Duff's show, and knew Tex and Dallas Williams from the Bel-Air Country Club and Republic Pictures, but our paths never crossed on that side of the fence. He'd made promises but did almost nothing for those "special ones" that put their trust in him. He bought them bottles of inexpensive cologne called Florida Water, a cheap imitation of the Jean Marie Farina he used lavishly. The young guys he didn't buy the cologne for, he turned toward the supply depot— the "revolving meat rack"—passing them from associate to would-be associate, starting with someone down the line, maybe an assistant producer or casting director, then winding up with a makeup man or someone fixing dresses. With dreams of fame, still chasing a career in Hollywood, many landed in the line of hopeful extras at the corner of Western and Hollywood Boulevard, and when that door shut, so went the dreams.

Not so in my case—born in Unit One, L.A. County General Hospital and raised in Hollywood, this was *home* to me. I'd acted as a child on radio and in movies, and later in television. My mother had been under contract to MGM as an actress, and my grandfather on my father's side was a carpenter for RKO Radio Pictures.

Doc Burkhardt, an old movie wrangler for Monogram Pictures before it became Republic, owned a dude ranch in the mountains north of Ojai. As a kid I spent summers there, and when Doc sold the ranch to movie star Rory Calhoun, I started working on the property as a hired hand, tending horses and wrangling when needed. "Diablo" was a crazy horse that belonged to Rory and was passed to me for special attention. Rory would visit occasionally, to swim in the pool or try to ride Diablo, who usually threw him off. The actor stayed for a week once, having brought Charlie Stoker, an LAPD cop famous for the prostitution busts of Brenda Allen and for contacts to Bugsy Siegel's pals in Beverly Hills. Stoker, who knew my father from the department, had just written a book, *Thicker'n Thieves*, an exposé on payola and prostitution in Hollywood and on Mayor Fletcher Bowron's questionable administration. Charlie Stoker was a hotshot and taught me to use a black-snake bullwhip so I could pare down a cigarette from someone's mouth.

Rory later turned publicly homosexual, but in those days he was married to Lita Castro, daughter of old Joe Castro of Ojai, who raised horses. Lita was singing under the name Lita Baron, and while I was working for Rory I fell in love with her younger sister, Marilyn Castro. I'd race an old Buick convertible back and forth between the ranch and Ojai, panting after her, and we'd go bowling in town or neck in the car. Sometimes she'd come up to the ranch and we'd sit on the verandah in a swing, eating green grapes off the arbor and passing the juice of the grapes from her mouth to mine and mine to hers.

Big sister Lita wanted to act, too, but played out most of her dramas in fights with Rory, throwing pots and pans and once even chasing him with a shovel, swinging it with enough force to kill a mule.

Henry Willson was Rory's agent, and I met him through Rory by chance in Ventura. Henry became my agent and told Rory, "The kid's a natural. He'll be working all the time. The important thing's to keep him suntanned, get him a contract and keep him stabled for a few years, then let him bust the town's seams as the next Robert Taylor or a young Gary Cooper . . ."

The first time Henry took me to his house in Bel-Air several people were there, including Rory and a woman screenwriter from Paramount. Henry sat me in his den to pore over scrapbooks he'd made of stars like Rory and Guy Madison, Rock Hudson and Tab Hunter, even showing me a picture of Guy Madison lying on a lawn somewhere without any clothes on. Henry said, "You see, that's a rotten shot of Guy. He looks like a dead Jap. But there's no reason you can't look as good as Guy when you get your teeth fixed." I asked him what was wrong with my teeth. He said, "They're too small, kid. You can't have small teeth and smile successfully. And there's something about your eyes—they're too far in, but there's really nothing to be done about that." He said they'd have to use a key light, a tiny spot that lit areas the larger lights tended to shadow. Henry said, "You should feel proud. If you have to use a key light on someone, you're talking about a special quality."

He sent me to Silverwoods on Wilshire to buy new clothes on his charge account that weren't "so damned baggy and horse looking." He said, "You don't want to go around like one of these New York characters." Then, with new loafers, a crew cut, a navy blazer and charcoal slacks, I began making the rounds of the studios.

"You're going to be a star," Henry told me. "It don't matter what the fuck anyone says about a star, even if they say you're a fucking asshole, a son of a bitch, it doesn't mean shit. A star's a star. A star's born a goddamn star, and it's like being born with green eyes or big feet. It's something you're born with, and only the one that's got it can take it away. I'm talking about drinking bad and being reckless and, especially, taking dope or eating your ass off and getting fat as shit. Even then, you're still a star, but it's all covered up. Sometimes you can still get it back, like putting something back in shape that's busted apart, and sometimes you can't put it back together and it's gone forever, though inside you're still a star. A true God-given gift that the receiver ruins by his own hand."

The woman screenwriter took me to lunch at the Polo Lounge of the Beverly Hills Hotel and convinced me Henry would land me a contract. She said, "More than likely at Universal, where his influence is terribly strong." The woman was staying in one of the bungalows. Paramount was paying for it, she said, inviting me to make myself at home while she made a number of phone calls. Instantly, she began massaging my neck with one hand, holding the phone with the other.

She rubbed my shoulder and chest, then put her hand inside my shirt and began feeling my stomach. When she hung up she kissed my neck and cheeks and asked if I'd like to get into bed. She did not take off her stockings, but put on a kind of Hawaiian sarong that opened up when she lay back on the bed, her upper body sinking into a mountain of pillows. She spread something like carbolated Vaseline on my cock and pushed some into her vagina. She had shaved herself with a razor, and said she used a small electric razor to keep the stubble from snagging her panties.

The only real sex experience I'd had with a girl was with singer Kate Starr's niece. But I'd gotten sort of scared in the middle of it and pulled out of her, then we'd turned around head to feet and kissed each other between the legs.

The woman screenwriter wanted me to put it in all the way and not move, just lay still on top of her while she did the moving from underneath. She made sounds in her throat like a bird—trilling and cooing in short gasps.

Another night we had dinner at LaRue's with some New York people, and then went to Mocambo to meet Henry Willson, but instead we were joined by Eddie Bracken and his wife, and the fan magazine writer Beverly Linet, also from New York. Later, we went upstairs to the Crescendo to sit at the piano bar, and a leading circus impresario from Ringling Brothers joined us. He bought rounds of gin and tonics and placed his hand on my leg under the table. I politely shifted position and withdrew my leg from the man's reach. A moment later, the woman screenwriter stared at him and said, "Jonathan is a promising young performer, John dear, but right now he is only a teenager."

One of Henry Willson's few adolescent clients was Natalie, even younger than I. He saw in the two of us "something special"—that is, money in the bank. Henry had paired Natalie and me as a "sweetheart duo," keeping Natalie in the news and waiting to spring me as his "new discovery." Natalie and I went to the movies together and had malts at a little Hollywood ice cream parlor—one malt, two straws. We attended a premier at the Egyptian Theater, then shared a hot fudge sundae at the tiny Pantages soda fountain, gazing puppy-like into one another's eyes. We went to the beach—with a chaperone—and watched Peter Lawford prance about playing volleyball with the gay actors, or actor Richard Jaeckel flexing his pecs at Muscle Beach.

Phyllis, Henry's confidential secretary, set up a date for us to be whisked away to the Santa Monica Pier. It's where Natalie would make *Inside Daisy Clover* years later, long after she'd dumped Henry Willson as her agent.

Some things about Henry were all right, even though he was a regular joke behind the scenes. His clients, they said, were "gorgeous" mannequins lacking personality, will, wit and even restraint, let alone talent. Henry said, "They say what they want—they're nothing but dumb fucks without any brains." The money Rock Hudson was making was no laughing matter, Henry assured me, and in time, when I "grew up," I'd be making as much as "solid as a rock" Hudson.

But first there were other considerations. One night Henry asked me to his Bel-Air house to look over photographs of Natalie and myself on one of our sweetheart dates. He told me to make myself a drink, then called me into another other room where I found him laying naked on a little towel. He looked like a skinned seal and wanted me to rub Johnson's Baby Oil on his fat body. His stomach was bigger around than any other part of him, and his legs looked short and bent. His face was red and swollen with booze. I was reluctant to even touch him, and he said, "What's the matter? You don't get excited by a naked man?" I said no, I wasn't excited and I didn't think I could get excited even if I tried to talk myself into it. Henry sat up. "Well, you can't talk yourself into it . . ." he said. "You *can* jack me off as a favor to me. You can put some oil on your hand and jack me off." I said no. His cock was small and he couldn't get himself hard. He said it was because he'd had too much gin. He sat there pulling on himself like a monkey.

I didn't want to offend him or make him feel worse, because it was obvious he'd been humiliated, and I looked away as he pulled the corner of the towel over his crotch. "You know what your trouble is?" he said. "You're not gay. You're not gay, and that presents a whole bunch of problems. I don't want to push myself on you, and if you're not attracted to me there's nothing you or me can do about it."

But, he said, he was not a "queer" who got his kicks by just going down on some straight guy that didn't give a shit for him. "So you see where this leaves us," he said. "Tab and Rock and Guy and R.J. Wagner have cared for me personally, you understand? You see where it's led them." He said, "I mean, it makes for a difficult relationship because of my being attracted to you. It may be possible to keep this on a strictly professional level, but that's not my way of doing things . . ."

I went on one last interview at MGM that Henry set up, and was invited onto the set of a picture. I saw the actor John Hodiak talking to some people, and I hung around, listening to them. I admired Hodiak, and actors like Robert Ryan and Sterling Hayden. After watching several takes, I went for my interview.

The casting director said he hated Henry Willson and made me feel ashamed that I was there as one of Henry's clients, especially since the guy had "heard" my mother's name in the past—a connection with Howard Hughes and Mervyn Leroy, and he knew she'd been under contract to the studio. He asked me if she had been able to "get the best of what seemed a drinking problem." I said that she liked to drink but to my knowledge didn't have a problem with it. He said that wasn't what he understood, and then, sort of laughing about Henry, said it was best if he didn't memorize my name since Willson would no doubt change it to "Flash Light" or "Jack Spratt" or some other silly invention.

After the interview I was heading out of the building when I saw John Hodiak at the end of a hallway, talking on a pay telephone. He was hanging up as I approached, and smiled, nodding hello. I stopped and said how much I appreciated the movies he'd made, and told him I admired his work and was a genuine "John Hodiak fan." He laughed when I said he was one of my favorite actors and that I'd learned a great deal from his performances. He said, "Even when it was a poor excuse for a picture?" I said sure, even in something like *Desert Fury*, which he'd made with Liz Scott and Mary Astor; I said I loved the picture. Hodiak shook his head, smiling, and I went on to say that as a young actor I could only dream about a role such as he'd played in *Lifeboat* with Tallulah Bankhead and William Bendix. Hodiak said, "Those parts come once in an actor's life, if he's lucky. But you've got to look for the silver lining."

Surprisingly, he seemed embarrassed by my admiration. As if trying to shift the attention from himself, he asked if I was working on the lot. I said I'd been on a interview, and told him about the experience.

When I got around to mentioning my mother, Hodiak apologized and said he wasn't familiar with her name, but since she'd known Hughes and Jean Harlow and had been a player at Metro, it was entirely possible that he at least knew some people who did know her.

Hodiak expressed some annoyance with Henry Willson's reputation, and with all "those people" who allow their private lives to get mixed up with their professional business. "The result can be a very negative view of the real nine-to-five movie world," he said. All I wanted was to work, I told him. He said if I had trouble getting a decent agent to call him at the studio, and he scribbled down the phone number for the production company.

I thanked him, and he said very emphatically, and surprisingly to me, that it was very important that I didn't allow negative feelings "to align with honest ambitions."

I felt impressed, flattered and on "cloud nine" thanks to Hodiak's interest, but soon wondered if he'd really been concerned about my plight, or just caught a little off-guard by my frank admiration. Maybe he was just a nice guy to his fans, even a little uneasy with the praise. He'd been married to Ann Baxter for a few years, and I was told they had been having problems and were separated. Hodiak had come back from New York, where he'd done a Broadway play that had folded in less than a month. He was involved in another Indian-ambush movie, but was talking about forming a production company to "get at something serious," just as his friend Ida Lupino, movie star, director and writer, had done earlier.

I quickly set out to test Hodiak's sincerity and called the company several times over the next couple of weeks. After leaving a number of messages, I did not think I'd hear from him, but one afternoon a secretary was on the line, inviting me to Hodiak's on Doheny for an informal smorgasbord the following Saturday. She told me an agent would be there that Hodiak wanted me to meet.

I showed up at Hodiak's apartment in a blue blazer, charcoal slacks and black loafers. A number of people were already there, including Ida Lupino and the agent John Darrow. Hodiak introduced me as "a talented young man in search of sound advice." Darrow had been an actor years before he'd turned agent. He'd worked at MGM and said he remembered my mother's red hair. "In fact," he said, "that wasn't her natural hair color." I said he was right. She'd been a blonde, but when she went under the contract-players arrangement, MGM suggested she change her hair to red. Darrow mentioned that she knew Jean Harlow and that he'd seen them together once or twice. I told him that, according to my mother they'd been "drinking pals." Darrow said, "Now I got it," and raised his scotch and water, rattling the ice cubes.

Darrow had starred in Howard Hughes' *Wings*, with Richard Arlen, which went on to win the first Academy Award for Best Picture. *Avalanche* was another movie Darrow made at Paramount, with Jack

Holt, and he'd been friends with Dolores Del Rio and Mervyn LeRoy. Not tall, but masculine and rugged, Darrow had short, whitish hair and a round, well-tanned face. He wore a black silk blazer and white trousers.

Hodiak said to me, "I was wearing white pants when John showed up, but I didn't want people thinking we're a bunch of medical interns."

Darrow was accompanied by a young actress named Elaine Stewart. Tall, dark-haired and well-built, Elaine was appearing in MGM's *The Bad and the Beautiful* as a bit player who shacks up with Kirk Douglas. Elaine had a soft, hazy quality—it was almost as though you were seeing her through a filter—and she seemed uncomfortable at Hodiak's get-together.

I told Darrow I was represented by Henry Willson, but that I was serious about acting, like Hodiak, and felt any connection with Willson was misrepresenting my purposes. "Plus the fact," Darrow said, "you've got to be romancing with Henry before he puts you to work." He asked me "quite confidentially" if I'd gone to bed with Henry, and I said no, I hadn't. Darrow grinned. "I believe you," he said, "or you wouldn't be talking to me."

There were a dozen or so people down in the courtyard of the two-story apartment building—another party taking place in the next-door apartment. Hodiak asked me if I'd ever met Marilyn Monroe, and I said no. He motioned me to the edge of his terrace and leaned forward on the rail. The sun was very bright, and one heavy-set young guy in the middle of the group was pulling his pants legs up and showing his socks or legs to others who were laughing.

"Hello, gorgeous!" John called down.

The blonde in the midst of them was laughing and looked up into the sun, waving. "Hi, John!" she said. Her teeth were sparkling and some saliva trailing between them caught the light and glittered. "Come on down!" she said. She named someone and said it was his birthday.

"I've got my own party going," John said. "Come on up!"

She said she was waiting for some more people. Her hair was almost white in the sunlight, and I couldn't see her eyes behind the big sun glasses. She looked small, her legs slim in the skin-tight white pants, and she wore high red heels with open toes. I remember the red polish on her toenails, and her feet and ankles looked white, as though they hadn't been exposed to much sun. John introduced me, saying, "This is Jonathan. He's a young actor friend of mine."

I said hello to Marilyn, and she said, "Hello! Bring your friend John Hodiak down and join the party." She said her party was better than the one we were having.

Hodiak said, "Different, honey. Different's the word."

"Oh, come on, John," Marilyn said, and something like, "They're all the same, aren't they?" She was laughing again, and he pointed at her, wagging his finger.

Hodiak said to me, "If you were a new sailor on board and I was going to advise you, I'd say here's these ropes and here's what they're for, and I'm not going to steer you to the wrong rope because we're all on the same ship. What you handle is going to affect what I'm doing." He asked me if I had "inclinations," if I was interested in other guys, and I said I wasn't. In fact, I told him, I'd gone briefly with Darrow's niece, Madelyn, as well as her sister, back in high school. I said I liked girls, and that I was straight, but kept getting in situations where guys were trying to get me into the sack. John asked if I'd been involved in any situations with any of these people, and I said at times I had because I couldn't seem to get around it without upsetting the people or putting them on the wrong side.

He asked, "But you haven't been active in these situations? That's what you're trying to say?" I said I hadn't. "You've never initiated the situations?" he asked, and I said that was right. He asked me, "How do you feel about these things?"

I was thinking about Irving Rapper, and I said I was uncomfortable with them. I said I'd left my father's house in Burbank because of the same problem with my stepbrother—a situation that had lasted until I was sixteen. I hadn't been able to say no. Everything was going wrong, and when I tried to talk to my father about it (my stepbrother was his second wife's son), I found myself in trouble with all of them. I just kept getting labeled as the black sheep, and I couldn't get the truth out. Unable to deal with it any more, I had packed my clothes and moved to Hollywood. I took up living with my mother, which I'd never done except for a couple of years on an every-other-weekend arrangement. They had split up when I was a baby, leaving me with my grandmother until I was around eleven. I told Hodiak I'd been an altar boy and acolyte in the church.

"Since you've been back in Hollywood," John asked, "is when these propositions have been cropping up?" Sort of, I said, but they'd been there before, and since I started going for movie interviews and seeing people in the business, even more so. Hodiak wanted to know how I felt about it, and I said I was bothered, that it wasn't right, and that I kept feeling it was some sort of invasion of me. Yet, at the same time, I wondered whether I had a right to bitch about it.

Hodiak said, "Sure you have a right to bitch about it, and I must warn you—or just pass it along—that it's possible such a situation as you've brought up could present itself between you and Darrow, if you understand what I'm saying." I said I understood. He said it would have nothing to do with the business—nothing to do with anything apart from a "social exchange," he said, but that it was nothing I had to do. I could say no anytime. He said John Darrow was a super guy, but that he had "his problems just like everybody else in this screwy town."

I found myself sitting with Elaine Stewart, and we didn't say anything—just sat there in Hodiak's apartment looking at one another until I started talking to Ida Lupino, who lit a cigarette for me by popping the match on the underside of the chair arm.

Despite Hodiak's warning, I didn't say "no" to Darrow. He sort of took up the slack in my life left by my father—still so distant to me, so emotionally unavailable. Darrow believed I was "some kind of protégé" and called me "kiddy car," because I was younger than his other clients who he also gave nicknames. One actress was "Miss Pussy Willow," and Scott Brady—Gene and Lawrence Tierney's younger brother—was "Slugger," not because he was tough and a drunk like his brother, whom Darrow admired, but "because Scott's a cream puff in the hay," Darrow said. "If he isn't nice, I give him a little spanking . . ."

He was handling the celebrated bodybuilder Steve Reeves—Mr. World and Mr. Universe—whom Darrow called "Miss Peter." He attributed this nickname to "Reeves' weenie—as soon as something squirts, Miss Peter runs downstairs to the refrigerator to drink all the fucking milk and suck up a few raw eggs to get back the proteins he thinks he's lost by shooting his little waddie."

He told me Van Johnson, another of my favorite movie stars, "squeals like a girl when he takes it up the rump." Johnson had lubricated himself in the bathroom one night without the light on, and picked up a toothpaste tube instead of the K-Y. The tubes felt the same, but the toothpaste was Ruby Red, an English brand, and the sheets and Johnson's ass were soon smeared blood red. In horror and panic, Johnson almost rushed himself to the emergency hospital, but then backed out fast, ashamed and red-faced.

I'd wonder why Darrow would tell me these stories about his clients and friends. He'd desperately wanted to be a star but hadn't made it, and instead made a great deal of money in real estate and the talent business.

Gwen Verdon, the dancer, was one of Darrow's prizes because she'd conquered polio to become a Broadway star. It was her will and determination, he said, that had boosted her from being a cripple, put her head and shoulders above the rest. Then he told me the secret: *The Power of Positive Thinking*. It was the link between Darrow and Hodiak. "Seek ye first the Kingdom of Heaven within yourself, and all shall be added unto you . . ." That's why Gwen Verdon was a star, the same way I'd realize my potential—becoming a star, bringing forth into the world that which was inside of me. Only through the "positive over-coming of the negative forces" could true power flow. Yet we'd drink—hours of bourbon poured into coffee while Darrow confided these awful stories about others that seemed thoroughly contemptuous of them, and were confusing to me.

The Darrow Agency on Sunset Strip was opposite the Darrow Development Corporation, an expansive reach into Westwood and Malibu Colony real estate including, he said, the property Lana Turner was "squatting on." He owned the Westwood apartment house where he lived, and where we drank, and where he'd show me compromising pictures of famous stars. He owned an apartment complex of several units on the beach above Malibu Colony Liquors—which he also owned—and occupied one of these on weekends.

Drinking wasn't new to me and I drank with the best of them, including Errol Flynn a couple of years later, and even Lawrence Tierney. My connection to Flynn came through the ever-present weekend guests at Darrow's in Malibu. When I was sixteen I was already having gin and tonics at Mocambo and Ciro's and the Trocadaro, and because of the people I was drinking with, I was rarely asked about my age. I was never sober when Darrow would go down on me or maybe stick his tongue up my ass, which was the extent of our physical relationship. Many times he'd be too drunk himself, and pass out. But for me, there was more to the friendship; the sex aspect was like a token of gratitude because it pleased Darrow, or so he said. There were times when it didn't even seem to me to be so much physical as as a sort of innocuous civil obligation.

One time, heading to Malibu in his Cadillac, we'd turned off Sunset onto Pacific Coast Highway as the sun was setting red and brilliant over the ocean, and Darrow reached down and took my hand and simply held it. There was nothing sexual in it, and a warmth sort of radiated through me. I felt almost a kind of love—secure and safe, as though my father had taken my hand, which he never had.

I kept calling Hodiak or showing up on his doorstep. He said he never minded my calls and I could come by whenever I wanted. He had become my mentor. I admired him greatly and listened carefully to his searching talks about the power of positive thinking. He said that negative floods were encountered whenever the door was opened to greatness, or when you were swept into situations like my own. Or like *his* situations: the marriage to Ann Baxter, the divorce, the lack of work, the lack of appreciation in general from Hollywood, due to its fear of superior talent—like that of Robert Ryan, or Sterling Hayden, or John Hodiak. Rebel talent. Despite everything, there was a power greater than the "undertow," as Hodiak called the ever-present negative forces that sought to suck one down. The pit was, first, shame, and then came the worst: to be forgotten. "Not me," he said. "Never me . . . I'll wage the war until I die." Smiling, he said, "There is a good life in Hollywood. There can be a good life here."

But I didn't want to be the pretty-boy stooge next-door with a tennis racket, no matter how Humphrey Bogart had made the grade. I didn't want to have bigger teeth or "flatter eyes." I wanted roles like Montgomery Clift's in *Red River*. Darrow told me everyone said I was too young and too difficult to cast, but that everyone wanted to go to bed with me.

Hodiak asked if Darrow had made a play on me. I said I hung around the beach place and that in town we'd gone to lunch a few times, but so far the relationship was fairly professional. I don't think Hodiak believed me, but I couldn't tell him the truth. I did say that something had occurred between a young actress and myself one weekend evening when Darrow had driven Scott Brady into Santa Monica for his car. He asked me if we'd made love, and I said, "Well, sort of," and he laughed. I didn't explain what had happened between us, how she and I were lounging around on the big corner studio bed in our bathing suits, drinking next to the fireplace, and how the actress kept looking at me in a funny way. The usual group had been playing cards all afternoon, this time with Nora Eddington Flynn, broken up with Errol Flynn, and Kurt Kazner, an occupant of one of Darrow's apartments in the same building. Everyone had been drinking since late that morning. The actress and I hardly ever talked. We'd sit around and look at each other, or she'd read or lay in the sun on the terrace over the water. She was there almost every weekend, though she didn't stay over as I did.

She kept looking at my stomach and rubbing at her own stomach in the two-piece suit, putting her finger into her belly button, and asking me if I'd had my tonsils out or other operations. I'd had my tonsils out, I told her, but no other operations. She asked, "Weren't you circumcised?" I said yes. "Well, that's an operation," she said. We were listening to a reel-to-reel of a Broadway show, and at one point she raised her bare foot to my shoulder and pushed me off the bed. "Did I hurt you?" she asked. I said no, holding her ankle. I moved her leg so I could get back on the edge of the bed and she said, "I have pretty feet . . . I really like my feet." I said they were pretty. "Do you want to kiss them?" she asked. I caressed her feet and then bent over and kissed them. She let me kiss her legs and her upper thighs, and then she pulled off her bathing-suit bottom and told me exactly where to kiss her between her legs, and where to put my tongue and what to do with it. She kept talking all the while I did it, and kept telling me to take my time. "Do it slow. Don't rush . . ." she said. "They won't be back for another hour . . ."

After that, we were like strangers again. She became "Miss Pussy Willow" once more, which is what Darrow called her because, he said, "her snatch is made of wood. It isn't real. She isn't real." She was a "knock-on-wood-virgin," he said. "When she gets married it'll be to the Wizard of Oz, or maybe a Pasadena gynecologist who'll have to *lance* her to get his dick in . . ."

Because my Hollywood High girlfriend's father was the cameraman for Gene Autry, Darrow kept after "Flying A" to put me in the series. They were doing *Range Rider* with Jock Mahoney and Dicky Jones, and Autry's assistant took me to lunch at Oblatt's by Paramount. He said, "Gene wants to feature you in a show as another actor's sidekick, since *Range Rider* is rolling along, and the new one's in the works." He wasn't sure when they would commit to it, but wanted me to sign some sort of "non-salaried availability" contract. I didn't even know what it was, and I called Ida Lupino from Oblatt's phone booth and asked her what I should do. She said, "If Autry wants you to sign a real contract with this guy, go ahead and do it. If he simply wants you to wait around until he makes up his mind whether he's going to do it or not, tell him to call you. If he wants you, he'll go to Singapore to sign you. If he wants you to wait around while he decides on drawing up a contract one of these days—then I'd say to hell with it."

Ida was involved in production, writing and directing. I'd talk at length with her because I also knew the producer of one of the television shows she was doing, and she'd taken an interest in me as "possibly something" for an upcoming production. Her intention was the same as it had been in the past—to "make real movies." After the phone call about Autry, she asked me to visit her at the studio.

Because of her show our meeting was brief, but she said it was clear that my friendship with Darrow had not led to a single day's work. She said, "You're in a kind of spinning-around situation that you ought to think seriously about getting out of." Hedda Hopper once told Ida to "get real" and change her life. "I'm suggesting the same for you." Ida said to me. She advised me to steer clear of those who would not be able to put me to work, "meaning those who want to wine and dine you instead of handing you a script." She said without a script the scene was bad, and could harm my reputation and my career. I would be going around on a wheel like a mouse, she said. I said I didn't want to do that. I wanted to be a serious actor, like Hodiak, who was going to New York to do another play—this one to be directed by Charles Laughton.

Ida told *me* to go to New York. She said, "In New York you'll get to know your craft. When you come back, I'll give you a script to read and that's a promise you can count on."

I mentioned what she'd said to Hodiak, and he told me she was on target. "You've got the time and the time's right," he said. "I wish I could cast you in something, but you're at an almost impossible time." I was too young-looking or baby-faced to be a younger leading man, and too tall to be a juvenile. He said I'd also be too demanding of attention when I appeared on camera, that I'd "stick out of a crowd" the same as if I was dressed in red. He said I was doomed and blessed at the same time. "You need a couple of years to get seasoned, so go to New York. It's what you want anyway, isn't it?" He said he'd see me in New York, and that with more experience, some self-assurance and a grip on the power of positive thinking, I'd come back and damn sure find the good life in Hollywood.

THE GREAT WHITE WAY

I REMEMBER LOOKING AT JAMES DEAN one day when he and I had been hanging around in New York—he was standing in the rain with his head tipped back and water running down his face. He reminded me of the famous circus clown, Emmett Kelly. Dean's eyes had the same look as the clown's: not funny or cheerful, more a sort of distant craziness, a controlled kind of craziness that kept you from knowing what he was thinking.

The first time I saw Dean he looked like a small scarecrow. I was at the counter in a drugstore at 47th and Broadway when he shambled in behind a guy I knew from Hollywood. Dean lurched into the place as though he'd tripped on the door sill and was struggling for balance. With that shock of hair standing out like straw, his hands jammed into the pockets of baggy trousers, and a checkered jacket that hung on him big and had leather patches sewn around the cuffs, Dean seemed like a burlesque character. He was all hunched down into himself, squinting through his brown-framed glasses.

The other guy, Ray Curry, introduced us, but Jimmy hung too far back for a handshake, so I nodded. He said nothing, just stood there staring suspiciously and bending slightly forward as though from a stomach ache. I was also wearing glasses, and he asked if I was near-sighted or far-sighted. I told him I was far-sighted. "You're lucky," he said, sitting on a stool. He glanced at what I'd ordered and asked the waitress to bring him the same: orange juice, coffee, an English muffin. Curry told her he'd have that also, then went to make phone calls with a big safety pin. You could stick the point into a mouthpiece, touch the clasp to the nickel or dime slot, and presto—a dial tone. Not every pay phone fooled so easily, but the drugstore and a booth in the Museum of Modern Art never failed to plug through free of charge.

While waiting for the juice, Jimmy twirled the stool between us, wanting to say something important. "Eyes can be a drag," he said. He'd been in a Broadway play, lost his glasses and had trouble seeing the other actors if they "got out of reach." He had seen them "only as shapes" and couldn't see how they were looking at him.

I asked him how he had managed to play it, and he said he had related to the scene in his mind, as opposed to "what the hams were doing on the stage. "I asked him what the play was, and he said it was "a shit-fucker with Arthur Kennedy." He didn't say anything else about it, which I figured meant it had been a rotten experience.

Leaning closer, he eyed the book I had open on the counter, Barnaby Conrad's *Matador*. "Why are you reading a book about bullfighting?" he asked. I told him I liked it. Had I read Hemingway's *Death in the Afternoon*? he wanted to know. "Now that's a fucking book about bullfighting," he said. Of course I'd read it, I told him. In fact, I had a copy at my apartment. He asked where I lived and I said, "Around the corner on 48th off Eighth."

"What've you got," he asked, "a room? You got to come here to eat?" I said, "No, there's a kitchen—part of one main room, and a bedroom."

"What about a bathroom?" he asked. "You got one in the hall?"

"It's in the apartment," I said. "A shower—no tub, you know."

"It's better to take a shower," he said, laughing, "or you start playing with your dick . . . So, no shit," he continued, "What's it cost?" I told him what I paid on a weekly basis, and he asked, "You live there by yourself?"

"Right now," I said and Jimmy nodded, logging in the information. When he asked to take a look at the Conrad book, I said, "It's a novel," and he said he knew it was fiction. He knew the book. I slid it down the counter and he picked it up. He held the book open in one hand. He hunched over the pages, touching the paper like someone reading

Braille. His lips moved quickly, and he'd glance off as if remembering something or mouthing lines.

That was how the friendship began: without wanting to know if I'd finished reading the book, he asked to borrow it. I remember the way he was holding it and looking at me with his mouth slightly moving with whatever thoughts were spinning in his head.

There would come a time when we'd talk about other books—Arthur Rimbaud's *A Season in Hell* and Garcia Lorca's plays. I loaned Jimmy my copy of *The Psychology of Interpersonal Relations*, and when we tried discussing the book, I could tell he hadn't read it. I tricked him on it; he didn't say anything at first, but later told me he hadn't had time, finally confessing that he read "slow." He said, "It takes me a while to get the gist of the whole thing." It was because he thought in "circles," he said, grinning.

I'd soon find out about his reading disability. Eager to talk about books, he'd absorb what was said, taking it in and quite consciously making it his own. An amazing trick, his sponging whatever you knew about a subject, kind of shaking it around with what he'd learned elsewhere and piecing together a rather original, persuasive presentation.

It took him a long time to actually read pages. He thought in pictures, not in words. Reading was an excruciating chore, and though he'd profess to be an avid reader—a "cosmolite," as he once put it—he rarely cracked a book. And yet he could evolve a spontaneous performance from what he'd heard and made his own.

In acting, Dean had to "swallow the script," as he put it, "take it into the stomach and fart it out." Without digesting the words, he'd mumble and stumble and say he was figuring out "motivations" and character—all of which was a ruse, of course, to hide the reading problem. He had to have the full play inside himself before he could relate to any of the parts. This would later create some serious problems for Jimmy, as his work became spotty, a collection of ticks and mannerisms that seemed to be jumping out of the picture. You'd be watching him pop through a series of bits like corn on a hot pan, and you wouldn't be taking in the character. At moments he'd appear as an isolated figure in a river of rush-hour traffic. "He'll have to control the idiosyncratic impulses," a television director said, "or go for a one-man show."

The 47th Street drugstore provided thick pats of butter with its muffins, and Jimmy helped himself to all the butter on his plate as well as Curry's, heaping it on the muffin, which he ate with one hand, sucking each finger clean afterwards. He'd gone down to Tijuana from L.A., he said, to see the bullfights, and the American matador Sydney Franklin had given him a cape during the filming of a movie there.

"Why did he give it to you?" I asked. Jimmy said he'd mentioned a particular matador by name and used the correct Spanish pronunciation, which is what had earned him the cape. I said I'd seen that bullfighter gored less than a year before, not fatally, but bad enough to put him out of the ring.

"He was probably high as a kite," Jimmy said, and slid the book back to me. He asked if I'd seen the horn go into the matador, and I said it all happened so fast I didn't actually see the horn sticking him. But he was on the ground in a second, and the bull was going for him.

I talked to Curry a few minutes after Jimmy walked out, hands in his pockets again, a cigarette dangling from his lips. Curry said they had met working as extras on a picture on the coast, and that Jimmy was a hot actor now. I could see Jimmy through the window, waiting near the curb, his head craned back as he looked up at the building. "He's an oddball," Curry said. "We're going to smoke some reefers with this spade drummer he knows . . ." When Curry joined him on the sidewalk, Jimmy glanced back and gave a little nod, holding up two fingers. I didn't know what he meant by that.

The drugstore wasn't a popular theatrical hangout like Cromwell's Pharmacy a few blocks away, but was right in the heart of the "the Great White Way." An acting school and dance studio were nearby, and performers ran in and out swapping news, grabbing lunch or coffee. The play Jimmy had worked in, *See the Jaguar*, had closed after six performances, but gained him a rush of television work. One actress from the drugstore said he'd been "the best thing in a bad play," but was "an asshole in every other way it's possible to be."

When I saw him again he was drinking coffee and dunking a Baby Ruth candy bar in the cup. He had a small cloth bag of dance togs from a class he'd taken with Eartha Kitt. I said I'd met her in L.A. at the home of Alfredo de la Vega when she was doing the Broadway revue *New Faces of 1952*. Jimmy said, "Shucks, I know that old queen. He wanted to suck my cock." Grinning, he said, "He must've wanted to suck yours."

Jimmy learned I'd bought an old Norton motorcycle and began talking about his high school days in Indiana, how he'd built a bike, then started putting together a hot-rod. But he'd gone to L.A., and he said, "I should've come straight here instead of getting groped by everyone out there."

Once we went to a 42nd Street movie theater to see *A Place in the Sun*, and I slept through the last part the second time through. When I woke, Jimmy was staring at the screen, missing nothing, his jaw muscles working as he chewed popcorn and Milk Duds, mixing them together. Other times he'd stuff his mouth with more than he could chew comfortably, and he'd gag and spit it out. A couple of times he flexed his lower jaw to loosen the bridge of his three false teeth.

His eyes were bloodshot as we left the theater, and he didn't say much on the walk to Seventh Avenue. Then he began talking about Montgomery Clift's performance, and how Clift had managed to keep his work consistent even though we knew it was "all busted up" by the continuity of a movie. But it was "pure," and Jimmy brought up a particular piece of sculpture at the museum that he considered "perfect," with open ends, the same as Clift's acting in the George Stevens movie.

In a cafeteria near Broadway, we used the men's room before getting in line and Jimmy laughed about some holes in the wall between the urinal and toilet. He asked if I knew what the holes were for. I said I had a fair idea, and he said, "Do you know how to tell a sissy by his eyes?" I said I didn't know. He said, "Because he's got highballs!" I grinned, but I didn't really get the joke. I'd never heard it before and I've never heard it since, so I suspected it was something he'd made up on the spot, clowning around—even throwing in a little dance step that had nothing to do with what he was saying.

Jimmy squinted at the holes in the partition and touched them. He said they had been drilled, not cut into the divider with a knife or some other tool. "Someone's come in here and drilled these holes!" he announced. Had somebody brought a brace and bit into the john, he wondered, sat there drilling holes with his pants down around his ankles as a cover in case someone came in? It seemed to matter very much to Jimmy how the thing had been done.

The all-night cafeteria was hot and stuffy, and Jimmy drank coffee and smoked one cigarette after the other, lighting each new one from the butt of what he'd puffed down to his fingers. He hadn't told me where he was staying, even though I'd asked, and after a couple of these cafeteria sessions, he told me about "the flake and the chick," a situation he'd extricated himself from as quickly as possible. He said they were baggage—"over-freight," is how he put it—that he couldn't "drag any further." He'd met the guy at UCLA drama school though the guy had switched over to writing since then. They had roomed together on the Coast, and then the guy followed him to New York, Jimmy said, where the chick he'd known hooked up with them. He said if one of them should die or "kill themselves," he'd be stuck with carrying the other farther than he wanted to. Laughing, he asked if I'd seen dead bodies in my travels, and I said only my grandmother in the coffin. He wanted to know what the coffin had looked like, and I said I couldn't remember exactly except the rails were shiny like the handlebars on my bicycle, and a different color than the casket. I asked him why he wanted to know, and he dropped the subject.

I didn't know what his intentions were or why he'd ask things like that. I only knew he wanted to be the "most important actor in New York." He'd lean toward me and tap his finger on the cafeteria table and say, "I'm going to be the most important actor in town."

Another time in the cafeteria I said that getting pulled into the Army could blow a pretty serious hole in someone's career. I knew a little about trying to get into Special Services, being an actor and doing shows in the service, but Jimmy said one could beat the draft by claiming to have bisexual tendencies, "which includes having homosexual tendencies," he said, but one had to be careful about being branded a queer. The Selective Service wasn't dumb, he said, pointing out that by telling them you were a bisexual they'd think you were trying to hide the real facts from them. "It's like saying you've got only a little bit of leprosy," he said. He hadn't been drafted yet because he was below 1-A due to his eyesight, but he was above 4-F because he wasn't blind.

"They're not going to make you prove it by asking you to suck someone's dick," he said.

On our way out he flirted with a woman at the cash register. He told some joke I didn't hear, and they were both laughing. Then, some time later in the drug store on 47th, he approached the waitress with the same playfulness, and suddenly she called him a jerk for acting up. It was as though she'd knocked the air out of him, and the brief incident bothered him a lot longer than it should have. He seemed to carry it around, a kind of nagging confusion he was working into some unnecessary grudge.

In Cromwell's he described the cartoon of a man in a small box who didn't like the world. He said it was the same as "an emotional prison" that few could escape. You had to "close up" and pull back in order to discover the truth about something, he said.

Jimmy also seemed to inhabit his own world, yet gathered me into that same world as though into a conspiracy against an "outside" he perceived better than I did. If you weren't paying attention, he could take you in without your knowing it. Eartha Kitt and I talked later about Jimmy's knack for pulling people into tightly episodic, one-on-one relationships that had a way of running disconcertingly, if not disturbingly, deep. He had few pretensions and seemed to demand that you join him to form some single purpose.

Maybe that's what intrigued me most about him. Eartha said she couldn't remember going through any sort of "figuring out" of how he'd climbed into her life, or whether she liked him or not. "He was just suddenly there," she said. "I felt he'd always been there—one of the strangest friendships I've experienced . . ."

I'd learn later that the intense, sporadic friendships Jimmy imposed upon certain people would be like replenishing rest stops—emotional banks from which he'd make withdrawals during bad times. Then he'd retreat to his box, maybe sticking his head out and making faces at the world.

Jimmy had his share of detractors, those who'd say, "Oh, shit," here comes that little bastard . . . Let's get out of here before he sees us." Of course, a couple years later these same people would rally around as his closest buddies, with tales to unspool like the ball on a runaway kite.

I'd met a girl named Miriam Conley who lived at the Barbizon hotel for women. For a few weeks I'd been taking her on my motorcycle for modeling jobs, and a couple of times we had lunch in Central Park. We were walking my bike along the trail on the Fifth Avenue side one day and saw Jimmy on a bench with another actor, Martin Landau. They were sitting at opposite ends of the bench, having some sort of argument. Jimmy was eating peanuts and had a camera strapped around his neck. He said he was taking pictures of the monkey—I thought he was kidding Landau, who looked angry.

As we talked, Jimmy tossed peanuts at Miriam, throwing basketball shots to sink them down the front of her low-cut blouse. She laughed, caught some and threw them back. Jimmy thought that was great fun, and giggled while Landau looked resentful and kept urging Jimmy to leave. He stood up, tried to pull Jimmy by the arm, but Jimmy said

"No," mouthing the word exaggeratedly and repeating it, rolling his eyes and acting silly.

Disgusted, Landau said, "Okay, okay," and walked away. Though they were friends, Jimmy shook his head and looked at us, saying, "Who was *that* guy? Some flake, man!"

Miriam had never met Jimmy, but she'd seen him on television and knew about the Broadway play and a radio interview where he'd talked about Aztec Indians. He wasn't at all shy about her flirting, and began to joke around, jumping up on the benches and almost falling. Pulling his jacket over his face to look headless, he ran lopsidedly up the path, calling out, "Ichabod Crane! Ichabod Crane! I want you!"

He collided with a woman and nearly knocked her over, scattering her packages on the ground. She was angry for a moment, but had to laugh as Jimmy, still headless, scuttled around picking them up for her.

The monkey house was a metal building with a tunnel through the center, bordered by cages. Jimmy was serious about taking pictures of the monkeys, and one in particular, a dark, noisy monkey that kept reaching frantically through the bars. Miriam said she'd heard of monkeys biting, and Jimmy gave the monkey a peanut, breaking the shell open with his own teeth. He wanted Miriam to be in the shot with the monkey, but then teased her by grabbing her hand and pretending to stick it into the cage. She squealed and laughed. He took pictures of the ceilings and walls because, he said, the light was "dancing" up there. I sat outside on the bike watching them, Miriam giggling in a kind of false voice while Jimmy's attention focused on the monkey and whatever he was seeing through the camera.

I know Miriam saw Jimmy again and snuck him into her room at the Barbizon, strictly against regulations. I'd made it upstairs to the Barbizon lounge with her, and we'd neck when no one was up there but I hadn't been to her room. She once said she wanted to "kiss it and take it into my mouth," and unzipped my pants. She put her head on my lap and I placed her coat over her head. A woman walked by and I said Miriam had been tired and fallen asleep.

Once heading down 8th Avenue, Jimmy told me Miriam had gone down on him and "gives pretty good head." I said I already knew that, and he said, "I hope you're not hung up on the chick . . ."

I wasn't, but I wanted to know if he'd fucked her, figuring he'd tell me if he had. He'd told me about a couple of girls I didn't know, one of whom worked at the Actors Studio. But he said he hadn't fucked

Miriam, because she'd said she was saving herself for marriage.

"That's a crock," I said. She'd mentioned a guy from Wisconsin who had gotten her pregnant and that she'd had a "dusting and scraping job" at Bellevue.

"They all fucking lie, man," Jimmy said. "Females lie." He talked about the girl he'd been seeing and staying with "half the time," together with the roommate he'd had in L.A. He said he should've played a trick on them by turning into a hermaphrodite.

In the late spring, he'd met a waiter who worked in a little Greenwich Avenue cafe. He slept on a slab door with a Japanese neck rest and, along with Jimmy, wore a motorcycle jacket and even a pair of black leather pants while visiting the bars along Third Avenue.

"These weirdos are fucking and torturing each other," Jimmy told me. He said he'd sleep on a stack of sofa cushions in the waiter's studio after wandering around. At night, when he was troubled, he'd amble through the city, hanging out in 24-hour diners, or he'd go to the 42nd Street movies and fantasize about acting the roles on the screen.

One night he called me, upset because he'd seen a dead guy loaded into a paddy wagon. He said the man's hand had been sticking up as if reaching for something.

Not long after we met, I'd been working on lines for a play, and I'd just fallen asleep when I heard someone knocking on the door of my 48th Street apartment. When I opened the door, Jimmy seemed surprised that I'd been asleep. He was holding his greasy hands up in front of him and said he'd been downstairs working on my motorcycle. I was on the third floor facing the street, across from a fire station, and I kept it chained to a pipe in a small alley between the buildings where the garbage cans were lined up. He said my carburetor wasn't original and that someone had "jockeyed it around getting it on the engine." "You do that?" he asked. I told him it had been like that when I'd bought it.

"A bad idea," he said, "using spacers like that." A friend in Santa Monica had used a part that wasn't stock and the bike leaked gas. "Burned the bike up," Jimmy said. He asked if I'd ever rebuilt a carburetor for a Norton, and I said I hadn't. He said it wasn't hard, then asked if he could use the sink.

After washing his hands, he stood in the middle of the room looking around at the walls. He said, "Where's the bullfight pictures?"

I'd told him of my photographs, and he said he thought I'd have them all over the walls. When I brought out the box I kept them in, he got down on the floor and went through all of them, studying each one, even turning them sideways. We were still there when daylight came. He found a picture of the matador we'd talked about, and mumbled something about men with mirror swords and eyes dripping blood, flowing capes and pinpoints of death in their pores . . . He said it was from a Mexican poem, but I imagined he composed it on the spot.

Again he wanted to talk about the matador I'd seen gored, and again I told him what I remembered—the horn hooking and nailing the bullfighter. He wanted to borrow the photo to put on his wall—"as soon as I get a wall," he added.

Once walking along 42nd Street, looking at the whores and nuts and movie placards—one for Brando's *The Men*—Jimmy said he had a snapshot of Brando with a cock in his mouth. The photo, however, has never been proven to be of Brando. He had another picture showing Brando in a room with a porthole window behind him. Jimmy mentioned the shot had been taken in a room on West 68th Street and, grinning, said, "I've got the place—the same apartment." Someone he met through Marty Landau, who'd worked out at Terry Hunt's with Brando, had given Jimmy the address of the apartment in the Brando photo. Jimmy said he'd dogged the manager of the building until the place became vacant. He believed it was the same apartment, the same porthole windows. "By the way," he said, "I've found out that Brando's fucked around with a couple of guys from Terry Hunt's, and one of them says Marlon keeps rolling over onto his stomach . . . So he loves taking it up the ass," Jimmy said, joking. He made a circle with his thumb and finger, then left saying he had a rehearsal in less than twenty minutes.

Later, Jimmy said he was sorry I was just a fan of bullfighting and didn't seriously consider doing it. Again, I took that as a joke, but he claimed that bullfighting was something he'd have to do someday— learn to work the cape and face a bull. "Maybe one about this size," he said, grinning, his hand held waist high.

He said he could see it—it was there, a speck in the back of his mind. He said it was a "black hole burned in one of those old-time photographs." He said whenever "the chick" said she was sick, he could smell the bull's breath. It was like "getting married or dying," he said. "Your life opens up in that one moment, and that's when you're the most complete you can be . . ."

The idea of cramming everything into one moment obsessed Jimmy. It was one of the ideas that nearly drove Eartha Kitt nuts. "He couldn't let go," she said later. He'd latched onto Eartha as a soul mate; there was nothing sexual between them. "We were like brother and sister," she said. Jimmy was convinced Eartha had "special powers" and knowledge she could deliver to him by some kind of osmosis if he hung around long enough. She had "a sense of magic, and the answers," he said, "were locked up in her." He'd badger her into long discussions, and while she enjoyed his friendship, she said at times it was almost painful for her. He'd devise some theory he knew she'd disagree with. "He'd play the devil's advocate. People had to get shook up. Sleepers had to wake up."

He was inclined to learn a little, she said, and then attempt "to teach the instructor." If Eartha thought he was wrong about something, he'd insist she didn't understand what he was trying to say: "It was one-sided. Jimmy wanted me to prove to him or demonstrate how he wasn't right. He believed that if I understood what he was trying to say, then I would agree with him." He'd go to great lengths to meet with her at such times and try to make her understand his ideas.

Such as his theory of "synchronization." He sensed moments in Eartha's performances when it seemed to him that everything she knew was fused directly into the moment. Even things that had nothing to do with performing, he thought, translated directly into one energy force—a magic connection. This moment of fusion was "synchronization."

He phoned her one night to meet him at the cafeteria. Jimmy had a small flask he used to spike the coffee, cup after cup, chain-smoking and sipping so intensely, she said, "he seemed to buzz with electricity . . . sparks flying off him."

The flask held brandy. He'd been told "by the gang Marlon hung around with at Terry Hunt's gym" that Marlon Brando drank hardly at all, but when he had to get to the meaning of something, he drank brandy. Jimmy wanted to learn everything and compress what he knew into one energy force representing "something perfect." He had to dance and sing, learn photography and bullfighting, because he knew that what he'd learn could come through in some other way, would make up qualities he would project as an artist—as an actor.

She told him she understood, "But whether or not all that can be 'fused' into a whole, some performance or art as a single energy, I didn't know. My logic inclines to say it can't, because life doesn't operate on single notes. It's a whole symphony." When she tried to tell him the "lessons of living" were orchestrated by God, Jimmy laughed.

"What bullshit!" he said. There was no God—there was only art, only the composer, the creator of the symphony.

"And God created him who creates the symphony," Eartha said. Jimmy laughed again. "He said I was passing the buck—shirking things off and not taking credit for my own perfection. He said that was why people go around walking in pig crap all the time . . . He didn't think I understood or was using my real knowledge to get at the answers he needed.

"He wasn't playing in anyone else's symphony," Eartha said. "He was a loner, a solo player, and those meetings with him were excruciating and frustrating and trying . . ."

A few years later, photographer Roy Schatt, from whom Jimmy had wanted to learn, displayed portraits of Jimmy in Rienzie's, a West Fourth Street coffeehouse, and told me Jimmy had bugged him mercilessly. "He was a miserable runt who was a genius at posturing in a different guise for almost everyone he came in contact with." Schatt said, "Alone and left alone, he was just that—miserable, a squinty-eyed runt. But he was like an electric bulb—you plug him in and there's all this light, a battery or something inside him, generating this incredible light . . . He wanted me to teach him everything about photography. I don't know why. I was the photographer. He was the subject, but he wanted to be as proficient as me. I said, 'What for? All you're interested in is yourself!'"

Jimmy's relationship with me was more fundamental. He told television director James Sheldon, whom I met through Jimmy, that I was a "kid iconoclast," a Rimbaud on a beat-up motorcycle. And others, particularly later in Hollywood, would say, "He's one of Jimmy's people—art-for-art's-sake." Jimmy's association with the Actors Studio was minimal; he was disliked by members of the board, and especially by Lee Strasberg.

Jimmy said that Strasberg was a "very ugly man" who kept no mirrors in his house for fear of chancing unexpectedly upon his own reflection. Neither Montgomery Clift nor Brando was affiliated with the Studio, and Jimmy felt that it was unnecessary for a talent such as his own to be criticized by the "ugly man" who had a "personal vindictiveness" toward Jimmy while favoring others who kowtowed to Strasberg's opinions or who fucked or sucked the members of the board. Jimmy said that Strasberg's ideas were "nothing more than personal opinions," and paraphrasing Nietzsche, Jimmy said, "It wasn't that they were true, only that they were held as being true." The instructor's opinions were, Jimmy said, "mostly hot air and hog shit." He mimicked Strasberg's self-importance; even the roundness of the man's bald head seemed to glint from Jimmy's impersonations. The voice was Strasberg's, mouthing silly, nonsensical statements or stodgy platitudes. "He sits there in this posture, this ugly man who is married to an ugly woman," Jimmy said, "and farts out these opinions while half of the people in the place run around goosing each other."

Jimmy delighted in the few times I became sarcastic and blasphemous, and he'd encourage me to get drunk and shoot my mouth off about people. James Sheldon said, "Dean aligns himself with the castigated. Point someone out as a mainstream reject or someone so wounded in some way they have a terrible negative attitude—a creep—and Jimmy goes out of his way to get close to that person. In that way you'll be caught off-balance."

Jimmy worked the angle of shock. He'd stir up ridiculous situations to upset people. Once he suggested I dress up as a girl before we went to visit some people. "The flake and the chick'll be there," he said, and he'd introduce me as a girl he'd met, and tell them we were "getting serious—going together." At the party he'd find out I was a guy. He'd be very upset and we'd fake a heated argument, but then we'd kiss and make up. The making up, he said, would "get them to the quick."

He asked me, "You ever had something to do with a guy, or just fooling around?" All I'd told him at the time was that when I was fifteen I'd gone to a Hollywood party at the Garden of Allah, and Tyrone Power, who was drunk, had squeezed my hand, patted me on the head, kissed me and said I was the most beautiful boy he had seen in a long time. Since then I'd gotten regular propositions, but I'd never had an affair with a guy. I'd just been experimenting and trying to get around.

Jimmy said the idea of us going to the party—me as a girl—was a "great idea." We talked a little about people being bisexual, and he said he didn't think there was any such thing. If someone really needed emotional support from a male, he would probably be homosexual, but if he needed the support from a woman, then he'd be "more heterosexual."

That season in New York, Jimmy began to deliberately shift his relationships. He was finding new supporters while breaking away from people who were no longer tolerant of his "bad boy" pranks. James Sheldon liked Jimmy, worked with him and helped him, but even Sheldon was taking a dim view of Jimmy's behavior. "He's changing for the worse," Sheldon told me, "and he can't even see it."

Meanwhile, John Hodiak was on Broadway in *The Caine Mutiny*, and I managed to join him in a restaurant one night after the performance. We'd talked briefly on the phone, and his voice had sounded far away. He was excellent on stage, but he had changed. He didn't look quite like he had in Hollywood.

With him was an attractive actress, Joan Loring, who teased me for eating the bread and part of the salad John hadn't finished, even though he'd invited me to take it. "The kid doesn't have any money," he told Loring, and then asked how one could expect an actor to have any self-determining abilities? I reminded him of what he'd told me about the power of positive thinking. He said success was an illusory state of mind, "a figment of the imagination . . . Success is simply one dog eating at the other dog until one is dead and the other one full." Then he said, "You go out and look for another dog," and they began to laugh. There were hard lines around his mouth, and he was losing his hair.

A few days later, Jimmy came to my apartment wanting me to teach him how to fence in an hour or two. I said it couldn't be done, but tried to show him how to hold a foil, as one would hold a bird, firmly but carefully. But he clutched at it, his moves sudden and jerky, and he couldn't bend one of his fingers. He was still in Eartha's body-movement class, and though she'd said the fencing was a good idea, Jimmy quickly lost interest in it. I didn't know why he'd wanted to learn.

Another time he asked if I had any marijuana. He wanted to get high and was sorry Curry wasn't around because he always had grass. I had cheese and soda crackers and a quart of beer, and Jimmy drank that quickly. He was restless and edgy, and seemed trapped in the space of the apartment. I'd been fooling around with a painting, a view from my window of the corner drugstore and the firehouse across the street. "There's no people in the picture," Jimmy said. I said I hadn't painted any into it yet. He said if it was his painting he'd leave it empty.

I put on Alex North's music from *A Streetcar Named Desire*, but it only made him jumpy. He couldn't sit still, bracing and tensing his shoulders and squinting through his glasses at everything. At one point, staring at me, he said, "If you put on a wig and dress you could play a chick." He made several phone calls, drank the beer and made faces because he didn't like the taste of it. Did I have anything else to eat, he wanted to know, something like cake or cookies? I said I didn't, but suggested going out somewhere.

"Like where?" he asked. He said he was starving. His belt was full of holes, he said. He was lying. James Dean never went without a meal in New York.

There was a pretty good French cafe on Ninth Avenue, but Jimmy said he didn't know much about French food, and he was broke to boot. He then said James Sheldon knew "all the French stuff," and had suggested dinner a couple of times. "Sheldon's got money," Jimmy said, and he could pay for the dinners.

He phoned Sheldon, who knew the restaurant and would be waiting in front for us. Spirits lifted, Jimmy bounced down the stairs. But by the time we walked over there, his mood had changed again. He sat hunched and guarded at the table, suspicious of what Sheldon had ordered. Once he tasted it, though, he dug in, wolfing the food down. He soaked the crepe with a sweet syrup before eating it, almost floating it, as Sheldon stared at him and said, "You're going to eat that?"

Jimmy picked up the crepe in his hand and squeezed it until the filling oozed out. He thought that was very funny, and at one point Sheldon said, "You're a knucklehead!" and rubbed Jimmy's head—one of those Dutch-uncle rubs, and said again, "This guy's a knucklehead!"

Sheldon ordered another bottle of wine, though he drank little of it. Embarrassed by our behavior, he paid the check and left early. Jimmy wouldn't leave until he had eaten all the crepes and bread, and finished the second bottle. As we walked back toward 8th Avenue, he told me he'd been in a show with actress Irene Vernon. They had been eating somewhere when she complained about the greasy potatoes; they were "swimming in grease," she'd said. Jimmy thought that was funny, but Irene was upset that the grease was spreading to the other food. He removed the potatoes from her plate, he said, and put them into a water glass where they could "swim properly," then used a napkin to wipe up the grease from her dish. She could spread the other parts of her meal, he told her, onto the place where the potatoes had been.

Heading north again, we stopped at Jerry's Tavern, drank beers and were smashed by the time we got to my place. And because the conversation got around to sex with guys as well as girls, I told him about the time an actor friend, Bill Smith, had driven up to a dude ranch where I worked, and how we'd stayed overnight at a country club. It had surprised me, I told Jimmy, when the actor showed me his cock in the room, how big he could get it.

I said I wasn't sure what I thought about seeing him like that. Jimmy wanted to know if I'd been in the sack with the producers I'd met, and I said no—except for a couple of them, but I hadn't liked it. It was something like the experience of a young relative of mine going down on me, having failed to persuade me to have sex with him from behind. "Butt-fucking him," Jimmy said. I said yes, and Jimmy asked me in a serious voice, almost like he was a doctor, if I'd wanted to suck the actor's cock. He went on to inquire whether I'd experienced any sort of pain. "Be honest with me," he said, "be as honest as all the days." What did I feel about the guy's cock, "because it seems to stand out in my mind." He laughed at the unintended pun, and asked me how come I hadn't done it?

I said the guy had surprised me and I had been scared. I said I couldn't say more about it than I already had.

Jimmy said it was probably possible for him to have a relationship with a guy, too—to have a physical exchange without it being labeled "homosexual," because he felt that something like that, like what the actor and I had come close to, was simply an extension of the friendship. "Just going to the edge of the friendship or sort of beyond it," Jimmy said. He didn't think any kind of sexual experience would push him or anyone else in one direction or the other.

He wanted to know if I had sucked my relative's cock, and I said I'd done that once or twice. That was what he'd done to me, had me shoot in his mouth, and fuck him in the ass. Jimmy asked me about another producer and how it had felt to have him kissing me. I said I hadn't liked it.

"Have you tasted jizz?" Jimmy asked. Did I know what it tasted like? "Sure, I know what it tastes like, I said, and told him I'd said—having tasted my own on my finger. Jimmy said, "You're like a little girl who puts her finger in her pussy and then licks it off." He said, well, did I like the taste?

I laughed and he laughed, too. I answered no, I'd had to spit it out. He said, "Is that why you were scared of that guy's dick, because you didn't want to have that stuff in your mouth?" That was the question he'd been driving at. That's what he wanted to know. It made me feel nervous, and I said, "I don't know . . . What about you?"

He didn't answer, but began to giggle. He said, "I'm not active. I'm passive. You are passive too, from what you have said to me . . ." But active and passive were terms that depended on what a person happens to be doing, he said. With my relative I was being passive, but by fucking him I could be said to be active, but only if it was what I wanted to do. He said it all depended on how it happened, and on what the person wanted. It was all about circumstances—the nature of the "interpersonal relationship," he said.

He was lying on my bed with his head hanging over the edge, and I was sitting in the wicker chair. At one point I tried to get up, but I was too drunk and ended up on the floor near Jimmy. I reached up and touched his head, then pulled on his hair. He said, "Man, you know more than just being kissed by Tyrone Power. You know things like I do, because you've been through the same shit . . ."

After talking for a few minutes more, there was a strange sort of vibration in the air, a kind of intimacy that was electric and exciting. He put his finger on my lower lip and started to giggle. Then he turned his head around and was sitting facing me, and he put his hand behind my neck and pulled my face toward his, putting his lips on mine. It was the first time I had ever really been kissed by another guy. He said, "Come up on the bed before I break my neck." I moved up on the bed and lay alongside of him and he kissed me again. Our teeth touched, stuck together in a strange way. I remember closing my upper row of teeth down onto his lower row, so that I could almost bite his bottom teeth by closing my mouth. I felt his tongue against the edge of my upper teeth, and then I opened my mouth and he put his tongue in my mouth, pushing it against my tongue. I put my hands up at the sides of my face and we stayed like that for a few seconds until we backed up onto the bed. He kissed me on the neck and bit—though not really hard—into the skin between my neck and collarbone, and then he was laying on top of me.

He said, "Can you be fucked?"

"Jesus!" I said. "I don't think so."

He said, "I want to try to fuck you. We can try it if you want to." He wanted me to put my arms around him—which I felt funny doing—and to hold him. He wanted me to kiss him while he moved his lower body against me, and to keep kissing him. He wanted to suck my nipples and leaned his face over and kissed me on the side. Again he bit me, and this time it felt sharp. He was holding himself and he said, "Am I going to fuck you?"

I said, "I guess we can try to. I don't how know successful it will be." At that I replaced his hand with my hand. We tried to fuck but it wasn't going to work. I tried to go down on him, but his cock was big and made me gag and choke. I didn't know what we could do. It wasn't going to work. Whatever the hell it was that had sparked such a situation between us was just going to be all bound up by the impossibility of getting it across.

This part of the friendship stayed in the background over the next few weeks, as if it had occured in another dimension and required no actual attention from us. For me, the physical thing was awkward. Though I doubted that either of us got much satisfaction out of it, the memory of it somehow held a wonder or excitement—and yet it still scared me. For Jimmy, the *idea* of doing it seemed more intriguing than whatever we actually did.

Caught up in our own ambitions, what we shared wasn't an affair by far, and what has been written about our friendship in books and magazines over the years is mostly mistaken. One book describes the relationship as "salacious" and "lustful," but it wasn't. It was a period of exploration. It wasn't so much a physical thing. I'd run into Jimmy and there would be an energy between us, even in the company of others, like a dark-haired girl he was seeing named Barbara Glenn, a young actress who cared sincerely for him, and whom he really liked.

Like one night in Jerry's, Jimmy was across from me in the booth, and we were joking around and drinking, and for a second our eyes met and that look was there, but just for a second. It was like something had run or flown across a screen—the bursting noise of a bunch of birds taking wing, so fast that unless you knew what it was, you wouldn't have seen it. But the feeling was there, and if either one of us had been a girl, we'd have gotten into a love affair, though it wouldn't have lasted.

Early that fall we were goofing around at a party on 45th Street, around the corner from the Algonquin and Iroquois. Jimmy had done another show with James Sheldon, who showed up briefly at the party. He said that he and Jimmy were momentarily at odds. It had something to do with Jimmy's attitude: the more work he got, the more he seemed to antagonize those he worked with. Playwright William Inge didn't want Jimmy in a particular production, because, he said, "his moods are so unpredictable and he scares the pants right off me."

At the party, in an apartment above a manufacturing loft, Jimmy was hiding in the kitchen. We were eating crackers and potato chips and drinking soda mixed with wine. I was watching Jimmy trying to open a can of salmon with a bottle opener when a young black actor named Billy Gunn joined us, prattling on about the Actors Studio, Geraldine Page and a play adaptation of Andre Gide's novel *The Immoralist*. Jimmy played dumb. He'd landed a good role in the same show, but pretended to know nothing about Geraldine Page starring in the play with Louis Jordan. Jimmy's part was that of a homosexual Arab houseboy, and Billy Gunn had been signed to understudy the same character. Gunn didn't know Jimmy except to nod hello at casting calls, and Jimmy once said, "He's got some good reefers, when he's got 'em."

In the kitchen, Gunn bragged about landing the understudy, and Jimmy just said, "Oh, yeah?" and "What play's that? Who's in it?" The fact that Jimmy was signed for the role hadn't been announced, but he finally told Gunn. "They're keeping it a secret," he said, "in case they have to fire such an asshole as me before we get into rehearsals."

"That's okay with me," Gunn said. "If they do, I'll go on in your place!"

He left the kitchen, and Jimmy stared after him and said, "What a fucking jerk, man." But Gunn would become one of the few people Jimmy was friendly with that winter—part of Jimmy's "uptown" group. Jimmy was still seeing Barbara, hanging out with her sometimes, but kept us all pretty separate from one another. If two of us who knew him appeared in the same setting, he'd sort of shrink up, or start acting up, pulling some kind of stunt.

Barbara and I shared a sort of troubled distance, because she thought Jimmy was paying more attention to me than he was to her, and that he turned to me to discuss more serious ideas. Billy Gunn and I were friends, though. We'd have coffee at Cromwell's or the Museum of Modern Art. Billy talked about wanting to be a painter and a writer as well as an actor.

I felt relieved that Jimmy had signed for *The Immoralist*, because I was afraid to tell him about the play John Van Drutin was putting together. The playwright told my agent he saw something in me of the boy he'd written in *I Remember Mama*—the character Nels—whom I'd played in stock. The play was projected for the following season, and with Van Drutin's support the role was within my grasp. Yet it was a role Jimmy would have been right for if the Gide play weren't taking him out of circulation.

At another party, Jimmy introduced me to a Park Avenue art dealer named Fredrick Delius—like the composer—and we joked about him looking "remarkably life-like." Jimmy had met him at a show he'd gone to with Leonard Rosenman, a musician friend, and Delius invited us to his gallery. Apart from free snacks, Jimmy wanted to show me two works—an old Spanish painting of Saint Sebastian with all the arrows sticking in him, and a portrait of Rimbaud "in drag" by a French Symbolist painter.

From a smaller room with a table and chairs off the main gallery, you could look directly at the painting of Saint Sebastian, almost life-size, bound to a tree, hands tied, head tilted back slightly with his eyes raised toward heaven as arrows pierced various parts of his body. Jimmy remained in a chair, smoking and staring, entranced by the painting while Delius showed me his latest acquisitions. The portrait of Rimbaud, he said, had been shipped to another gallery, but what he showed me was a peculiar work showing the Virgin Mary holding the infant Christ. The baby's face looked wrinkled and strained, its teeth like an old person's. The Virgin was how I imagined an embalmed Jean Harlow might have looked. As I stared at the painting in a kind of awe, I felt Delius' hand moving across my rump, and he tried to kiss the back of my neck. He whispered something in some other language, and I moved away. He implored me to come back for dinner, and I said I'd let him know. As I walked away from him, he said weakly, "I can help you . . . I can be influential . . . You can ask Jimmy if I am not sincere."

Jimmy had dozed off, chin resting on the folds of his sweater, which was spotted with cigarette ash. His eyelids were slightly open and the whites of his eyes were visible behind his glasses. He wasn't interested in the proposal Delius had made to me. "He's an old queen," Jimmy said. "He's okay, and who gives a shit?" The man had wanted to fly him to Spain to see the bullfights, he said, then added, "Fat chance." He wanted to talk about the bulls again, the gorings and the funerals of matadors, until the dialogue settled on how long it would take Saint Sebastian to die from those arrows. One sticking in his lower abdomen must have pierced organs, Jimmy said, and he had to be bleeding inside. "That'd kill him," he said with certainty. He talked about being hanged—about suffocation—and was trying to imagine being guillotined, and whether the eyes fluttered with any last-second sight.

Jimmy's talk of death, dying and dismemberment wasn't as exciting or interesting to me as it was to him. It was never morose, though, and at times he tended to become almost ecstatic. Things became important and purposeful to him, and his whole attention seemed to focus on particular details, like the arrow in Saint Sebastian's lower abdomen. Nothing else mattered.

I stayed at the gallery a couple of times on a couch in the alcove. After dinner at an elegant Italian restaurant, we drank old vintage wine like water. We listened to Taglivini records, and Delius gave me a black-silk Chinese robe with dragons on it. He said I was like Louise Brooks—like Lulu—and he wanted to kiss my stomach and thighs. He cried until I undressed and wore the new black robe. I was very drunk and Delius wound up fucking me on the couch, under the painting of Saint Sebastian. I remember afterwards sitting on the toilet in the huge white bathroom, the black silk and dragons shining on the tile and the fluid of the man coming out of me.

The company for *The Immoralist* was having a terrible time with Jimmy's "uncommunicative behavior," as they put it. He'd read slowly and sullenly, and with little apparent comprehension. What no one seemed to know was that until he'd commited the script to memory, he was unable to formulate what he'd say, so he'd mutter and mumble and make up words, or simply fill in the blanks with speech that had nothing to do with the scene.

Jimmy had other people read his parts until he knew the thing by heart. He couldn't deal with a new page, and it took him ages to finish a paragraph. He preferred simple books with pictures, and poetry, and if he'd heard it enough he could repeat it like a talking bird.

Louis Jordan complained that "Dean mutters obscenities!" Even then, it was not until Jimmy experienced the language of the play in rehearsals that he could get involved, and that didn't happen until almost the opening-night performance.

Frustration ran fever pitch. Other actors found Jimmy intolerable, impossible to work with. There were serious arguments that escalated to the point of almost getting him fired. But Geraldine Page rescued him by threatening to walk out if Jimmy was dismissed. She insisted he'd be fine by opening night. The truth was that he'd confided in her and made her swear she'd not repeat what he told her. Geraldine told me a few years later, "In some peculiar way, Jimmy's difficulties in dealing with the printed page somehow bypassed some other part of him, triggering the most intense concentration of any actor I've worked with. He was like a cat that jumps a great distance without the need to know how far he has to jump."

He attended rehearsals as though a reluctant viewer rather than an actor, wandering around the stage, turning his back to others or mumbling so nobody understood. Louis Jordan said working with "this monster" was the worst experience he'd had in theater.

The play was opening in Philadelphia for the out-of-town tryout when one of Jimmy's ex-roommates told me he wanted to talk to me. He said he was very upset about the breakup of his friendship with Jimmy. I met him for coffee, but wound up drinking beer. He believed Jimmy was a very lonely individual. "I thought I was a maladjusted, miserable, lonely bastard," he said, "but Jimmy takes the cake." He pointed out that Jimmy couldn't be his friend, and he couldn't be my friend. I wasn't sure I understood what he was saying. "He goes through people as fast as he does underwear," he said, "if he even bothers to put it on half the time." He toasted Jimmy's forthcoming success in the play, saying, "He'll steal the show, you know. Don't underestimate my lost friend, James Dean."

He told me that Jimmy's mother had given him the middle name Byron after the crippled poet, Lord Byron, because she somehow "knew" that Jimmy would grow up a cripple or have a crippled soul. It was fitting, he said, since both Byron and Jimmy *were* cripples.

"Jimmy has said, himself, that it's best to be a cripple," the young man continued. "Has he told you about his ball-game theory?"

I said no. He summed it up, saying that when someone is hurt in the ball game, he's called to the sidelines. "From that position, one is offered a vantage point of the whole playing field that can't be appreciated when one is in the game. "The injured one on the sidelines," he said," sees more and knows more than those on the field . . ."

He then told me that Jimmy was seeking in others the mother he lost as a child. "Though to these same people," he said, "he can be harmful, if not destructive." He said that it resulted from the fact that it was impossible for anyone else to fill in for Jimmy's dead mother. "No one can," he said, "and in the role he forces upon you, you'll always fail our troubled boy."

Attempting to tell me how much he had been through with Jimmy, he said he was leaving New York in despair, having thrown up his hands. He said, "Once Jimmy has finished with a person, that person ceases to exist. Finis! Kaput!"

The real reason for our meeting came out when he asked me if Jimmy and I had been sleeping together. People were saying things. Was that the reason Jimmy was being so hurtful to his friends? "Are you lovers?" he asked, with a kind of weak smile. At that, I finished our conversation.

"You're a sad character, you know?" I said. "You'd be enough to drive anyone to the sidelines."

He raised his glass in a mock toast. "The playing field is yours," he said, "and with it all the blessings and the curses."

I didn't see Jimmy's ex-pal again in New York. The play went well in Philadelphia, then successfully opened on Broadway. When the opening-night curtain dropped at eleven o'clock, Jimmy had delivered a masterful performance—as well as his three-weeks notice. Everyone was stunned, including his most patient supporter, Geraldine. She said, "It was the most unheard-of set of circumstances I'd ever witnessed."

Jimmy told no one of his secret plans to dump the play. Not even Geraldine knew the whole truth, though she had played an unwitting part in the chain of events. A writer she knew, Paul Osborn, was doing a screen adaptation of John Steinbeck's novel *East of Eden* for Elia Kazan and Warner Brothers. Geraldine had talked a great deal about Jimmy's antics, but stressed his peculiar intensity during rehearsals. After Osborn went to the Philadelphia tryouts, he realized Jimmy was the perfect actor for the part of the boyish troublemaker in Steinbeck's story.

Osborn told Kazan, and the director went to take a look at Jimmy. "I got to know him," Kazan said, "and he was an absolutely rotten person. Right away, he was a real cocker and an asshole. But he was the most perfect fucking actor for that part—all bound up in himself with his neurotic problems, lashing out at inappropriate moments. A sulker, an asshole, but absolutely perfect for the role. There wasn't any question in my mind that he'd bring it off—all he had to do was be himself. The problem I faced was convincing Warner Brothers that I should go with an unknown, starring him in the movie."

I hadn't seen Jimmy since he'd left for Philadelphia, but I went to the play after it opened at the Royale Theater in New York. He kept talking about plans that were in the works, and he said he couldn't tell anyone why he'd given his notice on opening night. In one scene, he did a seductive dance as the homosexual houseboy enticing Louis Jordan. Using a pair of scissors like castanets, Jimmy improvised the snipping sounds to accompany his dance. "It was the strings, man," Jimmy told me, "and Louis Jordan didn't even know what was going on." Jimmy was snipping away at the invisible strings binding Jordan's character to the safe middle-class morality he'd left abroad. In the blaze of the Middle Eastern desert, surrounded by rampant sexuality, Jordan becomes helpless, and with each coaxing step of the dance, Jimmy's snipping cut more and more at the man's hopeless respectability. The rigid European gives in, then finally commits suicide.

Jimmy told me his thoughts about the scissors when he called with a vague, muttered story about money being hidden in his apartment. He was going out of town on something important and had to alert me that he might need a favor, someone to get into his apartment and and take care of a couple of things, maybe send something out of town. I later learned that he'd called Billy Gunn, and a girl named Chris White who worked at the Actors Studio, with a similar story. It was his way of saying "See you later" without giving away any secrets. Kazan had warned him not to talk to anyone about the movie until they had completed tests in New York, and until the studio had rubber-stamped the director's decision. With hardly anyone knowing it, Jimmy had fulfilled his prophesy—he had become the most important actor in town.

Though we'd get together in Hollywood, that was the last time I talked to him in New York. Soon, with most of his clothes and belongings stuffed into paper sacks, Jimmy was on a plane heading west "to shake the shit out of Hollywood . . ."

BLINDSIDE

JIMMY'S FASCINATION WITH THE SPILLED BLOOD OF MATADORS escalated
during his brief year-and-a-half of stardom. He'd stage endurance trials
of bodily pain, sticking himself with safety pins and staying up for days
on end, while quickly skipping over whatever emotional anguish happened to get tangled up in his relationships, which bottomed out one
after the other.

From those lean and hungry days in New York to his sudden success,
a part of Jimmy tried desperately to undermine his fame—as if any
Hollywood foundations were cast indestructibly. He could not twist himself free of the emotions surrounding his mother's early death, and he
clung to these painful memories as one might perpetually clutch a
child's jack with sharpened points in one's palm. He sought to remain
constantly aware of the pain. The image of his mother's coffin was
indelibly etched in his mind—the idea of dwelling in caskets in general
obsessed him—and this was somehow mixed up with his own sexual
ambiguities.

He was not a homosexual, but dallied in it as an "opportunistic
explorer," as he called himself on occasion, engaging in heterosexual sex for
similar reasons. One of his early so-called romances was with the young

actress Pier Angeli, under contract to Warner Brothers. Way back in her past, controlled by a zealously Catholic mother, Pier had developed a constant, though outwardly unseen, morbid streak that caught Jimmy's attention immediately. The kind of "delightful romance" the fans so gullibly chased was conjured up between them by the studio publicity department. So little has been shown of Pier's gloomy side that any revelation seems a shock, except to those who were exposed to Pier's escalating mental turmoil and drug use.

The trouble was there long before her "discovery" by screenwriter Stewart Stern, who also wrote the script for *Rebel Without a Cause.* Something churning in this incredibly lovely young woman with the dark doe eyes—and a nature so wildly sexual that she sought to be punished for her defiance of those past Catholic bonds—would eventually push Pier to suicide.

Even though she believed committing suicide was a sin, she still hoped that she'd find peace in a death she'd bring about herself. Never having found happiness or joy, she gambled for everlasting solitude. She claimed that the only love she knew, which had cut her to the quick, was the love she'd experienced for James Dean, though he could never have given her what she needed.

Jimmy had become an "overnight star," the envy of everyone in Hollywood. Many were so bitterly jealous of his success that it would eventually poison their own careers. Within only months of Jimmy's death, Steve McQueen in New York would be looking at it as a personal convenience. And back in Hollywood later that same year, I'd be living with Dennis Hopper in a small house off Laurel Canyon, and he'd be chain-smoking reefers and saying that "cosmic configurations" had manipulated fates so that Dennis, another Warners contract player who'd acted in the shadow of Jimmy, had by Dean's sudden death been given a "mantle" to fill. I said to Dennis, "You worked in *Rebel* and you worked in *Giant,* but you didn't know Jimmy. You didn't know him."

Dennis said, "But fate knows us both, and fate makes the decisions, not Warner Brothers. I'm the one to play the empty parts Jimmy left." I thought, "You might play the roles, pal, but you'll never fill in for Jimmy."

There was something similar about the people Jimmy shared himself with. Together they functioned as a refuge, a kind of cove into which he could escape for varying periods of time—minutes, hours, a phone call, a fast ride, whatever he required. It was not the person, but the "sanctuary." (I'd heard him use the word two or three times, imitating Charles Laughton in *The Hunchback of Notre Dame.*) To Jimmy, people were almost interchangeable. From Eartha Kitt and other celebrities to Rolf Weutherich—the young auto mechanic who accompanied Jimmy on his last ride—the qualities that attracted him would gradually rise to the surface, converging. Getting a clear picture of Steve McQueen, Natalie Wood, Jack Nicholson, Jane Fonda, Warren Beatty or Dennis Hopper was an easy task compared to even focusing on Dean. The work he did will always be there. He proved in the very short time he had that he was one of this century's consummate artists. The other side is in shadow—the flesh and blood Dean has been dead more than four decades now, and only exists in the memory of a group of people who are rapidly dying off themselves. Jimmy—the mercurial clown who dances, sparks, outwits and is outwitted, and who never stands still—was in search of "the moment of truth," not as it was or as others saw it, but as he wanted it to be.

It was this "glorious" compulsion that found wings in the racing that led to his death. He had to go further than the others, and finally to surpass himself. "Dying," he told me, "is at the vanguard of limits. It's a symbol like a stop sign. It's an implication and a matter of interpretation . . . "If you're chicken, you can't make the discoveries."

I hadn't seen Jimmy in about a year. I'd come back to Hollywood from New York with John Darrow, to work out a contract with Paramount. I was about to be drafted into the Army, but volunteered for induction instead, signing up for paratrooper school. I was doing okay in the Army until I got picked up and accused of going AWOL, and was stuck in the old stockade at Fort Ord, across the bay from Monterey. After a summary court martial, I was back in the stockade instead of being sent overseas. I talked to the chaplain and a couple of army shrinks who stressed the necessity of being candid. I remembered that Jimmy had told the draft board he was "afraid of being inducted," afraid of his own "inner inclinations" toward other guys. When I told them I'd had some bisexual experiences, they claimed I could be emotionally unsuited for military training and urged I be discharged.

At first I decided to use what G.I. Bill money I got to go to France and study painting. But instead of living in a garret in Paris, I was soon back in Beverly Hills with a black 1947 Jaguar sedan and an apartment on Cañon Drive. I was acting in *Season in the Sun* at the Geller

Playhouse and seeing a blonde carhop at Jack's Drive-in on the Strip. She was a part-time artist and movie extra with big breasts and a skinny waist. She introduced me to the blonde actress Irish McCalla, who was taller than I was. Irish and I got along beautifully. She wanted to paint, and we talked about art. Though she was starring in the television series *Sheena, Queen of the Jungle*, she didn't talk that much about acting; it was like she didn't really want to do it.

Through another agent, I got a few jobs while going to the Geller Workshop Theater. The Jaguar quit on me, and I sold it and got a rigid-frame BSA motorcycle, cheaper than a car. I dumped the ascot and the fancy vests and started hanging around in a leather jacket.

I'd wanted to see action in the Army. Too late for Korea, I had still hoped there'd be something else—somewhere, some battle I'd be able to sink my teeth into. I even thought of joining the French Foreign Legion since the U. S. Army had stamped me a misfit. I kept thinking about the poet Alan Seeger and his love of combat, the glory and sense of immediacy he'd experienced in battle and written about in his diary and letters. It was something Jimmy and I talked about in New York. He'd read and reread Seeger's poem *I Have a Rendezvous With Death,* and he'd recite it—once stoned on pot from Billy Gunn. But what I was after wasn't verse so much as a rendezvous with fortune.

Sally Kellerman was still in Hollywood High School, as was a cousin of hers, Hooper Dunbar, a very lean, pretty-faced boy acting in Hollywood High plays the same as Sally, while also studying modern dance. We met in a book shop on Hollywood Boulevard and started hanging around together. His body was like a slim girl's, and I was attracted to him, though he'd had no experience with boys.

One spring day, I pulled into Googie's' parking lot on my bike and saw Jimmy sitting on the seat of his own bike, a Triumph. He was wearing an expensive black leather bike jacket with a fur collar, and tan cowhide gloves. A photographer named Phil Stern was taking pictures of him. Jimmy had clip-on sunglasses over his regular glasses and stared at me as I stopped in a space near his bike. He gave a little salute and said, "Hey, *atado*, what's happening, man?"

He seemed cool and distant, untrusting maybe, but that disappeared during our first few talks. He was running around with an odd bird named Jack Simmons, who held a reputation as "one of the most notorious faggots in Hollywood."

Jack has been described as being an "unknown" screwball who

attached himself to Jimmy after the making of *East of Eden*. Actually, when *Life* magazine's huge spread on Jimmy had run the previous March, Jack had made up his mind to meet Jimmy and become his closest friend. Begging and badgering his way onto the Warners lot, Jack had succeeded in cornering his new-found idol, and laying himself down as Jimmy's personal doormat.

"What's 'atado'? What's 'atado'?" Jack asked me.

Then later he said, "It's got to do with a fucking bull. Tying it up or using a rope so it means some kind of state of *peace*—what bullshit! Why does he call you *that?*"

Rarely quoted, Jack would remain a "mysterious character" in Jimmy's history, with most of the tidbits coming from another mutual friend, Maila Nurmi, the would-be actress and self-professed "witch" who called herself Vampira at the time. Dressing in black like Morticia of the Addams Family, Maila hosted a television show of old spooky movies—the forerunner of many late-night TV horror gimmicks to come. While Simmons was reticent, Vampira freely concocted stories about Jimmy after his death, crediting herself via movie magazines and other publications as having been a lover of Jimmy's. She created publicity for herself and her television show, and unwanted notoriety for Jack, who was chauffeuring Maila around in an old black hearse. It was through Jack's possessive attachment to Jimmy that Maila was briefly ushered in as part of the "night watch," as we were called—or, by some columnists, the "crew of creeps."

Many of the all-night jams at Googie's, the bikes and stunts, were construed by reporters as crazy antics to shock and deride Hollywood. Jimmy was reveling in the publicity, creating a language of physical and psychological impact, a dangerous image that radiated from the screen and tabloid papers. The stories read, "The crazy kid is going to kill himself." It was a fear shared by the studio. Jimmy loved it.

Enhancing the public's curiosity were Vampira's innuendoes to the press about the "romance" between her and Jimmy, which he'd chuckle over. Most of all, however, it was the "morbid" appearance of his "crew," which included myself, that kept the bad publicity cooking. No one knew where it would lead or what Jimmy intended to do with these "jackals" he'd gathered around himself.

Jimmy's penchant for secrecy kept Jack Simmons initially half-ignorant of the relationship we'd shared in New York. At the same time, Jimmy showed no more than a passing curiosity about the fact that Jack and I had been friendly two years before. He did ask, "Did you and Jack get anything going?" I said no, absolutely not. Jimmy said, "He's a very nervous guy," and laughed. He asked how we met, and I told him it was in front of the Tropical Village, a gay bar on the boardwalk at Santa Monica. Jack had long dark hair and a big hook nose in those days. They called him "the Hawk," and when I met him he was wearing pink bathing trunks, cut high on the sides, and some sort of Indian beaded belt. He had on a pair of white sunglasses and was trying to dance with Rock Hudson or George Nader. The bar was usually jammed on weekends, and it wouldn't have been unusual to spot Hudson or George Nader or Dan Dailey dancing somewhere deep in the place. Someone I'd worked with on a show invited me in for a sandwich, and Jack stopped me on the boardwalk. He said he recognized me and wanted to buy me a drink. I said it wasn't a good idea because I wasn't even seventeen yet, and the whole place might get into a jam. He insisted on a Dr. Pepper and we talked outside the bar. After that, he was chasing me, calling at night, driving me places I'd have to be, but he never seriously tried to put the make on me.

Then he'd had his nose bobbed and combed his hair like Jimmy, who'd landed him a small part in *Rebel*. While the "New Star" halo was shining over Jimmy, it was people like Jack—as well as myself—who puzzled Hollywood. A reject, tabbed a pitiful fringe-nut in Hollywood's substratum, Jack had captured Jimmy's interest with an unwavering, dog-like devotion. Like myself, he wasn't one of those "fat numb people" who criticized Jimmy, but quickly became a member of the crew with whom Jimmy surrounded himself, "frequenting Sunset Boulevard's night hangouts, racing cars and motorcycles, and what gaucheries Dean doesn't think up, these sycophants do . . ." It was a very short-lived moment, long-remembered by Hollywood.

Jack would later claim that he was in love with Jimmy—the only love of his life, he'd say—and even decades later he'd break down and sob over Jimmy's death. Jack said he had not only lost his "one true love," but his "soul as well." Years later, Jack would try to purify his relationship with Jimmy, even telling writer Val Holley, "I never touched his organs," by which, of course, he meant Jimmy's cock.

One night in Googie's, Jimmy said that the line he wanted on his tombstone was from the poet Alan Seeger's diary about "one crowded hour of glorious life" being "worth an age without a name." A telegram was quickly sent to Jack Warner, suggesting an engraved headstone.

The front office didn't appreciate the prank and promptly clamped down on Jimmy's reckless motorcycle racing around the studio lot. They began to keep tabs on the "oddballs" Jimmy was palling around-with. These "tabs," actually file cards, soon became a sort of blackball list of potentially troublesome people—those who might cost the studio unnecessary expense. Following Dean's death, the word "unnecessary" would be changed to "grievous."

The night the telegram was sent, I ran into Irish McCalla in Googie's. She was in a front booth with a couple of people while Jimmy and the crew were in the usual rear booth. We were heading out when Irish looked up at me and then at Jimmy, and I said, "Hey, this is Irish McCalla, who's Sheena, Queen of the Jungle." Jimmy took her hand as if to shake it, but brought her up out of the booth. She was much taller than him and he started to giggle. She was still holding his hand as he mumbled something to her, bowing a little in mock-acknowledgment of her station as Queen of the Jungle. Then Jimmy said, "I'm gonna come swing in your tree, Sheena." She said that would be all right with her, as she had a lot of slack in the vines. I remember her looking at me and grinning.

When Jimmy asked your opinion, or how something might be "handled from a different perspective," as he'd put it, he was really seeking approval for something he'd already figured out. If you were critical of his unvoiced decision, or showed that you were no longer at ease with his antics, then you would be cast into the chorus of what he called "inconsequential grownups" and no longer of service to him.

People like Eartha Kitt and others whose particular intelligence or talents he valued were allowed to be critical of his behavior, but they could never be members of the the "night watch." We were, as one writer put it "the small handful of malcontents quite isolated from the mainstream, whose necessity to Jimmy so disturbs the studio front office that these hangers-on encouraging his rebelliousness are being noted in a way that assures what is called 'blackballing' in Hollywood . . ."

Jack's apartment was just west of Fairfax an old second-floor building with a large living room separated from a dining room by a serving divider, where a pair of Jimmy's old boots sat enshrined inside a clear plastic box. An unmade double bed was in the living room, and another bed and several stacks of boxes occupied the bedroom where Jimmy stayed when he didn't want to be chased down. Jack volunteered some ambiguous statements about his closeness to Jimmy, hinting at sex—"I won't say yes and I won't say no," he chirped. Even then, he claimed that he both loved and worshipped Jimmy, but that they were "friends first." It was bewildering to many, how important Jack was to Jimmy, over and above any of the members of the *Rebel* cast. Jimmy even suggested that Jack play Sal Mineo's role and had Jack tested for the part, though Jack, being not nearly as experienced an actor as Sal, would certainly have had a difficult time with it.

The test was shot one night on location during a break for another setup, and I'd ridden over with Jack in the hearse. It was the scene in the mansion with Sal and Natalie Wood, and tension quickly developed between Jack and Jimmy and myself. After the filming, Jack drove me to Hamburger Hamlet on the Strip, where we would later be met by Jimmy and Rolf Weutherich. They drove over in Jimmy's Porsche Speedster, at moments hitting seventy miles an hour along Sunset.

Jimmy drank milk at Hamburger Hamlet. He didn't smoke that night, complaining about a sore throat. The two of us talked about bikes for a while. Jack hardly spoke. After Jimmy left for his apartment on Sunset Plaza Drive, Jack said Jimmy had told him that he'd met me through James Sheldon—which wasn't accurate. I said I'd met Sheldon through Jimmy. That was the end of the conversation, though Jack wanted me to come to his place that night and talk to him. I said I couldn't. I had an interview first thing in the morning and I wanted to get to sleep. He asked me to meet him and Maila at Googie's the next day, and I said I'd call him, or talk to Jimmy. That upset him.

For days, Jack kept calling me and trying in every way he could to get me to talk about Jimmy and New York. Everything he said seemed to be an attempt to pry out some information about anything sexual that might have happened between Jimmy and myself.

A few nights later I was with Jimmy in the Speedster and he said Jack was driving him crazy. He said he thought Jack would take sleeping pills or cut his wrists. He told me Jack had said some things about me, even though Jimmy had claimed that he wasn't interested in the subject.

This was the night I saw Bill Smith on La Cienega at Melrose. Bill's sister had been an actress, and Bill was doggedly chasing a career of his own—years later he'd star with Clint Eastwood in *Any Which Way You Can*. I introduced Bill to Jimmy, who did not get out but reached across the passenger side to shake Bill's hand. Jimmy said, "Nice to meet you," then giggled a little and made some sort of face about Bill's forceful grip. I got out and Bill said, "I love this car." I went into a liquor store for cigarettes while Jimmy waited at the curb. When I came out, Jimmy had the hood open and they were standing at the rear of the car looking at the engine. I remember Jimmy nodding and Bill saying something about having worked on a Volkswagen engine, but never having seen a Porsche's. We got back in and Bill bent down by my side of the car, saying he was glad to have met Jimmy. When we drove off, Jimmy chuckled and asked, "Is that the guy you told me about, with the hard-on?"

I said yeah, to which Jimmy said, "What if he showed it to you now? What would you do now?" I said I didn't think he'd do that.

"That wasn't what I asked you," Jimmy said. "I said what would you do?"

"Nothing," I said.

Jimmy said, "We both know what Jack would do . . ." I said he wouldn't wait until Bill showed it to him, but I was sure Jack wouldn't survive to blab about the attempt. Jimmy laughed. He took my hand and put it on his crotch and said, "What if he did this?" He said he'd bet Bill wouldn't do something like that. He imagined Bill was all muscle without a whole lot "sparking between his ears." If Bill jacked off with the same strength he'd shown in shaking Jimmy's hand, he said, his cock was probably carried around in a sling. Jimmy had his hand around my left wrist, holding my hand on his crotch as he drove, moving both our hands to the shifter when he put in the clutch, guiding us into gear and saying, "Hey, I'm teaching you to drive, man."

A girl who had lost a leg in a motorcycle accident had been coming into Googie's, and said she really wanted to meet James Dean. She knew he liked talented and unusual people, and that he wasn't a phony like so many other movie and television assholes she claimed to know. I was sitting in a booth alongside Jimmy one night when he nudged me with his elbow and pointed across the aisle. The girl was sitting at the counter, looking right at him and smiling. He said, "You see that girl? She's a nice girl. She's only got one leg." He told me her name was Terry, though that wasn't her name. This girl, who also sang in clubs on the Strip, would later write an autobiography in which she described Jimmy coming to her apartment and asking her to take off her clothes, and when she did, telling her how beautiful she was and kissing her stump.

One night, we rode to a party at the home of Samson DeBrier, a Hollywood "character" and actor rumored to have been the homosexual lover of André Gide, author of *The Immoralist*. Samson's house was a museum of pirated movie relics and antique set decorations. He usually held what was called an "open house," a kind of revolving door party. Kenneth Anger's film *Inauguration of the Pleasure Dome*—featuring DeBrier, Anaïs Nin, and experimental filmmaker Curtis Harrington—had been filmed in the house. Jimmy was eager to meet and talk to Samson.

Among the people there that night was another young and struggling actor I'd seen around town, a nice guy named Jack Nicholson from New Jersey. He was all smiles when he saw Jimmy and asked me to introduce him. I said to Jimmy, "This is Jack Nicholson," and Jack reached out his hand, but Jimmy mumbled something and turned around to talk with Samson. The snub had nothing to do with Jack personally, it was something Jimmy did, but Jack was embarrassed and I made up some excuse, telling him it was the wind and the bikes that did something to Jimmy's eyes and ears.

Jack nodded and turned to a cute girl. He never let on that he'd been bothered by Jimmy's snubbing, though in the instant it had happened I could see him caving in right in front of me.

I'd met Dick Clayton, Jimmy's agent, at Famous Artists while he was handling Tab Hunter, following Tab's flight from Henry Wilson. Dick was also handling a kid actress named Tuesday Weld and living in a single apartment with a Murphy bed, on Norton just north of Santa Monica Boulevard. There was no connection between Tab and Jimmy as friends, or even acquaintances. In fact, Jimmy rarely socialized with other actors, especially members of the *Rebel* cast—not even Natalie Wood. He was not friendly or on talking terms with other Warner contract players like Sal Mineo or Dennis Hopper. In time, Sal would be one of the few people to publicly state his distance from Jimmy—while still desiring to have been closer in any way possible. Following Jimmy's death—others like Dennis and Nick Adams—would not be able to resist fabricating personal friendships with Jimmy that had little to do with real life.

During the filming of *Rebel*, Jack Simmons stayed close at hand. He was excluded from Jimmy's celebrity hobnobbing, though Jimmy only put in the occasional, obligatory "flash in the pan" appearance. His real, vital private life was being played out no differently than in his night wanderings through New York. Sammy Davis, Jr., for one, was always tickled by the bad-boy stories circulating around Jimmy, and openly fawned over the "hottest actor in town."

Jimmy's Hollywood career spanned only eighteen months and three motion pictures, two not yet released at the time of his death. In that brief time, everyone wanted to meet him or get close to him, but Jimmy shied off into the shadows of his own notoriety.

"I only have this one life to live," he said, "and there's too many things I don't know yet . . ."

Though he'd signed on to play Billy the Kid in *The Left-handed Gun* and Rocky Graziano in the prizefighter's life story, and to star in *Somebody Up There Likes Me* alongside Pier Angeli, Jimmy's "movie star" abode was a cramped furnished apartment above the Sunset Strip. It had one room, and a kitchen littered with paper cups and takeouts from Googie's or Hamburger Hamlet, plus stacks of papers and spools of reel-to-reel tapes. His clothes were thrown into the closet—he'd scoop up some shirts and pants from a chair, open the little closet with a partitioned door like a folding screen, and throw the clothes in on top of whatever else was there. "Hollywood is not my home," he said. He still kept a small apartment in New York, but claimed that that was not his home either. He'd been back again to Fairmount, Indiana with photographer Dennis Stock, who took those prophetic pictures of Jimmy sitting in a coffin, but neither was Indiana his home, he said. And neither was Santa Monica, where his estranged father still lived, remarried to another woman that Jimmy stayed away from.

One time he wanted to ride to Tijuana and had me race up to his place. He was leaning against the sink in the small kitchen, eating sardines from a can and looking sick. He'd been cut during the filming of a knife fight for *Rebel*, and he'd also been accidentally tapped on the cheekbone by Mushy Callahan, an old prize fighter who was showing Jimmy the ropes for the Graziano story. I asked him if the slight stab had hurt, and he told me that the pain was good, because it "clarified direction." He said, "Any pain is like misdirected energy." He said it was important to read Gerald Heard's *Pain, Sex and Time*. "You know, atado, Strasberg in New York and these fuckers at the studio are afraid of pain," he said. "But without pain, no discoveries would be made. It was the fear of the pain of death," he continued, "and not death itself that kept the fat numb people from making discoveries."

The discoveries Jimmy wanted to make were in some unknown territory a good distance from the conventions accepted by someone like Pier Angeli. While making *Eden,* Jimmy was having sex with Pier in the dressing room he occupied during most of the filming on his first picture. He said she'd been a little "tight," but tasted "good like a pizza."

When the picture was finished, he didn't want to leave the studio and stayed holed up in his dressing room. Loaning out Jimmy to star in *Somebody Up There Likes Me* would give Warners the chance to further play up the romance between Jimmy and Pier. Any connection between the two short of marriage meant additional box-office for Warners. But no one anticipated Jimmy's volatile mood swings or the depth of the personal confusion that was being kindled by his sudden success like a heat ray through a magnifying glass. Though the studio drummed-up the studio romance between Pier and Jimmy, no one could have anticipated the peculiar chemistry that passed between them in that short, intense time.

Pier later said, in characteristically dramatic fashion, "I brought out in Jimmy the small boy that he kept locked in his heart, or in his mind. This small boy was a very troubled one. He wanted me to love him unconditionally, but Jimmy was not able to love someone else in return, that is, with any deep feeling for that other person. He wanted to be loved. It was the troubled boy that wanted to be loved very badly. I loved Jimmy as I have loved no one else in my life, but I could not give him the enormous amount of love that he needed. It emptied me. Loving Jimmy was something that could empty a person. There was no other way to be with Jimmy except to love him and be emptied of yourself . . ."

Jimmy never had it seriously in mind to marry Pier. To people he thought the idea would please, he suggested the "possibility of matrimony." But on the practical side, he was more concerned about the horse he'd bought and what it ate and where it was stabled.

When Pier rushed into a sudden marriage to her ex-boyfriend, singer Vic Damone, the head-hanging attitude adopted by Jimmy drew sympathy from those he wanted to feel sorry for him. But to others he said of Pier and Damone, "Fuck them both—who the fuck needs them? People who nobody needs, they find each other."

There were the rumors of a few brief "romances," rumors that have been drastically exaggerated over the years, elaborated in the fantasies put forth as fact by those claiming to have been "involved" with Jimmy. What relationships he had following Pier's marriage to

Damone, Jimmy handled as carelessly as he did the sports cars he raced, with the same recklessness as he rode his motorcycle. Back in New York, he'd used my bike a couple of times, but he wasn't good at handling it. In Hollywood, he traded in his Triumph and bought another one with a bigger engine. He was impulsive, taking more chances than he had two years earlier, yet he still rode a motorcycle like a farmer. There wasn't really anything copacetic between Jimmy and a machine, like there was with Steve McQueen. Though I'd never like McQueen or get along with him, I had to salute his handling of cars and bikes. Steve knew machines.

Jimmy didn't. He wanted to, but even if there had been more time it would have remained another thing Jimmy claimed he had to do, had to know. He would have lacked the discipline and focus to follow through. When he entered his Speedster in races, he wasn't there to race, but to win. Winning with Jimmy was more important than the race.

His one-month relationship with the young actress Ursula Andress was going nowhere. Jimmy told me her mouth reminded him of Miriam's in New York, "but Ursula and me can't get an intelligent situation going, and her perfume chokes me," he said. "But we're getting our pictures taken and it's hotsy-totsy time in Hollywood! We're all going to the moon!" he sang.

Some publicists claimed Jimmy rode his bike to the church where Pier was marrying Damone, and that he sat across the street and then gunned the engine and took off dramatically. In truth, Jimmy described himself as an "existential pencil" who felt nothing about Pier marrying Damone. There was no sense of loss, he said, though he'd act the "poor injured soul" to the hilt for those who'd understand the "conventional approach" and readily applaud Jimmy's performance of "Woe is me, oh, woe is me!"

The pain that Jimmy felt could not be understood by others. Kazan had eyeballed it instantly and tagged it as "a crazy streak in the person who's always jumping around without any provocation from the outside." And then there were the discoveries Jimmy had to make. "Discoveries can be inside the person," Jimmy said. The thing about making them was that you had to pit yourself against the outside, and the only way to get inside yourself was by putting yourself in situations that were risky, that you couldn't back out of once you got into them.

The religious shadows hanging over Pier's life seemed to bind

Jimmy up in contradictory feelings. He played out a kind of "I've been converted" role for some of those close to Pier, but was far more clearly intrigued by "those destructive influences of beliefs based on torture and blood and crucifixion." Later he said, "I believe in freedom, not God. If you want to call freedom God, then you can say I believe in God, but I say I believe in freedom." He claimed he had "a lot to discover," and that maybe others would prove that he was wrong.

He said riding bikes and driving race cars, sex, photography, bullfighting, and people like the one-legged girl were the real "avenues of discovery." Ursula Andress, he said, while she was cute and sexy, seemed to question nothing about the role Hollywood had stamped onto her. In fact, she'd bypassed Jimmy in favor of an actor of "shallow talents," John Derek. The only good thing about Derek, said Jimmy, was the line he'd delivered in the Bogart movie *Knock On Any Door*, "Live fast, die young, and have a good-looking corpse." With that, Jimmy gave a little two-fingered salute and stepped off into infinity.

AN ACTOR'S LIFE FOR ME

"I'M GLAD DEAN'S DEAD," said Steve McQueen. "It makes more room for me." We were on the sidewalk of 14th Street, and I was facing McQueen as he straddled a British motorcycle backed against the side of the stoop of the old apartment house where I occupied the rear first floor overlooking an alley. It was the first conversation I'd had with McQueen since the girl he'd been living with broke off with him and moved in with me. Gena, a black haired, dark-eyed dancer and actress, still wanted to be friends with Steve—a "no hard feelings" sort of thing. She told him that I'd hung around with Jimmy Dean, but instead of being impressed, Steve hated even more the idea that since Gena had left him, she'd started sleeping with me, and had moved in with me as she'd once lived in his flat a few blocks away.

McQueen's comments bothered me because Jimmy hadn't been the only friend I'd lost that year. Dean had died at the end of September at twenty-four, and less than a month later John Hodiak died at forty-one. John had married again and had a house in the Valley. Though his career was in trouble, he still had hopes of grabbing the good life in Hollywood. What he'd feared more than death was being forgotten. "*Lifeboat*," he said one of the last times we talked, "is the

84

only picture they'll remember, but it's Hitchcock's picture they're talking about. It's *Hitchcock's* movie . . ."

"If I was superstitious," I told McQueen, "I'd say you might buy a curse from the gods with a statement like that about Dean's dying." I sort of laughed a little to let him know I thought he was joking, when I knew he wasn't. His excitement over Jimmy's death making more *room* for him was a reflection of McQueen's bedrock, almost absolute self-absorption.

He was eating poorly, stealing food from grocery stores even when he had money in his pocket to pay for it. "He's been a thief so long," Gena said, "he's forgotten how not to be one. Everywhere he goes he steals something." He wore a ratty black raincoat with inside pockets he'd wedge full of what he'd steal, and his thinness and the weight of the coat pulling downward made the ends of his shoulders stick up like knobs. Nights he'd hang around Louie's Tavern, a basement bar next to a coffee house on West Fourth at Sheridan Square called Pandora's Box. He borrowed money from actors like Ben Gazzara and Anthony Franciosa, and I'd see him stealing tips from bars and from tables in coffeehouses.

McQueen's mother would partly fall down the stairs into Louie's to beg Steve's friends to buy her drinks. She'd say she'd show them "a good time." Once I saw her pass out and drop from a stool to the sawdust floor while Steve made a fast exit up the stairs. Stewed to the gills, his mother would press against some guy drinking with Steve and make a play for drinks. McQueen told Gena he wished his mother was dead— that she'd just disappear from his life and "quit hounding" him. His only escape, he said, was in making it as an actor, hitting it big and getting out of New York. He *had* to make it. He told Gena he'd do anything to get on top.

"He'd kill for a part in something," she told me. "He said, 'Name me a Jew or a wop and give me a fuckin' shiv and I'll eat his gizzard to get in a show.'" Gena told him she was a wop, and he said he was talking about "*them*—in show business." He told her he'd thought of killing his mother. She was a "drunken slut," he said, and if there was any way to boost his career by having her dead, she'd "already be laying in a morgue."

And he hated horses. Whether he made that clear to me because Gena had told him I'd worked with horses and Jimmy Dean had had a horse, or whether it was because he knew that Jimmy's concern for a horse was greater than for "a piece of ass," McQueen said that horses "disgusted" him. Watching the way a horse's ass puckered when it shit was something that turned his stomach. He told Gena it gave him nightmares.

I'd come to see that McQueen was riddled with hate. He said he hated "niggers and Jews and wops," and he hated me because I had blond hair and blue eyes and chances were we'd show up for the same part, though McQueen was a little older than me. He hated other actors, too, even those *without* blond hair and blue eyes, especially if they were working and he wasn't. Then his thoughts of murder included all those who were employed, if only in a bit part or a walk-on. He said he couldn't understand why God would let someone else get the job when it was so important for McQueen to make it.

His dislike for me turned to something even more sinister when he learned that I knew the actor and director Frank Corsaro, who was then on the board of the Actors Studio and conducting his own classes outside the Studio. While Gena had lived with McQueen, he'd told her he'd suck anyone's cock—he didn't care if was a Jew or a nigger—he'd get fucked or fuck anyone who'd get him a part in a show.

I was ambivalent about McQueen and wouldn't have known him if not for Gena wanting the three of us to be friends. But it would surface that Gena talking to me about McQueen was a dreadful source of worry to him. He'd confided his secret thoughts to her, and for this information to get out was more frightening to him than if he'd stuck a knife in someone instead of putting their cock in his mouth.

The notion that anyone might think McQueen was "queer" kept him in a state of turmoil. He told Gena that if he ever had to "suck on a dick" to get work, then he'd wish—he'd *pray*—that person would get "a heart attack or a stroke and die," and there'd be no way for anyone to know how McQueen had got the part, except by way of the talent he longed so desperately to possess —or, for that matter, how he'd managed to get hooked up with the Actors Studio later that year after our awkward conversation on 14th Street.

Gena had broken it off with him after traveling to Maine, where he was appearing in a stock production of *Two Fingers of Pride*, directed by Frank Corsaro. When Gena found Steve in bed with a young female member of the cast, she screamed for a few minutes and headed back to New York. She packed up what she'd moved into Steve's and ran off to a girlfriend's in the Village.

The first time I talked to Gena was at the end of a warm, bright day. An evening breeze was coming down the Village streets carrying scents of lemon and espresso, sausage and pizza. Along West Fourth the lights sparkled in the clear air, and Gena was sitting on the sill of an open window at Pandora's Box. I stopped and looked up at her. Her long, black, wavy hair, parted down the center, was moving in the breeze, and her face was like that of an exotic Hindu princess. She was staring down at me. "Are you coming in?" she asked. I smiled and went up the steps.

Looking back, I don't know why I got involved with Gena—I suppose I never loved her, though I thought I could. She'd tell me in time, "I saw you and I wanted to be with you, and if you hadn't been an actor and didn't look like you do, I'd never have made a play for you. But I did want you, and then when we were together, I knew it was going to be a mistake to go as far as we'd go . . ." We actually got married.

While living with McQueen, she said, he told her he wanted to marry her, but first he had to make it as an actor—that is, unless she got famous first. "Then, baby," he said, "you just watch us fly." Being a hard worker, Gena found herself carrying the burden of McQueen's unemployment. But he didn't like people to know she was paying the bills, or even that she was living with him. He'd check the hallways to make sure no one would see her coming and going.

Stephen Ross, another actor and a mutual friend, said McQueen didn't want anyone to know he had a woman living with him. "Steve wanted people to think he balled a lot of chicks," Ross told me, "that he'd fuck'em and boot 'em out. That's the image he wanted. No chick was going to stake a claim on Steve—the loner." There were two other young girls living in the building that McQueen was chasing while Gena worked nights as a waitress so that he wouldn't have to steal food. He didn't want Gena and the girls running into each other.

McQueen's MG sports car had a canvas flap that could zipper over the seats, dash and steering wheel when he wasn't using it, and a center zipper to close off the passenger side while driving. Gena said, "It was important that people thought of him as a loner—a sort of lone wolf image was what he wanted. A couple of times we went to the auto races in New Jersey, and when we came out of the parking lot he had me crawl down on the floor so he could zip the canvas over the passenger side. He'd cruise out of the parking lot, looking like he was alone in the sports car. He wanted people to say things like, 'There he goes, the loner, a guy alone, the Lone Ranger, that guy . . .' That's what he wanted."

For hours McQueen would stare at himself in a mirror mounted to the wall. "I've *got* to make it," he'd say to his face. "You're *going* to make it," he'd answer. "You have to make it, man. You *have* to!" The dialogues often became rages, and neighbors complained about the shouting. They'd knock on the walls.

Sometimes McQueen seemed drained of life, sucked dry and gray. Wasted, he'd stare into the mirror, hunting for that possible flaw, the thing that was holding him back from fame. He'd stare hungrily at pictures of James Dean and Marlon Brando, trying to ape and emulate their expressions and gestures in the mirror. He'd constantly grill Gena on how he compared to Dean and Brando, and what the differences were. "It became an obsession, or else it always was," she said. "It was confusing and strange. There'd be fights—actual fights where I'd be slapping him and he'd be punching me. I'd kick him, try to kick him hard. Once I burned a jacket of his in the oven."

McQueen's mother tracked him down to where he lived and she'd wait on the stoop or lay unconscious in the hallway, blocking the door. Gena said she once could barely get out of the apartment because Steve's mother had passed out against the door. At those times, McQueen would "run away," Gena said, "maybe for a day or two days," until his mother would drift off somewhere else. "But he'd be out there and trying to find some girl—any female—to have sex with."

When Gena found out she was pregnant, she said, "Steve made me go get a scraping and dusting at the hospital. I bled for a week, and chunks of coagulated blood and tissue were falling out of me. I was still working nights and sending him money up to Maine. I'd paid for him to join Actors Equity so he could get into the play. When the bleeding stopped, I took off for a weekend and went up to see him. That's when I found him in bed with one of the girls . . ."

Susan Oliver, an actress I later worked with in television and became very close to, attended the Neighborhood Playhouse with McQueen before he started hanging around the Village. Before starring in *Look Back in Anger* on Broadway, she went out with Steve a couple of times, but got sick of his bugging her for money. "Loans here and there," Susan told me, "for gas money, for a motorcycle he'd wrangle off someone, for coffee money—like getting a cup of coffee with Steve, you'd wind up paying the check for something he'd eat as well. He wanted to make out with me but I wasn't interested, so he put the tap on me. I got damn sick of it.

"I wasn't a girlfriend of Steve's. I told him he should get a girlfriend; one who had some extra money and didn't mind footing the bill for everything. I wasn't anything to Steve, and he wasn't anything to me. He was a pain in the neck and a moocher . . . I didn't know why he was taking acting lessons. He said he was doing it to get the money from the government to support him while he screwed around the Village."

Stephen Ross appeared in *End as a Man* at the Theater de Lys and hung around with McQueen a good part of those New York days. One night Ross was in Louie's Tavern when Steve repeatedly poked a young girl's stomach whenever she walked past, suggesting that they could have a swell time in the sack. She was with a young guy who became annoyed with Steve's poking and attentions, and as McQueen walked past, the young guy poked him hard in the stomach, knocking the air out of McQueen. "At first," Ross said, "I thought Steve was going to retaliate, but instead he backed down. He had every opportunity to take a swing, but you could see the kid was ready for it and looked like he'd lay Steve flat out if he threw a punch. He was shorter than Steve, too, but Steve bowed out. He was afraid. The only time I think he was tough was when he was belting some chick around."

For all McQueen's talk about longshoremen and being a "hardass," he was actually "chicken," Ross said. His pal wasn't as rough as he bragged to be, and Ross had learned something else about Steve. "He was soft in the belly. He couldn't take it in the belly. Even scuffling around a little, he'd get himself crouched forward sort of, shielding his gut as best he could, but that'd leave his kisser wide open. He liked to talk about street fights and get it across that he'd been a tough kid, but he wasn't. It was a role he played better than anything he ever did as an actor. That, and being a friend. I knew Steve for almost half a dozen years. We'd been through a lot of crap together, a lot of thin spots, you know, like they say, thick and thin. It was mostly thin, and I laid myself on the line for the guy a number of times.

"As soon as he got that television series in Hollywood, he told me to come out there and he'd get me work on the show—help me get straightened out. A lot of New York actors were heading west. I sold everything I had, gave up my apartment and everything to take up Steve's offer. When I got out there, I couldn't get through to him. He had this office set up that screened people. When they got my message through to him that I'd made it to L.A., Steve said he didn't know me."

McQueen had been so taken with James Dean after the release of *East of Eden*, he'd spend hours poring over movie magazines with stories on Dean. He'd study the photographs, attempting to ape the "smoldering, brooding look," as it was called, while at the same time dismissing Dean as another "Brando imitator," which was exactly what McQueen had tried to be before Jimmy's success.

"He'd read about the MG Dean bought," Gena said, "and that's why he had to have that car, like the motorcycle. Everything had to be like James Dean."

McQueen hung around Roy Schatt's studio, reasoning that the photographer would find something in Steve reminiscent of Jimmy. But Schatt only found McQueen "a bore, no different than the hordes of others who showed up wanting me to take pictures of them after Dean was dead."

Gena believed it was a "mental quirk" of Steve's, this desire to have people think he was like Dean. But after she found Steve in bed with another girl, Gena didn't want to finance Steve's obsessions any further. That was a couple of months before I met her in Pandora's Box. When the bill for Gena's abortion showed up in McQueen's mailbox, he sent it to her, saying, "This is your problem. I don't pay for nobody's problems."

I'd been preparing a scene from an original teleplay for the Actors Studio and needed someone to audition with. A girl I knew was attending the Neighborhood Playhouse and suggested a fellow student for the scene, James Earl Jones. He'd never worked professionally, but was seriously studying and wanted to be an actor.

Jones told me had no illusions about "living a grand life as some star," only that he wanted to act. He said, "It's like someone who wants to fish or tinker around with mechanical things. I believe the need for that is inside, and you have to follow it or be unhappy in your life." We met a number of times to talk and work on the scene. Jones would portray a young black detective, and I was the sullen juvenile delinquent accused of car theft and robbery.

We'd sometimes meet in the Mayflower Coffee Shop on the east side, often talking for a couple of hours. Jones told me about his background, where he was from and how he'd overcome an early problem with stuttering. We talked about some John Wayne movies and a picture Tex Williams had made. We talked about jazz, and Jones said he knew a musician from Kenya, Africa—a Kikuyu who had operated a little puppet theater. Jones said he believed the guy had been with the Mau Mau, trying to drive out the Europeans and give the government back to the Kenyans. I told Jones I hadn't been bothered by the Mau Maus' views. He said he believed in what Mau Mau stood for, but until he became famous he'd never admit it out in the open. He claimed he could hide some of his "deeper" beliefs, but he couldn't change the color of his skin.

Frank Corsaro said Jones and I worked really well together, that the chemistry between us was "fiery and arresting." We were called back for the second audition before Strasberg and Kazan, but we weren't accepted. Rip Torn, another young actor who'd been hanging around Broadway and politically working his way into the Actors Studio, presented a scene that night from Tennessee Williams' *This Property Is Condemned*. Though Frank Corsaro said it had been a "toss-up" between the Williams scene and ours, I had trouble convincing Jones that we weren't turned down because he was black. He said, "I've been told Strasberg has tried to keep Negro actors out of the Studio. I think that is a shame," he said, "if such a thing should prove to be true."

One night after I'd started seeing Gena, McQueen lost control of his motorcycle and crashed down into Louie's Tavern. He plummeted down the stairs into the barroom, and a couple of big, gun-packing Italian guys Louie had hanging around carried McQueen and his motorcycle back up onto the sidewalk and laid them both against the curb.

Not long after, McQueen and I wound up interviewing for the same part. He had one foot still bandaged, and was rocking back and forth on the seat in the waiting room, staring at me. His eyes were distant as though myopic, and he bit his lips and twisted his hands. Gena was still living with me, and McQueen cornered her in Pandora's, wanting to know "what the hell" I was doing showing up for a part he was being considered for. He told her he'd have to cut my throat. He said, "It's nothing personal, you understand. I'll cut anybody's throat, so you can tell him for me . . ." All McQueen and I had in common were the same sort of casting looks, Gena said, and we'd both been brought up in the East Hollywood or Silver Lake section of L.A. I got the part in the television show, and according to Gena, Steve had watched it, and told her he would've been far better than I was. After that, he wouldn't look at me, even if we were face to face on the street.

She'd tell me she'd see Steve in Pandora's, or uptown, or while I was on an interview, or in Frank Corsaro's afternoon class. They seemed to be running into each other all over the place. I didn't know it at the time, but the meetings weren't by chance.

Corsaro claimed to have been friendly with Dean from the Theater de Lys, where Frank had directed a play years before. But what Corsaro said he first saw in McQueen was a "sluggish mimicry of Dean . . . a kind of travesty." Frank said Jimmy stayed with him for a short time, but after Dean's death, his attention shifted to McQueen, who'd been in the road company of a play with Melyvn Douglas, directed by Corsaro.

Frank brought Steve in as understudy in the Actors Studio production of *Hatful of Rain* with Ben Gazzara and Tony Franciosa. At this time, the Warners film *Somebody Up There Likes Me* was in production with Paul Newman having taken over Jimmy's lead. During some New York second-unit shooting, McQueen was one of several actors hired for bit parts.

In a short time, Corsaro would distance himself from McQueen, claiming that Steve had been "openly begging for anything to come his way. . . desperate to be connected to Actors Studio and quite willing to take any shortcut to get what he was after. . ."

Though he'd moved out of the downtown flat and had a small apartment uptown, McQueen kept coming down to the Village to see Gena. I didn't know they were meeting, and during this time Steve and I made an awkward try at a friendship. But when he saw books in the apartment, he demanded to know who they belonged to and how long I'd had them and if I'd read them—and if I had, what had I learned that was supposed to make me smarter than him?

He sent Gena complimentary tickets to the play when Ben Gazzara left to do a movie and Steve stepped into the leading role. We had choice seats, but could hardly hear his lines—a few rows from the footlights and he *still* wasn't audible. He gave a stiff, cardboard performance, and his movements seemed to blueprint the blocking and staging as though he were walking through a rehearsal. Harry Guardino, standing in for Tony Franciosa, gave a stunning, brilliant performance that rendered McQueen invisible.

Two days later I saw Steve and Corsaro arguing at the bar in Jim Downey's Restaurant. McQueen was complaining about his throat and that he didn't want to go on that night, while Corsaro insisted that he had to go on. "You have to adopt at least some basic rules of theater," the director said, but McQueen kept shaking his head. No matter how Corsaro tried to convince him that "the show must go on," McQueen balked. Another actor from the play said McQueen was terrified of the audience: "He wasn't an actor like you'd think. He was afraid of the audience, of the theater, and of the rest of us on stage. My God, I'm in the middle of a scene and I'm looking into this terrified face that sees nothing and just stands there. I had to cue the fucker under my breath almost every one of his lines. He couldn't remember anything, and he was plain rotten. It was almost impossible to hear him from the third row. He was Corsaro's choice for understudy, and by default went on stage. He ruined the production—quite apart from personally being a fucking asshole."

McQueen was fired from the show, but was not without resources. "One thing about Steve," the same actor told me, "he was always going to land on his feet. Didn't matter if he happened to land on *your* feet—just so his were on the ground."

He'd met a dancer named Neile Toffel who had a part in the musical *The Pajama Game*. She was giving McQueen modest amounts of money for his expenses, although he was still trying to get money from Gena. When Neile was to sign with Robert Wise to work in the movie version of the musical, McQueen quickly moved in with her and began to talk seriously about marriage—and about being introduced to Robert Wise. He was positive that someone as important as Wise would spot the parallel between McQueen and James Dean.

Meanwhile, I married Gena in Connecticut. She'd been married and divorced once before, the year before she took up with McQueen. She claimed that she loved me, as Neile now loved Steve. But what neither Neile nor I knew was that McQueen and Gena were getting together in Neile's apartment while Neile was still doing the musical on Broadway and while I thought Gena was working with a new dance company.

SUBTERRANEAN HOLLYWOOD

I WAS CALLED BACK TO HOLLYWOOD about a part in a picture at RKO, and Gena and I sold the lease to our West 68th Street apartment and bought two one-way tickets west. I sold books, bullwhip, guitar and mandolin, and with a little extra we got a berth on the plane and curled up for the flight. At one point somewhere over the Grand Canyon, I was making love to Gena from behind while she had her chin raised to the airplane window.

In L.A., we stayed a few days with my mother before taking a place on Beachwood up toward Hollywoodland, and after a couple of weeks we were on the Strip hanging out with her father, who was now writing for the movies and living at the Park Sunset across from Ciro's.

Tops Restaurant was in the building next to Otto Preminger's office, and Hollywood's favorite gangster, Mickey Cohen, was in and out of Tops almost daily with a goon or two at his side. Gena's father was chummy with the hood, affording me the opportunity of some hit -and-miss dialogue with Cohen. We chatted about some of L.A.'s famous crimes, like the Black Dahlia murder. Cohen said he'd talked to the beautiful black-haired victim at the Florentine Gardens nightclub not long before her death. He told her she was hanging with a bad bunch and gave her a fifty-dollar bill to take a hike. He talked about his late close pal Johnny Stompanato—stabbed dead, supposedly by Lana Turner's daughter. But Mickey Cohen said, "That's a crock. The kid took the rap to save the bitch's skin. No matter what Lana puts her mitts on, it turns to shit in front of your eyes." Mickey knew my father was a cop who'd been pooled in on the Black Dahlia investigation, but he didn't hold that against me since I was an actor.

Life with Gena that spring in Hollywood bounced between the Park Sunset and Schwab's drugstore—sometimes Googie's, but for me, the place was sort of haunted. So we buzzed around the Unicorn, a beatnik joint where Lenny Bruce was hanging out along with some poets, folk singers and a gaggle of struggling actors like Warren Oates, Jack Nicholson and Dean Stanton (who wasn't using "Harry" in those days). Sally Kellerman had finished Hollywood High and sat around nursing coffee in Schwab's, the West Coast equivalent of Cromwell's.

Everyone kept track of everyone else, but there was a marked distinction between "working actors" and those who hadn't landed something, no matter how small. If the part was something good, you rarely hung out in Schwab's, and the friends you'd had were no longer your friends. The endless stream of revolving-door hopefuls from Idaho or Houston who'd never get a part usually went unnoticed except by people like Steve McQueen, who would frequently pluck out a morsel for his never-ending romps.

Nobody cared about these people from other places who'd never work in Hollywood, and it was not unusual for some of them to be put to use as small sacrifices to what Jack Nicholson jokingly termed "the insatiable bitch goddess." And it was good to keep her looking the other way! What's been called "subterranean Hollywood" by some writers hardly presents a whole or accurate picture, however, nor was there any kind of allegiance to a sociological sweep or a countercultural movement such as the Beats; all that mattered was who was working and who wasn't, and a textbook adherence to the mechanics of cutting someone else out of work to jockey yourself in front of the camera.

No one was ever "discovered" in Schwab's. None of the hopefuls nursing coffee at the counter, like Sally Kellerman or Warren Oates or Harry Dean Stanton, expected to be discovered, because no one came into Schwab's looking for talent—only to mooch money or try to get laid.

An exodus of New York actors in search of work was crowding L.A.'s casting calls, and that particular flood of Manhattan bodies brought with it some heady thinking that would indelibly color the Hollywood scene. Dedicated actors wanted to do meaningful work, but they had to survive first. The hunger was more apparent on the faces in Schwab's than it had been on Broadway.

The East Coast actors believed they had the God-given task of shoveling some integrity into the failing movies. But hard-line Hollywood wasn't fooled by their elitist patter. "She takes her pick," Warren Oates said, "and dumps the others at the side of the road, like you throw a bag of rotten bananas out the window."

Aspiring actor Jack Nicholson had the distinctive quality of lacking allegiance to either coast. Jack was a young man constantly vacillating between what was called for and what he hoped for. Always on the fringe, he'd prove more complicated than they were giving him credit for. Some thought he was a little simple-minded, that he couldn't measure up to a serious actor by any means, but unlike McQueen, lacked the cut-throat ambition. He was like a crow, waiting for the jackals to take their fill. Some braver souls set aside survival, turning down the low-budget garbage that got ground out like fat. They sought out only the lean and meaningful. But not Jack Nicholson, who never fretted over "contaminating" his career. Clearly, he lacked the inner barometer of a New York actor—that ability to sniff out the difference between the putrid junk and the art. Failing to make these distinctions, Jack simply dismissed what he did, saying he barely remembered one day from the last.

Some said it was all the dope he smoked. You couldn't take Jack seriously; he was more like a spectator than a participant, patiently waiting for those of finer sensibilities to turn down a dead turkey so he could swoop in to scavenge the bones.

He took the dumb jobs serious actors turned up their noses at. Jack was always "along for the ride," for the fun of it—if any fun was to be had. Like Janis, later, he just wanted to get stoned, kick around a laugh or two, and maybe get some ass. He wasn't interested in art or Method Acting or the Moscow Art Theater, and Stanislavsky could have been an exotic vodka for all Jack cared. He bored quickly with the avant-garde unless it offered a couple of bucks or some grass—harder to come by than Idaho ass. He once told me, "I don't care who I fuck, as long as it isn't Gravel Gerty—" He stopped and reconsidered, saying, "Unless she's in the dark." If he had to pretend to know something about theater or art, he said he'd give it a shot. "After all, I am an actor," he said.

He was impressed with McQueen's lucky streak, and admitted he'd "sell off twenty" for a chance at the girls McQueen was racking up on the sly from his wife. Usually somewhat of a quiet guy, Jack was just sort of there, hanging around, a pothead, a smiling face in the upstairs quasi-Zen existential book shop of the Unicorn, pretending to be reading as he smoked grass with a few of the regulars. He wasn't impressed with Lenny Bruce, though Lenny once shot out a stinging monologue about his marriage problems that had Jack crying with laughter—a rare moment when Lenny hadn't intended to be funny. He asked Jack rather seriously, "What the fuck's the *matter* with you, man?"

Jack laughed at that as well. He thought a lot of things were funny, and he'd often tell jokes nobody else laughed at, or he'd try to stir up conversations around subjects nobody cared about. He was like a store-window mannequin at times, as though someone had come in with this Jack Nicholson dummy and set it down in a booth at Schwab's and just left it to sit there, smiling.

There was something phony in his adulation of successful actors who'd happen into Schwab's for prescriptions or cologne or toilet articles or anything else, and have these charged to their accounts. Jack wanted an account at Schwab's. He said, "When I open one here, I know they'll think I've made the grade."

He said he'd seriously wanted to work in *The Blob,* a grotesque science fiction cheapie that gave McQueen his first starring role. Marty Landau, later teaching Actors Studio-style classes in L.A., said, "No one says they want to be in such a monstrosity, but you gotta live, so you always apologize for making a fool of yourself. You don't *hunger* to be a fool."

While *The Blob* made a killing at the drive-ins, McQueen's acting was compared to the blob itself—"a shameless aping of the late James Dean." But Steve's aping landed him the lead on a mediocre television Western series. Career on a roll, McQueen bought thick-knit sweaters by the dozen, a 1600 Porsche Speedster, the same as Dean's, to accelerate his "cunt chase," he told a stuntman. Steve picked up girls wherever he could. "Get in," he'd say. "Shut the door . . . You know who I am, right?" He told one girl he didn't like to talk—she could see him talking in the movies—but had some dope to turn her on. Though never a brilliant conversationalist, McQueen spun together makeshift lies about loneliness, about his wife, Neile, who was in New York or

Vegas or someplace else. He prowled the Strip hang-outs, making arrangements to meet his dates out of sight—around corners or behind buildings.

It was only a matter of time before Gena and McQueen linked up on the Coast. One night after she met him secretly behind a bar on Santa Monica, Steve managed a moment of insight, confiding that he felt like he'd gone to bed a flop and a failure and awoke to hard success, though inside he remained a flop and a failure. It was like Brando's line in *Viva Zapata* about a monkey in silk still being a monkey. McQueen thought he could never be that person everyone was seeing on the silver screen. He was afraid his life was going to collapse on top of him. He was empty, he said; it was the reason he needed so many things—so much dope, so many girls, cars, motorcycles—you name it, he *needed* it. His life was a hole that had to be filled.

Perhaps this self-conscious episode was just another lie—a kind of mating call—because McQueen quickly talked Gena into furthering the affair they'd had in New York, even though she was married to me. The fact that a woman was married never had any significance to McQueen.

Back in New York when Jimmy had been in *The Immoralist,* I'd met the playwright Leonard Kantor. He'd been an artist before turning to theater, and I spoke with him a few times. He'd known McQueen "back then"—had loaned him money, he said, for "favors best left unsaid." Kantor was then in L.A., writing scripts for *The Untouchables,* starring Robert Stack. He said McQueen was still hustling, a "habit he'll never break . . . it's what he'll always be." Only now, Kantor said, McQueen had the stamp of middle-class approval, and his crazed and tortured side couldn't cope with his success. "He'll never *have* the good life he lives with every day." He agreed with Gena—McQueen's inability to accept himself, his past, was creating a terrible rift in his life, a constant void. Worse, it was eating him up like an enormous ulcer, demanding appeasement by any available means. Gena shared the booze and dope with McQueen, she said, because she felt sorry for him. She said she knew I could never understand her pity. And she believed for a short time that she was the only one he was sleeping with, as he was cheating on his wife, while Gena cheated on me.

With a sly smile, Kantor said on the subject of McQueen's constant tomcatting, "How to convince yourself of your desires for the opposite sex is to never let a gleam in an eye get by without knowing you gleaming right back." Of course, Kantor said, he'd never known Steve to sustain solid relationships with women—or even with the men he sometimes struggled to feel comfortable with. His marriage was a lost cause. Sex had fallen off with his television success, according to Kantor, who also knew Neile from Broadway.

To ease the gnawing sense that he'd never be taken as seriously as a Dean or a Brando, McQueen binged blindly on drugs, sex and ostentatious buying sprees. He picked up girls on the streets, at bus stops, and at phone booths. Waitresses were easy targets, undemanding, as were the would-be actresses and teenage fans.

He rented an "office," as he called it, in a building off Santa Monica that had concealed parking. McQueen used this hideout to prove his prowess with the girls, most of them one-shot situations, a hop in the sack and out the door. When girls found their way back to the pad, McQueen would have a stooge vacate the premises and find another "office" for booze, dope, sniffing coke and humping the pick-ups.

Hiding the fancy Ferrari was the important ploy, and keeping it out of sight—especially hard to do when he was seeing Gena again. We'd broken up following a fling she had with Brando, and when she rented a small guest house off Harper below the Strip, McQueen made night calls by sneaking through a side window. He'd park a block away in a garage rented for this purpose, then sneak back up the street to Gena's.

For a while before we split up, I'd had trouble having sex with Gena because she kept wiggling upwards, struggling and pulling to the top of the bed. If we reversed our positions on the bed, she'd be going over the bottom until her head was on the floor. It seemed she was trying to get away. Or she wanted to be fucked laying across the kitchen table while I was standing. She later told me that was how McQueen liked to "take" her—face down on the table with her hips and legs hanging over the edge.

She worked as a waitress for Herb Cohen at the Unicorn, and at Cosmo Alley where Allen Ginsberg and some Frisco poets read to jazz, and where the Kingston Trio was also playing. For more than a month Gena was sleeping with no one except McQueen on frequent visits through the window. Then she got a "germ or something" from him, and when she told him she had it, and that she wanted to see a doctor, McQueen told her she hadn't caught it from him. He wouldn't even pay for her medical expenses. "It was the same situation as back in New York," she said.

When I found out she had gonorrhea, I gave her the money to see a doctor and had myself examined. I didn't have the disease, though I'd heard through the pipeline that McQueen's personal doctor was treating him for it. I figured it would be the last time Gena and McQueen would be sleeping together.

I was wrong. They resumed their middle-of-the-night or early-morning rendezvous a month later, after I'd moved into a house off Laurel Canyon with Dennis Hopper. I then heard that Brando's best friend, Sam Gilman, thought he had contracted a disease from the same girl Marlon had slept with, and had come down with the infection—some kind of inflammation of the eyes.

My chumminess with Dennis Hopper had started two years earlier during *Rebel Without a Cause*. Though Jimmy Dean had not been sociable with Dennis or others in the cast, their paths would eventually cross with others who had been close to him.

One night I arrived with Jack Simmons at Maila Nurmi's house to find a few of the *Rebel* cast lounging around on the floor. Maila didn't have any furniture in the living room or dining area, and the light came from a low-hanging wagon wheel with at least a dozen candles mounted on it, burning and dripping wax onto the yellow shag carpet. Without her vampire costume, Maila seemed shorter and more compact, and beneath the long black wig, her blonde hair was trimmed down to less than a crewcut. She was lying on the floor in tight jeans and had said something to Dennis like "Kiss my ass, stupid," which he saw as an invitation to pull down Vampira's jeans and literally kiss her ass. She was pushing him away, but he kept it up, and had her jeans down part way when he noticed that she wasn't wearing any underpants. She was embarrassed and mad, and socked him in the face with her fist. The wax had been dripping from the candles and was matted in Dennis' hair. He tried to laugh off the blow that turned into a black eye the next day.

In one of our first brief talks, Dennis said he couldn't see what Jimmy saw in "the witch," or why he was hanging around with Jack Simmons. I said Jack was around because Jimmy liked him; I didn't say anything about Maila. Dennis quickly became docile around Jimmy on the set, apologetic and sometimes silent. During the filming of *Giant*, however, Dennis got a little closer to Jimmy, who was encouraging anyone to take his side against the "others," who were making problems for him on the Texas locations.

It was after Jimmy's death several weeks later that Dennis began to change. His agent and mine at the time, Bob Raison, said, "Dennis has undergone a metamorphosis. He's lost who he was, and he's being replaced by this troublesome, unbalanced person."

Dennis was peeing in the long trough in a men's room on the Warners lot one afternoon, telling me how he saw in some way that the duty to carry on Jimmy's enigmatic rebellion had fallen upon his shoulders. Very much alone in this presumption, he said, "Only they don't know it yet," and wagged his penis in the direction of the front office. "But they're going to find *out*, man . . ."

His later claims of sexual prowess stemmed from a convoluted need to be viewed as a Lothario—a pint-sized "nut" with a Casanova complex. Women chased Brando,and they'd been literally crazy for Jimmy. Dennis publicly fabricated his sex life to the point of gross overemphasis in an attempt to attract the same kind of adulation from the ladies, but those goo-gooers he stumbled across were mainly fringe wanna-bes, groupies and toads. For this braggart, imaginary partners came and went in a fantastic blur while his thumping hand refused to lay still.

He'd been late on the set, and Warners sent a letter detailing the expenses this had cost the studio—from producer to director, from actors and stand-ins to the grip and mixer, right down to the makeup man. The waste amounted to a considerable sum, not to mention the inconvenience to everyone involved in the production. Satisfied that they were at odds, just like it had been with Jimmy at the end, Dennis framed the letter and hung it next to a small painting Vincent Price had given him of a round, sickly green, grotesque face, like a freak or a wind-god, with distorted, blown-out cheeks and crazy, sleepless eyes.

Relishing the nickname of "Dennis the Menace," Hopper rode to town on a cockhorse, through a haze of dope and booze, disregarding the warnings from Warners—ultimatums which he misconstrued as nothing more than scoldings.

The trouble he caused the studio was all part of Dennis' "break for freedom," as he put it, bragging that Warners understood they had another volatile talent on their hands who needed "special handling—the same as Jimmy Dean."

Jack Nicholson, always ripe for free dope and vino, was at the house listening to Dennis' condemnation of the moguls. But even soused or stoned, Jack couldn't applaud Dennis' "mumblings about rebellion," which he saw as rationalizations for an "ill-chosen course of action."

When Dennis went outside to where he'd hidden the dope to roll another joint, Jack said to me, "Man, this is suicide! What the fuck's he *doing*?" He stared apprehensively at the studio letter on the wall.

Sally Kellerman, though physically bigger than Dennis, said she was afraid of him. "It's like something you may hang around too close to," she said, "and everything that's bad about it will affect you the same."

Considered pretty much of a clod at the time, Sally was too tall, her head too big, and she never wore makeup. A farm girl with Cadillac tits, she was running around with a sandy-haired hopeful named Roger. In a thick Texas accent, he said he thought of "things in a Texas way," but no one cared what he thought. He paid me to shoot some pictures of him, and I snapped off a roll at the Frank Lloyd Wright house on the hill. Sally wasn't exactly his "girlfriend," he said, since he'd never "done anything" with her. He believed as "sure as God" she'd never been laid; maybe a couple of kisses, but she was cold, he said, "like there's no juice in her battery." She didn't warm up, and she wasn't going anywhere because she didn't have any personality. He said she'd asked him if I'd take some pictures of her as well, since she didn't have any photos to show anyone.

I saw Sally a few days later in Schwab's, eating a sandwich and drinking milk. I mentioned Roger and the pictures, and we agreed to take some. She had on a plain skirt, a sweater buttoned up the front, and was almost dowdy-looking. There wasn't anything really interesting about her.

We drove around and I took shots of her in the car with the top down, parked in the shade for contrast with the bright daylight. Down on Doheny, I showed her where Marilyn Monroe and my friend John Hodiak used to live. Sally wanted to see the courtyard, so I parked and we entered the outside door to the foyer, an area with a gold-veined mirror above the mailboxes. It was a portal-like structure with both ends opening into the sunlight. I asked her to open her sweater a little, and after two or three shots she had it unbuttoned almost to her waist, her generous brassiere showing, with me reflected in the mirror behind her, looking down into the camera.

I saw Sally a few times after that, and we'd talk or drive down Sunset. She thought I was still involved with Gena and said Gena had told her that we were married after she'd spotted us driving past her one day. We weren't together, I told Sally; we'd split up. One of us would be filing for a divorce pretty soon. Gena had even told Sally she had a kid, but hadn't told her it wasn't mine.

We were in a drive-in one afternoon when I kissed Sally, just leaned over and lightly kissed her on the lips. I said I supposed I shouldn't be doing that with Roger still on the scene, but Sally said she didn't have anything to do with Roger, or anyone else. She was looking at me very evenly and said, "I don't want to have anything to do with anybody because I'm saving myself." I asked her what she was saving herself for. "For the right situation," she said. "I'm saving myself for myself."

Producer Michael Garrison suggested I see about a part in 20th-Century Fox's *Compulsion*, with Diane Varsi from Jerry Wald's *Peyton Place*. Diane had been married twice, once when she was fifteen, again at seventeen. She'd kicked around L.A. a little after leaving what she called a "rotten" life in the San Francisco Bay area. She'd even played drums in a coffee shop before landing the big time. But she was quick to downplay any seriousness about acting as a career. They'd say to her, "Stop bitching, Diane, you're a big fucking star."

In Garrison's office, Diane said, "This isn't going on forever. It isn't going very far. I don't like this town and, I don't like what it's making me feel about myself." I asked her what she meant, and she said she felt like she was being "poisoned slowly, like how you can do it with arsenic over a period of time. You don't even know you're being poisoned."

I stopped into the Sea Witch one night when Gena was working there and asked her to sit down with me for a couple of minutes. The radio guy was broadcasting from the glassed-in booth, playing Bobby Darin. Troy Donahue was in the corner by the window with the girl he hung around with, and kept looking over because the last time I'd seen him we were both with Henry Willson. I said to Gena, "Can we come to some meeting of the minds about being separated and what we're doing?" She stared at me. I said, "About what we're presenting to others that isn't really true?"

She looked at me for a few moments, then got up and walked away. When she passed the table again, she said, "Dennis Hopper came in here last night looking for you. I didn't realize he's as short as he is. He asked me if I wanted to fuck."

"What'd you say?" I said.

She smiled and said, "I told him I'd stick it on the back burner in case of emergency."

Driving with Dennis in his little red Austin Healy sports car could be scary. Always giving it gas when the light was turning yellow, he never looked both ways before racing ahead. At a bus zone he'd block traffic to tell the waiting commuters he'd seen the bus several blocks back and it was on the way. They would thank him and he'd pull away laughing. I never understood the prank—one of many he'd claim he was pulling to "put people on."

One afternoon we hit downtown Main Street to catch the burlesque girls. Hopping signals, he had to blow a couple of joints on the way, then sat stiffly anxious when the short, big-nosed comic in baggy balloon pants teetered around the girls, stepping on a fart bag for laughs. The comic's voice was shrill and hysterical, and the girls he "gastered" tittered and giggled, swinging the little cones that hung from the ends of their tits like glass balls on a Christmas tree.

The strippers pranced and bumped through the show to a half-empty house—mostly winos, staring at them distractedly. Dennis displayed near-apathy until the last girl came out. Bony and dark-skinned with a face pitted as though from smallpox, she bore scars on her stomach like she'd had some sloppy surgery or someone had tried to stab her to death. She stumbled about in gaudy Carmen Miranda platform shoes, barely able to dance, but something about her so enraptured Dennis that he began at once grabbing and pulling at his crotch. A couple of bums edged off, thinking he was some sort of queer, and soon the assistant manager came down the aisle and asked us to leave the theater. In the lobby, Dennis yelled, "I'm Dennis *Hopper,* man. I'm with Warner Brothers and I'll have your fucking job!" The guy said that if he was such a hotshot he wouldn't want the job in the first place, but if Dennis didn't leave the lobby immediately he'd call the cops. "We don't allow no jacking off in here!"

Frequent parties took place in Hollywood at a small alleyway house on Melrose Place near La Cienega. Jazz and rock and Elvis were mixed on the reel-to-reel with Arabian music or Bach or Hank Williams, and the sounds of water dripping or toilets flushing, and the banging of a hammer or drumsticks on a sheet of metal. Everyone was stoned and cheap wine flowed by the gallons. Jack Nicholson usually showed up early for the booze and grass, and the sex orgies just happened—no particular cue—blooming on the big old movie-prop couch or on the mattress in the narrow step-down bedroom where the plaster walls were painted with black sunrises and people hanged by the neck and women being skinned alive.

Jack shied away from the hardcore action, though years later he'd be prone to glamorize his past. Looking back at those "wild and crazy times" and "existential stunts," he recalled himself far more involved in the scene than he'd actually been. In reality, he was more like a shadow with gloating eyes, his "killer smile" just sort of hanging there like a half-witted grin.

Dennis was the one impelled to crash the "front line," to walk the razor's edge. Like Hank Williams, he was drawn to the high side, and only partly afraid of charging further across than he'd be able to get back. Blonde Tuesday Weld was barely fourteen but made her appearance at these gatherings, as did producer Norman Jolly's daughter, Judy Jolly, an energetic girl who was drawn to Dennis's "torn and twisted monologues."

One night Dennis was urinating on the side of the kitchen range while tapping his foot to the music. Squatting alongside me against the wall in the living room, Jack watched Dennis and said, "A guy that keeps telling you how sick he is and doing numbers to make you think he *is* sick, for whatever reasons. I mean, this guy doesn't have to knock himself out to *prove* it . . ."

Sometimes it seemed Nicholson guzzled more wine than he could handle. Cowboy folk singer Jack Elliot and I once picked him up off the sidewalk in front of the Ash Grove, a folk hangout down the street on Melrose. Jack had fallen down on the sidewalk, and Elliot nudged at him a little with the toe of his cowboy boot to see if he was conscious. We picked him up and propped him against the iron pole of the awning. Jack was gripping the pole and weaving back and forth.

"You got a good hold there, son?" Elliot asked. Nicholson nodded, but his eyes were clenched shut. Elliot helped me get Jack into my car, and I drove him to his rented place off Santa Monica. He'd lost the key and I couldn't get him into the house, so I left him laying outside to sleep it off.

One night I took Sally up Laurel Canyon in Dennis's red Austin Healy. We were having some hot tea in the house when Dennis showed up with two girls he'd picked up at a party—one for him and one for me. They'd come up in the girls' car, which I then used to drive Sally back down the hill. She wasn't the kind of girl to get into any of Dennis's "funny" scenes.

Another car swerved past us on the left, forcing me against the canyon embankment. There wasn't much damage, but there was some. Sally caught the license number of the other car, and when I got her to Fountain we sat in the car talking and I gave her a few kisses. I then headed back up the canyon, worrying about the damage to the car.

One of the girls was naked on the mattress on the floor where I slept, with Dennis kneeling between her spread legs, examining her by candlelight while puffing a joint. The other girl was sitting on Dennis's bed against the wall beneath the wind-god painting, still dressed and sporadically emitting a nervous laugh. Dennis looked at me and said, "She's waiting, man," and I sat down next to the clothed girl and began to undress her. She said she didn't want to take off her things, so I sat back, lit a cigarette and held her hand. After a few minutes, Dennis blew out the candle, and the girl and I sat in the dark, listening to the sounds coming from the mattress. As Dennis's partner began to cry out over his grunts, I leaned over and kissed the other girl's ear and told her the car had been forced against the side of the hill—not much damage, but I had a license number and the other car was responsible. She listened partly to me and to the gasps and moans from the mattress, and finally said it didn't matter—it wasn't her car anyway. It belonged to the other girl's mother, she said, and then she took off her clothes.

Dennis said, "What the fuck's a car?" He'd buy them a new car—not the following day, perhaps, but soon, with the escalating salary on his Warners contract.

I told Nicholson about the girls and the car, since Sally had already talked to Jack about my getting sideswiped. I was on an interview at NBC on Vine Street, and Jack was there along with Robert Redford, who was talking about some things he was doing. Redford always talked about himself; I don't think any other subject held any interest for him. I'd always found him to be somewhat dumb. When he went in for the interview, Jack slid over onto the chair Redford had been sitting in next to mine. We talked briefly about the car incident, and then Jack told me he'd heard from someone at Warners that Dennis' option was being dropped. I said if Dennis knew anything about it, he was keeping it a secret.

The slogan *Movies Are Better Than Ever* was campaigned frantically by die-hard moguls clinging to the notions of big-studio control and longevity. But the stranglehold of television's rapid advance was on. Movies had to survive—they had to draw the moviegoers back , fill the empty moviehouse seats. There was no need for unnecessary trouble. The so-called "rebels" were weeded out, those "misfits" who could create unbalance in the flow toward picture prosperity. The troublemakers were sifted out through a kind of blackballing that had quickly gone into effect after Jimmy Dean's death.

The industry was lenient, and forgave unspeakable things in the name of genuine, saleable talent, but the consensus was that Dennis Hopper didn't have any such talent. His pranks had cost the studio money that couldn't be backed up with any sort of commercial delivery, and so he was simply dumped. It was all very easy—no one cared. But Dennis hit the unemployment line hard, joining the rest of us out-of-work actors in a crowded, desperate town.

Lenny Bruce and the Bunny

HE CAME INTO CANTER'S DELICATESSEN on Fairfax, where I was sitting with Gena and some others from the Unicorn—one a doper pal of Jack Nicholson's who was bragging about a chunk of opium he'd wrangled from some pusher. We'd driven down Fairfax in a couple of cars, my red Ford convertible and someone's beat-up Chevy, blowing grass on the way from the Strip. Gorging themselves on whitefish and blintzes when the munchies set in, everyone kept hooking these smirks to the secrets they shared. It was harder for me to get into the loony-tunes mode when Gena's pupils were as big as keyholes.

I wasn't a real pothead—or into smack, coke, or mushrooms—so I was the oddball, sitting next to my estranged wife who'd been balling half the guys at the table. They all knew a lot about one another, things they thought I didn't know. It made me jealous and angry and sad. I kept thinking about the New York days with Gena after she'd split up with McQueen—her face like the face of a Hindu princess, reflecting candle light in the little Italian joint where we'd eat spaghetti, and drink Chianti, while we talked about Fellini or Jean Louis Barrault or Marcel Marceau. She'd practiced pantomime with Lionel Shepherd in the Village coach house he'd converted for his troupe. As a mime, she moved like a white-faced Shiva, and she'd also been studying Balinese dance while I'd been making the rounds.

The fights we'd been having seemed far away from those good times. Now I didn't know the person I was sitting next to in Canter's. I wasn't really with her anymore. I had been labeled a "square," the brunt of their hip jokes. Only a part of me was sitting there—the rest had already walked away. I knew it wasn't going to be long before the other half of me followed. Lenny Bruce saw that other part in a flash. He was sharp, like he was walking around with his antennae out, like one of those sacrificial characters, a human pincushion. When he walked into Canter's and spotted us, he said, "You're all a bunch of sissies" and winked at me. Gena and I had met Lenny in New York, and he'd told me he wanted to be an actor and that he had gone to Geller Workshop in Hollywood about a half dozen years before I'd gone there.

He was already stoned—just floating by—when he slid into the booth beside me. Looking across at Gena, he said, "Why don't you and Jonathan come back to the closet with me and get a shot of something good?" I didn't know what he meant, but he took my hand like I was a child and led me through Canter's kitchen, Gena behind us. Someone said something to him about his not being allowed back there. Lenny said, "It's okay, it's okay. I'm Jewish."

A guy in a dishwasher's hat passed Lenny a bottle of twelve-year-old Scotch, and we all stepped into a small area around a time-clock and shared a drink. A guy named Gordon who'd come into Canter's with Lenny found his way to the kitchen and told Gena her friends were splitting. Lenny quickly passed me the bottle, and when Gena left he said, "You want to get high with me and the bunny?" I asked who the bunny was, and he said, "A girl I know, but don't tell my wife." Then he said, "Oh-oh, I don't have a wife—I mean, I did but I don't . . . *You* do." But you're a cute guy, and the bunny likes cute guys, so it's okay if you want to get high with us. Or do you want to go back in there for a little more matrimonial crucifying?"

Grateful to be singled out for a mission, I left Canter's with Lenny and the other guy. Once in my car, Lenny kept looking at his watch and screwing around with the car-radio buttons while Gordon slumped on the back seat. We picked up the bunny on a side street off Santa Monica, then drove to a house on Larrabee, a couple blocks south of where Maila Nurmi—Vampira—had rented a house.

After a stint with Liberace, she'd hit on hard times and found herself working in a cheap movie called *Grave Robbers From Outer Space.* She told them as long as she didn't have to say anything, she'd do it for the bread—as paltry as that was—and hoped nobody would spot her in such a "piece of shit." It was produced, written and directed by a guy named Ed Wood—shooting from the hip on empty pockets and a five-day schedule. Vampira had said, "He's fucking nuts. He's a transvestite on top of it, and he isn't even a *queer* . . ." Wood had resurrected drugged-out Bela Lugosi—thought dead by half of Hollywood—to lurk through the scenes with Vampira in search of fresh-blooded victims.

Poor Maila. She'd wanted fame, and gone around expanding broadly upon her friendship with Jimmy Dean, but found only Ed Wood and a taxidermied Dracula. A couple of people I knew who were desperate for any sort of work were hounding Wood, but unfortunately for them, his particular vision encompassed only a few favored oddballs who worked for peanuts, or the promise of pay, and didn't criticize Ed's penchant for dressing in women's gaudy used clothing.

Lenny, Gordon and I came to a small, dark house. The curtains had faded red-block designs on them, and the kitchen was painted an emerald-green enamel. When Gordon pulled the chain on the bulb above the sink in the kitchen, everything took on a greenish glow, even our faces. The bunny was a big girl with a lot of brown hair and high cheek bones, a wide, pretty mouth with thick lipstick, and enormous false eyelashes. She was as tall as I was, slim, but with very large breasts held up in a black brassiere under a sheer white blouse. When she stretched, her reach was longer than mine.

Some patio furniture and a big portable television sat in the other room, where Gordon had snatched up the bunny's purse and was digging through it. She paid no attention. She was as tall as Irish McCalla, and looked like one of those women in Amazon movies—all shoulders and tits.

Lenny watched eagerly as Gordon gathered together a few crumpled sacks and a small yellow box. They broke into broad smiles that looked green from the reflection off the kitchen walls, and Gordon let the purse drop to the floor. He and Lenny snuck down a short hall and disappeared into a bathroom. The bunny scooped up her purse, and flopped into a round wicker chair, her legs spread apart and her breasts almost coming out of her blouse. She wore a cream-colored skirt over

110

black leotards, and with her legs apart I could see the whiteness of her panties showing through the tights at the crotch. She nodded toward the bathroom. "What the hell are they doing in there so long— giving each other blow jobs?" She stared into her open purse as though it were some object she didn't recognize. "You like Gorgeous George?" she asked, her eyes moving in thought. "Do you like him or don't you?"

I said I hadn't watched wrestling for a long time, but that I remembered him and the Baron and Argentina Rocca. She asked me to turn on the television because she was too tired to get up and her "chest hurt." After several minutes I got the knob to stay still on the wrestling channel, but the set hummed and dull shapes flickered across the screen. "The tube's bad," I told her. "Who's house is this, anyway?" She said she had no idea, maybe some joker sucking up to Lenny. The screen went black and there was only the sound.

"What did you do to it?" she asked. "You bust it?" I said I hadn't done anything—the tube was bad. She said, "That must've made it go off the air." I tried to adjust the set, but the screen kept going black. I noticed her reflection in the screen—she had her breasts out of the brassiere and blouse, just lifting them out like she was trying to figure out the weight of two big cantaloupes.

I turned around, staring at her as she cupped them, comparing one against the other. I said, "Very nice," but she didn't seem to hear me. Her nipples were large and pinkish amber, her skin two tones lighter within the outline of a bikini top. She didn't even look up from them.

"Shit, man," she said. "Shit!" I asked her what was wrong and she said, "I got to *piss* and they're hoarding the fucking john." Scooping her breasts back into her brassiere and blouse, she said, "What the hell are they doing back there?"

I didn't know. "They took some stuff with them," I said. I wasn't sure what I was supposed to do with her while Lenny got high in the can. Since she'd delivered more than either of them planned to shoot, Lenny had to talk her out of having some when he finally came down the hall. He didn't want her to get high on anything except the grass or the scotch from Canter's.

He passed me a joint which I nursed to be sociable, sitting half-stewed by then and sick to my stomach. The bunny stayed in the chair watching the black television screen, listening to the sound until she passed out, pitching forward out of the chair. Her head made a hard, thudding noise as it struck the floor. Lenny laughed. He was a bright-eyed new man since his visit to the john. "Well, well," he said, "She's out of it, eh?" He stirred and I thought he was going to pick her up and put her on the couch, but instead he was only settling deeper into the chair. "Are you high— or should I say, do you want to get higher?" he asked. I told him I was pretty high already. "You've never shot any real shit, have you?" he asked. I said no. He said, "It's the closest you come to seeing the face of God without kicking the bucket. There's no experience like it," he said. "Simply as a sensitive, intelligent guy, you should try something once to see what it does . . ." I said I was kind of afraid of it. He liked that. "Afraid of getting sick," he said. "I still get sick. I'm sick half the time, but there's times I don't get sick and I can go a long time without getting sick. *Then* I get sick . . . Oh, man, I get so sick—and bang! I'm like dead and laid out with silver in my shoes. Not dead like you think *dead*, man, but dead like to what's unimportant . . . Dead to even *sex*—when you're looking into God's eyes, you don't want Him seeing dirty pictures in your head . . ."

The bunny's lips were parted and she was gasping, hands opening and closing, sort of fluttering like her eyes. Lenny was staring down at her. "She was like your old lady Gena is now. She had that same touchy quality—*fine*, you know, like a dark side, a dark quality that's got a brain attached to it. And that means you get connected to it, so now you've got all that stuff in you. Am I right?" Then he said, "You and Gena still getting it on?"

"She's stayed with me a few times out of convenience," I said. "To her, that is. Not to me."

"So what's the scene?" Lenny asked. "How tight are you?" I said we weren't tight anymore. She was seeing a couple of other people—like she was still seeing McQueen. Not Brando anymore, but his pal Sam Gilman, and Brando's other buddy, Carlo Fiori. "Who's a junky," said Lenny. "I can't stand the guy. He's a fucking bad junky. Junk gets in him and it turns to shit."

I told him Gena still wanted to sleep with me, like the last time when she stayed over and put in a diaphragm. I hadn't known she'd wanted to, and instead we argued about her kid from a previous marriage, who I believed Gena was turning inside out. And then she reached down into herself—her face twisting up with the effort—and yanked out the diaphragm. She threw it straight up in the air, and with the jelly on it, the diaphragm stuck to the ceiling for a moment. Both of us were staring up at it, then it fell to the floor.

Lenny and I were looking absently down at the bunny. "Gena's a good person," Lenny said. "I dig her. I'm not balling her, man, but she's got a sensitivity I can groove with." He nodded to the bunny. "This one's all fucked up, you see. I thought we had something tight, but now it's just the dope. I mean we did, you dig? We had something close after I had to bust off with my old lady, but I can't make this an end unto itself." He grinned. "I'm in the market," he said, "so tell me, if I make a move on Gena, it isn't going to put you up a tree?"

"You've got women coming out of the walls," I said.

"But they're just chicks," Lenny said. "They got this cute little hole in the middle of their geezo and this cute little hair all around it, and you stick in your finger and your prick and you la-la-la for a while and you change the sheets, man. And stupid. Stupid chicks. Can you believe this bunny on the floor is bright, man? Has a fucking college degree? Can you believe it? I should say *was* bright."

We both stared down at her. His eyes were like glass. "You get so deep, man, you got to come out the other side of things. That's what's happened to the bunny—you go caving, man, you go digging deep, and then getting in, and you lose sight of where you got in . . ." He started to laugh, then coughed, then laughed and coughed and I asked him if he wanted some water. He said, "I'd appreciate it, man, 'cause I'm too stoned to move."

I found a glass in the kitchen. It was dirty and I rinsed it a little in the cold water, which looked rusty. When I brought the glass back, Lenny was already on the nod. Spit dripped from his mouth, and the way he was sitting—chin on his chest and his hands curled in—he looked like a photo I'd seen of someone executed in the gas chamber.

The bunny hadn't moved, except for the muscles of her wrists and hands, still flexing like little shudders in her tendons. Both her and Lenny were out of it, so I went to look for Gordon, who hadn't come out of the bathroom. I found him on the tile floor lying in his own vomit. He looked green, like he'd absorbed the green color from the sticky kitchen walls. I thought he was dead, and when I felt for a pulse, I heard a clicking noise in his throat like a chicken. He started changing color, from green to a sort of dead man's gray, a cardboard shade, and his eyes were rolling up into his head.

Back in the living room, I shook Lenny and said Gordon was going belly-up in the john. I had to shake Lenny pretty hard, so his head was snapping back and forth. Then he jumped up, springing into action.

"Call the fire department!" he said.

It took me a minute to find the phone, and as I called, Lenny walked outside saying he was going for help. He never went down the hall to the bathroom. When I followed to tell him the fire department was on the way, he was gone. He'd walked out of the house and down the street, leaving me with the conked-out bunny and Gordon croaking in the can.

I had visions of being stuck there with these two when the cops arrived, trying to explain what had happened without implicating Lenny or myself. There was nothing I could do for Gordon, but getting the bunny out of there seemed the next best thing.

Putting her on her feet wasn't easy. I found her purse and steered her out of the house and into my car. She was neither light nor maneuverable, all dead-weight on rubber legs. I turned the car around as a fire truck pulled south on Larrabee, then I headed toward Santa Monica looking for Lenny. He'd disappeared. Smart.

What to do with the bunny was the next problem. I kept shaking her and asking her which way to go. She'd point one way and I'd go that way, then she'd say, "No, no" and point me in some other direction. We were going in circles. I finally drove to an apartment building where I used to live and stopped the car in the basement parking area. I tried to wake her, but it was no use. She stayed curled up on the seat, but her breathing was okay. I didn't know where she lived or where Lenny was staying, so I decided to let her sleep it off. After smoking a couple of cigarettes, I put my head back and slept for what I thought was maybe twenty minutes. When I woke up, another car had parked next to us. It was still daylight, and the bunny hadn't moved. I nudged her and said, "Can you hear me?" She nodded and I said, "I don't know your name. Lenny called you 'bunny' . . ."

"The fucker!" she said. "Lenny Bruce—Lenny *Bruce*! Did he die?"

"No," I said. "He took off. I don't know about the other guy. Lenny said to call the fire department."

"The fire department . . ." she said, sitting up. "That's a joke he tells, the fuckin' fire department . . ." She was fumbling through her purse. "Shit!" she said. "*Fuck* both of them." She sat back, focusing on my face as though for the first time. "He took everything out of my purse," she said. She looked around the garage. "Where the hell are we?"

I didn't know where to take her, so I just stayed parked until she came around. "Where do you want to go?" I asked.

"I need some coffee," she said.

We drove to Huff's restaurant, off the corner of Fairfax and Sunset, where I helped her out of the car because she said her legs had gone to sleep. I asked if she wanted to eat, but she just drank coffee—poured it into herself. She was shaking, and I asked if she was cold. "No," she said. She needed to get straight. "Where's that scotch we were drinking?" It surprised me she remembered the bottle. I told her I thought it was gone, and then mentioned Gordon turning grey in the bathroom. She said she didn't care—he wasn't going to be a loss to anybody. "I gotta go to the john," she said. She got up shakily, and I wondered if she'd make it. I ordered some toast—something to put in my stomach.

The bunny was gone for at least ten minutes. I imagined she'd passed out, and I was about to ask someone to check on her when she came back, made-up and looking less like a zombie. She sat back down and said, "Lenny didn't give me any of that *shit*, did he?"

"No," I said.

"He hoarded it," she said. "That *ass*hole. When he split he took the rest of it with him. That's what he does. The asshole! He's a fucking asshole . . ." She gulped the coffee. "Give me a cigarette. The cocksucker left me without any money—I had money in here! He took the fucking money out of my purse and left me without any dope. That asshole."

I gave her a cigarette. "I wish I could take you somewhere," I said. "Where do you want to go?"

"To fucking hell," she said.

"You want to go to the beach?"

"What beach?" she asked. "What the fuck's there?"

"A friend of mine's got a place, and he's usually got a stash. There's a big bed, one of those round ones, if you want to catch up on some sleep. My friend's in New York right now. I mean, it's okay. It's in Malibu."

"Yeah . . . Malibu," she said. "I thought it was maybe friggin' Redondo Beach or somewhere where that fucker goes. Do me a favor and don't talk about Lenny anymore. I never want to see the son of a bitch again."

We got in the car and I turned the radio on. Frank Sinatra's "Witchcraft" was playing. The bunny snapped her fingers. She had a fair voice and sang for a while before falling asleep again, tipping over with

115

her head on my leg the rest of the way to the beach. Once she put her hand in my crotch and felt around, touching me in her sleep.

I woke her when we got to Malibu. She followed me dutifully out of the car and along a kind of gangplank to where the key was hidden. Inside the house, she didn't even look around, wasn't curious at all, but went straight to the liquor cabinet and grabbed the nearest bottle. We both took a few swigs, and it burned all the way down. I showed her the bedroom, and she took the bottle with her. I figured she'd crash, but she turned to me and struggled out of her skirt—fought, actually, to get out of it—and then her blouse and brassiere. She pulled down her black tights, kicked them off and, only in her panties, stood looking at me.

"I don't even know who you are," she said and laughed, "and I like that. That's the best part . . ." She took a few more swallows of booze and went into the bathroom, leaving the door open to stare out at me as she peed. I sat on the bed, and when she finished she dropped her panties aside and lay down on the bed.

With my pants still on but unzipped, I got on top of her. She didn't move much while we fucked and I thought she'd passed out, but she was sort of conscious, her hands above her head, the fingers opening and closing again. When I finished, she didn't seem to have noticed that anything had happened.

I saw her again a couple of times at the Unicorn when Lenny was around. She was still hanging onto him, as was Gordon. The fire department had saved Gordon, who'd spent a few days in jail. Lenny said he was sorry for taking off, but couldn't get into any hassles because of his pending legal matters. He was getting the bunny a job downtown as a stripper, where she had some kind of floral, beak-like things affixed to her breasts. It was called "exotic" dancing because of the music, he said, not because of the way she danced.

One of those nights at the Unicorn, I sat down at a small table with Lenny, the bunny and Gordon, listening to Judy Henski sing. I liked Judy—she was something special. Gena was waiting on tables and was overly chummy with Lenny because I seemed to be there with the bunny. It was almost as if Gena could smell if people had had sex. But I wasn't exactly *with* the bunny, who had only a vague memory of me. I didn't think she even remembered the beach. She'd studied me over her cappuccino with which she chased some pills. I said, "It's good to

Jonathan Gilmore, Hollywood, 1954

Blue suedes and '50 Mercury

Gilmore and stepbrother,
Balboa Island, early '50s

Hank Williams,
under the influence

Dallas and Tex Williams of Riverside Rancho

Gilmore in New York, early '50s

At Mocambo on the Sunset Strip

Caricature by Cal Bailey,
on the Strip, 1952

Actress Elaine Stewart, "The bad and the beautiful,"
fellow client of John Darrow

The Garden of Allah Hotel on Sunset Boulevard

Marguerite LeVan
(Gilmore's mother), 1940s

"The Black Dahlia,"
Elizabeth Short,
Hollywood, 1946.
Murdered the
following year.

Robert T. Gilmore, Jr. (father)
LAPD, 1942

Actor John Hodiak, Gilmore's mentor in the early '50s

Gilmore, New York, 1953

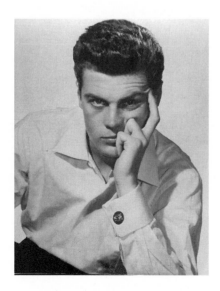

Gilmore, theater publicity still,
New York, early '50s

Gilmore at Museum of Modern Art,
New York

In his Greenwich Village apartment, mid-1950s

James Dean on the Warners studio back lot

Dean and Pier Angeli, Hollywood

Eartha Kitt appears at Mocambo

Sal Mineo in Beverly Hills

Natalie Wood, Dean, Ann Doran on set of **Rebel Without a Cause**

Natalie heading toward the deep end

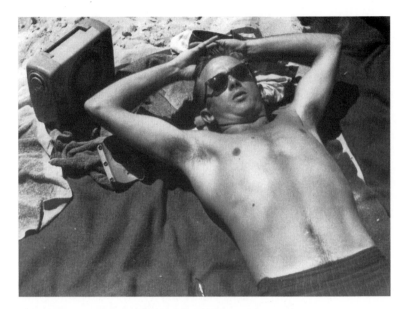

Dean at Santa Monica Beach

Googie's, home of the "Night Watch,"
next to Schwab's Pharmacy

Vampira (Maila Nurmi)

Maila Nurmi (sans wig)
with pet monkey, Hollywood

Lenny Bruce

Director Curtis Harrington

Sally Kellerman

Irish McCalla
"Sheena, Queen of the Jungle"

William Burroughs in the Beat Hotel, Paris

Brigitte Bardot
"The one that almost got away"

Jack Nicholson
"I wanna be a star no matter what they say"

Diane Varsi
"I quit Hollywood"

Gilmore and Regina Gleason in
William Inge's **Loss of Roses**

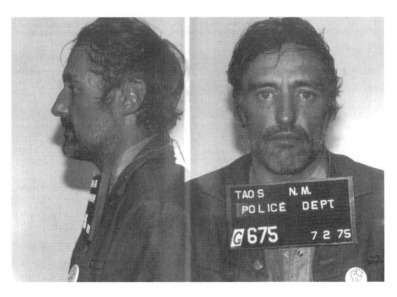

Dennis Hopper
"Hey, man, it's **my** head, you know?"

Jane Fonda
"Falling in and out of love is easy"

Roddy McDowell and Jane Fonda

Gilmore and Susan Oliver in CBS program
Run to the City,
directed by Stuart Rosenberg

Cecilia Madach,
Gilmore's first "legal" wife

Susan Oliver
"From Broadway to Hollywood"

Shooting **Blues for Benny**, lost film
directed by Gilmore (left), with
cameraman Andrew Janczak

Lining up a shot, California Studios, Hollywood

Director Ed Wood, Jr. with
Criswell of "Criswell Predicts"

Pat Barringer in "Astra Vision"

Jean Seberg
"A flame that burns on"

Steve McQueen and Neile Adams

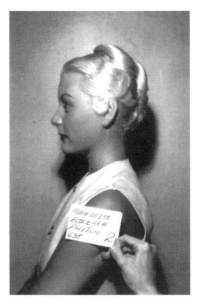

Barbara Payton

Tom Neal
"Blow their brains out"

Payton and Franchot Tone

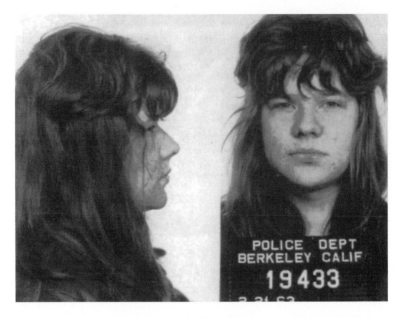

Janis Joplin, 1963

Joplin during Frisco coffeehouse days

Joplin at the top

Jayne Mansfield
"Waiting for nothing"

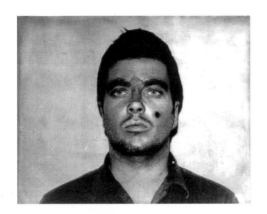

Thrill-killer Charles Schmid
"The Pied Piper of Tucson"

Gilmore and F. Lee Bailey
Tucson, Arizona airport, 1966

The Last Ride: Gilmore's Harley chopper and high-performance Camaro

Today: Gilmore and atomic bomb "Fat Man," New Mexico

see you," and she nodded. "I'd like to see you again sometime," I added.

"Man, you're seeing me," she said. Then it wasn't long before she started to fade. Lenny leaned over to say something, but he couldn't get through to her. She was nodding off, then slumped forward. Lenny shook her a few times and laughed about her being like a rag, all wobbly, then asked Freddie the bouncer to help get her into the back of the place. It was fairly crowded, but they managed to angle between the tables and through the small kitchen. One of her shoes came off, and I picked it up and followed the three of them outside. Lenny and the bouncer laid her down on a bench that was built around the trunk of a tree. She didn't move. I put her shoe on a flagstone beside the bench. "It's kind of cold out here," I said.

"Oh, that doesn't matter," Lenny said. "She doesn't feel anything." He picked up the shoe and tried to get it on her foot, but couldn't, so he left it on the ground. He went back into the cafe, and when I turned to follow, Gena was standing in the doorway staring at me. She looked astonishingly lovely in the half-light, and I smiled at her. She didn't smile back. It had just been a moment, just a second, that she had looked so lovely and I had thought maybe I still cared for her.

"You like the town whore?" she asked.

"She's out of it," I said. "She's a goner."

"Yeah, no shit," Gena said. "She's a goner, all right." She gave me a hard smile and said, "She's the town whore."

I didn't say anything. I wondered why she couldn't see herself in the bunny. Gena's eyes were beautiful. Strange. Her pupils looked as big and black shiny as marbles. I wished we were somewhere else, somewhere on the Left Bank or somewhere like that. But it was like a trick of the mind, like a light that snaps on and snaps off.

LOOSE NIGHTS IN GREENWICH VILLAGE

ONE MORNING HEADING EAST across Route 66, I saw the sun rising over a vast desert, and as I drove down a long, gradual descent, the sun suddenly swelled up above a distant mountain. I felt as though I could let go of the steering wheel and the new '57 Coupe de Ville would lift from the road and fly to that burning ball of light.

My heart knew only the excitement of heading to New York again— leaving Hollywood and Gena and all that shit behind. She'd spent a couple of hours with me in a place on Vine sharing mugs of beer and saying good-bye. She drew a picture on a napkin of a cute bug drinking beer to keep me company on the long ride east with a guy I didn't know, who was just joining me on the drive-away car.

Gena had stayed at my apartment on Harper a couple of weeks, and I'd been sunning myself on the roof with a tinfoil reflector when I heard her scream from the rear top-floor window. My blood ran cold. Thinking she'd jumped, I raced down to the hall and into the apartment to find her standing behind a door she'd pulled against herself, hiding from some shape she'd seen rushing through the room.

It was the same as back in New York—she'd told me about the shadowy things chasing her during her first marriage, to a guy in the

Bronx. She'd started seeing a shrink named Lawrence Hatterer, especially after the kid was born. The marriage busted up and the little girl went to live with Gena's folks. That was a couple of years before she'd moved into McQueen's cold-water flat.

When the shapes started chasing her again, I knew she was going off the deep end and that if I didn't get away, she'd pull me into her crackup.

I'd hit a fallow point anyway, and all I could think about was getting back to New York—getting into *theater,* even waiting on tables or washing dishes till I landed a part in a play. Through John Stix, I knew I had a lead as the leprechaun in a stock production of *Finnian's Rainbow* the following season if I could get to New York. The idea of singing and playing fantastic characters thrilled me. By reaching beyond the pretty-boy mixed-up kids and neurotics I was perpetually cast as, I felt I might catch on to what I was after in my life. I had to do it through the work—I'd never figure it out on my own.

It was the third time I'd traveled Route 66 from L.A. to New York, but the first time in a brand-new Cadillac. There were moments when I felt I was going only fifty miles an hour, though I pushing closer to a hundred. We slept for a few hours in a concrete teepee at Wigwam Village in Arizona, then ate chicken-fried steak and french fries in Albuquerque's Coney Island Cafe. We switched over driving every few hours—the guy was popping bennies, and I dropped one after Albuquerque. He gave me a few pills for later, which I tucked into the top of my army duffel bag. Tanking up in the east of New Mexico, he told the Indian attendant, "Fill it up, chief."

A couple of days later, at dawn, a joy went through me as we drove over the bridge against the early morning Manhattan skyline. From the bridge, sweeping down into the city, I gazed up the walls of its canyons and thrilled to its dawn noises—policemen with silver whistles clenched between their teeth, horns, taxis, garbage trucks. Among the people streaming over the streets and sidewalks, reflected on the glass buildings, I spotted the Cadillac—my own face reflected back on a New York window. It was like I was snapping a shot of where I'd found home; the happiest place I'd ever known.

We got coffee and doughnuts, and I called my friend Norman, getting him out of bed. He invited me to his place on 79th off Broadway to pick up the key to the 17th Street apartment where I'd be staying.

As the guy dropped me off uptown and pulled away in the Cadillac, I had the feeling it wouldn't be long before I'd be behind the wheel of my own Coupe de Ville, getting a grip on the good life in Hollywood John Hodiak so often talked about—the good life I could only find by dedicating myself to work on the opposite coast.

"With half the New York actors looking for work in L.A.," Norman said, "you got the competition cut down a little." I had more coffee at his place while he told me about the girl he was living with. They had to show separate addresses as a term of probation—they'd been convicted on drug charges earlier that year while living at the 17th Street address. He was happy to have me paying half the rent downtown while he stayed uptown with his lady.

The 17th Street place occupied the front two rooms on the top floor. It was bright, sparsely furnished and spacious, with hardwood floors and an uptown view. I came up the elevator with my duffel bag and overnight bag loaded with books, opened both front windows, flopped onto the bed and stared at the skyscrapers.

Within days, I'd looked up most of the people I'd bummed around with in the past—painters like Donato Manfredi and Barbara Lehman, a poet friend, some actors and a couple of directors I knew. A hunger was stirring in me that wouldn't stop. I ate and ate—bacon and eggs and biscuits, steak and potatoes and rare lamb chops, thick soups and salads. I didn't gain a pound and even tried to quit smoking. In a few weeks, I landed a part on a Sunday morning television show and was up for a role in a Broadway play.

In a sense I was living in a theater of the absurd. I was ridiculously conceited, uncooperative and lost—unlike McQueen, who stared into the mirror desperately trying to see into his pain, I searched out the pain in others I'd find myself close to. But I did not know I was on such a search. When I'd first begun seeing Gena, I'd chanced to meet Burgess Meredith, who was then on Broadway in *Teahouse of the August Moon*. He said a successful actor must first learn to take instruction well, to set his ego aside. One had to play against the obvious in one's own nature, he said. I asked what he meant by the obvious, and he said, "That which is obvious to yourself . . ."

The bitter lessons weren't behind me—they were on the road ahead. How, I wondered, could one learn to play against the obvious in one's nature? Would it be through Jean-Paul Sartre, Camus and Kierkegaard, or the Actors Studio and Harry Stack Sullivan, or Buddha, or Mozart, or Jimmy Dean, or, later Janis Joplin? Could one come closer to God by way "a three-ring circus of thrills and chills", could one come "nearer my God to thee" as they'd say.

But with all that jumble going on around me, I kept scrambling, committing to nothing because I thought I had a foot on both roads. Jimmy's desperate desire to fuse all of himself into a single reflection seemed at heart nothing more than craziness, piling wood at the foot of your self-styled funeral pyre.

I wanted to survive, but I didn't know how.

It never occurred to me that I might not even want to be an actor. It would be another few years before I'd even allow myself to tip the mirror in some other direction. *Finnian's Rainbow* was set for the following season, and I was having frequent dinners with John Stix and Geraldine Page. I'd become secretary of Stix's acting class, held in a loft on 56th near Sixth Avenue, around the corner from Carnegie Hall. I was working on a scene from *Hatful of Rain* with Brooke Heyward, the daughter of producer Leland Heyward and the late actress Margaret Sullivan, who'd committed suicide. Years later Brooke would write a bestseller, *Haywire,* about herself and her parents.

She wanted desperately to be a Broadway actress, she told me, but was so troubled by other things she wasn't able to give herself wholly to the work. There was much about Brooke that reminded me of Ida Lupino, from her constant nervousness and awkward mannerisms to the way she'd stand at times, or dress, or fool around with a cigarette. But there was nothing *physical* about her, as there was with Ida Lupino. Brooke had a plainness that Gore Vidal would describe to me as "New England wash and wear."

Except for Brooke, I was having sex with girls I worked with professionally or in class, and I was also seeing the painter Barbara Lehman. There were lots of Greenwich Village parties—we'd drink gallons of cheap red wine and make love on the rooftops, or on the fire escapes in the rain. When Dennis Hopper arrived in town to do the television version of *Swiss Family Robinson*, he wanted me to fix him up with Barbara because I'd told him she was a kook, that she took off her clothes at parties and liked to hump in the middle of a room with people watching. But she wasn't interested in Dennis, so he suggested I introduce him to a few of the other girls I was seeing. He was staying with me on 17th Street, and I always had a room in Stix's place if Dennis wanted my apartment to himself for the night. But Dennis was just after a quick jump on a mattress, with few preliminaries. He believed that any romancing was unnecessary. He said, "I just want to get my rocks off, man. I'm not looking for any involvements or a fucking wife!"

Just before he showed up, another actor, Tommy Gilson, called to stay a couple of days while he was in town. Tommy had worked in *Rally 'Round the Flag, Boys* at Fox with Paul Newman, Joanne Woodward and Joan Collins. Gilson's marriage was busting up, and there were a lot of problems. His wife accused him, according to Tommy, of having an affair with Joan Collins, which he said he hadn't, of course, grinning hopefully. I knew Tuesday Weld had also worked in the picture, and I asked him if he'd gotten chummy with Tuesday. He shook his head and said, "No, man, this past year she's been under lock and key." A tall blond guy like a tougher-looking Troy Donahue, Tommy was trying out for a show and hoping to land something to keep him in New York. He told me about the play for which he was trying to get auditioned, and it was the same show I was up for. I didn't say anything, but it reminded me a little of the situation with Jimmy Dean and Billy Gunn.

Gilson had also been friends with Tom Pitman, another Jimmy Dean imitator who'd been one of Gena's serious flings the year before. Pitman wore a red tanker jacket and raced around Hollywood in a Porsche Speedster until he killed himself. He'd also been pals with Dean Stanton, who later told me, "Pitman had a chance at a good career, but couldn't shake his need to be another James Dean. He said he'd rather die and have people say how much he'd been like Dean than go on living without people making the comparison."

I found out from Gilson while he was at my place that he, too, had slept with Gena. "Just a passing thing," he said, right after he had separated from his own wife. Though I really didn't know Gilson well, just as part of the Schwab's crowd, I felt sorry for him. It wasn't pity as much as kind of sadness. Nothing much was to happen for him in New York.

I remember Gilson sitting in my apartment in jeans and tee-shirt, talking about his future with an intense hopefulness he tried to hide beneath a casual facade. He said, "Acting's a lark anyway. It'll be easy, and once I'm over the hump, there's Beverly Hills and sports cars and women." He acted as though he could read the future like a book or a crystal ball.

But when nothing happened in New York, Gilson packed up and headed back to L.A. There he only experienced more hassles with his wife, with the separation—and then came something he hadn't seen in his crystal ball. While trying to get into his house through the screen door, his wife shot him in the chest with a shotgun—straight through the screen.

Dennis said Gilson had been dead before he hit the ground. The future was a joke, according to Dennis, who was loaded on dope and booze. While he stayed with me on 17th Street, he ranted about a personal "all-encompassing present" that had him in a kind of bear-hug, and about how the world was just shit. He was surrounded by shit, he said, "submerged in shit." He ate shit for breakfast as his Breakfast of Champions. The only chance of creative salvation was to shake free by changing who he was. It was like tailoring a new suit. Once he'd shed the skin of his present, he'd slide into this new one and step right out of the shit.

He anguished over what the Beats had already harped on long before: that the only way to one's truth was to turn the head inside out through dope's disorganization of the senses and overall craziness. Flipping the lid and letting the steam fly was the only route Dennis could imagine to what he called the "holy grail." But in time, this personal grail would become nothing more than a tin cup—his desire for an okay from Hollywood, rubber-stamped by the big wigs, validating Hopper as a bona fide movie actor, equipped with the perks of mediocrity—the divorces, the drugs, the blue-ribboned salvation—and an allegiance to the evocation of emptiness.

Following his dump by Warners, Dennis had managed to scrounge up some jobs here and there through the graces of his gay agent and friend, Bob Raison, who kept his own body shaved hairless with European razors. Raison was one of those few remaining with any interest in Dennis's survival, if only out of a kind of maudlin pity.

The first night on 17th Street, Dennis had a blue BOAC bag stuffed with marijuana. He wore a striped polo shirt from Sy Devore's in Hollywood, US Keds sneakers and a gold St. Christopher around his neck, inscribed with the names "Paul and Joanne." He smoked a handful of fat joints until the whites of his eyes were red, and droned on about Hollywood's failure to see "the truth." In his dope-addled haze, he fumbled out some new aspiration to get even. Warners would be sorry. He'd *make* them sorry.

123

While I was working on another scene with Brooke, from *Le Ronde*, I introduced her to Dennis in a coffeeshop on the corner. He happened to be tagging along West 56th, and I had no thought of pairing them or playing Cupid, since Brooke was married—unhappily—to an investment banker with artistic pretensions named Michael, and they had two kids.

Twice I'd met Brooke's younger sister, Bridget, an astonishingly beautiful girl but with a kind of misty quality at times, as though she were only half awake. On another occasion I saw Bridget alone in a health food restaurant near Carnegie Hall, and she was bright and vivacious, and bubbling over with energy. I was very attracted to Bridget and yet felt nothing in that way for Brooke—just a friendliness. We talked about her sister once, and Brooke said that Bridget had some emotional problems, yet to be resolved.

After meeting Dennis, Brooke said he was "one of the most completely self-indulgent people" she'd ever encountered. Dennis put the make on her within minutes, and though Brooke said she wasn't impressed and that she felt she couldn't get through his self-importance, a relationship would later develop between the two of them—largely manipulated by Dennis—leading to marriage.

Stewart Stern wrote the script for *Rebel*, and was close friends with Paul Newman and Joanne Woodward. Dennis became a kind of "bad boy" character hanging unshakably in their midst. I remember a long-handled silent butler on Stewart's coffee table that had a big dent on its bottom. Joanne Woodward told me she'd become so impatient with Dennis's "moaning drivel" one night, she'd grabbed the silent butler and smacked him on top of the head as hard as she could. "Hoping in some way," she said, "to knock sense into him . . ."

Dennis and I talked about Tuesday Weld and the parties back in Hollywood on Melrose Place, but I didn't introduce him to a new girl I was seeing—Susan, who was very young and who had been a model with Tuesday and another girl, Carol Lynley, also trying to get into the pictures.

Stumbling through the Village, desperate to get laid, Dennis would stop girls on the street. "I'm Dennis Hopper," he'd say, blocking their path. Did they "want to fuck?" They'd laugh or huff or just glare with indignation. "Who the fuck's Dennis Hopper?"

One older crippled woman with albino-like eyes stood right against his chest and said, "Where you want to do it?"

Dennis grabbed my arm. "I'll take her back to the apartment . . ." I glanced at the woman and asked if he was kidding. He said, "No, man, this is what I've been *telling* you . . . This is the way, man!" I gave him the key and he ushered the crippled woman into a taxi. It pulled away with her leaning on him and Dennis kissing her, his tongue going into her mouth.

Following that episode, he drunkenly tore the St. Christopher medal from his neck and threw it out the apartment window, yelling that the only "path" he needed to be protected on was "against the powers that battle with the fates."

He seemed to peak one night when a few people drifted over to empty some wine bottles and smoke up Dennis's dope. A chubby, good-natured guy I knew from a few years before at Normandie Village on the Strip, an unemployed operatic baritone, was filling in as a singing waiter since coming to New York. The gig was across the street from a convent, two blocks north of the Coney Island subway. That night the singer, who was himself a Catholic, had collected two nuns on his way to my place. They asked if Dennis and I were brothers, and I said, "Certainly not."

Both nuns wore black habits decked with rosaries. One was sort of heavy-set, the other, younger, prettier, with a bright face and blonde eyebrows. The singing waiter had coaxed them on a mission— "not exactly saving souls," he'd told the sisters, but to meet a challenge, a difficult personality caught between "faith and the abyss," as he put it. It had to do with the destruction of the spirit brought on by one's own volition. He meant Dennis the Menace, of course.

Not to disappoint, and like a geek going for the chicken, Dennis swung into awful form. Sufficiently puffed up on dope and weaving with booze, he began to unwind his weirdness. Mocking celibacy as a "fantastic notion of marriage to someone who doesn't exist" meaning Jesus—he shamelessly offered himself to the younger nun who he said would be blessed by a romp with a "live pulse" like "Dennis Hopper. "

The singing waiter stepped in when Dennis started pawing the young nun. "Excuse me, sister," he said, picking Dennis up in both hands as though he were a pizza, then tossing him to the far corner of the bed against the wall. "Cover your head!" he ordered. "The shame of your face!" Dennis couldn't grasp what was happening, and the waiter threw the blanket over Dennis's head and pushed him down, warning, "Don't move a muscle." We all watched for what was going to happen next. "I'm escorting the sisters out of this place," the waiter said, "but first you're going to apologize to them."

Dennis couldn't apologize. He pretended to pass out. I made excuses to the nuns, and again assured them that Dennis and I were *not* related. "He's in a television show," I said. "He's only staying a few days." The younger one kept nodding with a sad smile, and the older sister went to the bed and placed her hand on Dennis's shoulder. She said, "I can see he is in pain, and we will pray for him . . ."

"And I'll pray for you," Dennis mumbled from beneath the blanket, but later claimed to have no memory of the incident. Every time the subject came up, he'd tighten his face like a child at the dentist's.

Finished with *Swiss Family Robinson*, Dennis quickly left New York to hook up with a new dope connection he'd made through a Broadway dealer. Before he left, we were having a cup of coffee with John Cassavetes at a knish and hot-dog stand. John and I were talking about his 16mm film *Shadows*. He mentioned that he was still cutting it, when Dennis suddenly burst out, "An artist does crazy things . . . He's got to break free, man, he's got to get out of the trap by breaking the fucking molds. That's what an artist has to do . . . "

Cassavetes nodded and said, "Like who're you talking about? Anybody around here we know?"

By the spring I was signed to a big role in a movie to be shot in Paris, starring Jean Seberg. What they wanted was a young Marius Goring, an American "starving artist." I fit the bill, according to my agent at William Morris, George Litto, who went on to produce films like Brian de Palma's *Dressed to Kill*. He sent the contract over by Litto to my personal manager, Howard Austin, then handling Tony Perkins along with me. Howard was Gore Vidal's live-in secretary and spent weekdays in Gore's Upper East Side apartment and weekends upstate in Gore's mansion on the Hudson. I often saw Tony Perkins in the apartment, once with an attorney helping him out of a vice jam. Tony was on a day bed, wringing his hands and crying.

When he left, Howard told me about Tony's exploits in the subways and movie theaters. He couldn't stay out of the back rows and public men's rooms, and was in hot water for groping a cop staked out to collar "sex offenders."

He told me Tony was anxious about that term—that he believed he was not an "offender." How on earth could he be a sex "offender," he said, when the other party had been asking for it?

"It's called entrapment," Howard said, but he had not been telling me Tony's troubles for the sake of gossip. He wanted to instruct me on the dangers of indiscriminate hanky-panky—especially, he said, with the large number of young ladies who came my way, and the possibility of one or any of them being "underage." He said, "In your seemingly limitless devouring of pussy, you're risking the sinking of a career before we're out of the bay, no matter how they're asking for it or instigating it . . ."

We went up to the Hudson house that weekend with Gore. I stayed in a big room normally occupied by the writer John Latouche and surrounded by books, as were most of the rooms. Gore spent most of his time in a circular library huddled in a blanket while he worked at an ornate, gargoyle-legged table.

I took a long morning walk with Gore down a dirt road past a few scattered houses, and we talked about Joanne Woodward and about his friend, Franchot Tone. We talked about Henry Fonda and his children, and the suicide of their mother, who'd slashed her throat in the bathroom.

He talked about Leland Hayward, and Margaret Sullivan's suicide, and I volunteered my concerns about Brooke's marital problems. Gore said, "It's in the blood—all this grouse-shooting in Scotland, this Harvard and Yale and Vassar back-boning . . ." He said it "dries one out," and if one wasn't cautious, "one might snap more easily than one could seriously anticipate . . ." A dog was barking up the road and Gore told him to hush up, but the dog wouldn't hush up. "You see," Gore said, "he doesn't have to listen. He doesn't have to do what he's told."

I'd been rehearsing a scene, directed by John Stix, with Brooke for the Actors Studio. We practised either at Stix's house or in the loft, where I was still secretary of the class. I was temporarily living at Stix's, since leaving Norman's on 17th Street. There had been such a commotion when Dennis left, I had been locked out of my apartment.

Stix was friendly with nightclub singer Libby Holman, who'd married the painter Louis Schanke. They held weekend parties in East Hampton, gatherings for poets and actors and artists. Another close friend of Holman's was Montgomery Clift, whom I found myself talking with one afternoon in East Hampton. Clift, I supposed, had been drinking since the preceding day or earlier, and I reminded him that I'd met him in Coffee Dan's on Hollywood Boulevard years before. It had been the middle of the night, and he'd been sitting there with Burt Lancaster and James Jones, who was decked out in Indian jewelry, and all three had been pretty pie-eyed. Clift had been nipping from a flask and acting out the scene from *From Here to Eternity* where he plays "Reenlistment Blues" on a bugle.

The conversation with Clift in East Hampton got around to Jimmy Dean. "I have great admiration for the work he did," he said. "I've been quoted as saying I resented Dean, and that's a fucking lie. I never said anything like that, and they'll tell the same goddamn lies over and over until you think it's the truth . . . I didn't know the guy, and I didn't know what he wanted from me. . . I would've answered the guy if I'd known he was going to die, for god's sake . . . So I've been told he was an admirer of mine, and I think that's great, and I'm appreciative of his admiration . . . It's a mutual admiration society, or we're all lost . . . I'm sorry he's dead like that, wrecked in a car . . . I only hope the guy didn't suffer, that he didn't feel any pain. There's nothing fucking worse than pain . . . Do you agree?" he asked, swallowing his breath. He coughed and I stared at him as his face turned white. He seemed to gag, and a stream of vomit poured out of his mouth and nose.

Not long before I took off for Paris, I played Michael J. Pollard's older brother in Saroyan's *The Human Comedy,* a special program on the *U.S. Steel Hour.* Part of it was taped, but most of the show was live, with Burgess Meredith narrating. For the few days we rehearsed and blocked scenes, I again talked to Meredith, who now called acting an "imprisoning avocation" not "too dissimilar from being sentenced to Alcatraz." He seemed to be joking, but I could tell he wasn't. You had no choice in the matter, he said. Once you were an actor, hopelessly committed as were James Earl Jones and Jimmy Dean and Burgess Meredith—there were few other possibilities.

He talked about memory, the immune system, psychoanalysis and perfecting dialects. Again he talked about "the obvious in one's nature." He said, "Many people are spending a fortune for someone else to tell them what would probably be obvious to them if only they could view their miserable hides from a different angle." Meredith said he had conversations with himself—or, as he put it, "dialogues." He said, "I've allowed characterizations to evolve through these dialogues" without revising "one iota of the language." That would be cheating, according to him.

We talked about his work alongside Franchot Tone in *Man of the*

Eiffel Tower, which he had directed, and he introduced me to an actress named Sylvia, who he said had been chasing him around the set. Burgess suggested I take her for dinner to a Chinese place down on Mott Street. She drank vodka with Coke and Pepsi, and told me she got in the habit from the singer Mario Lanza. "He went for the extras, the bit players," she said. "He didn't have regular sex with me but wanted oral stimulation, whenever he was in the mood." The singer had a sort of trailer dressing room at one time, constructed against the outside wall of the sound stage.

"He wanted this 'oral stimulation' frequently," Sylvia said, but usually didn't complete the act. "I don't mean to say he was impotent," she continued, "just that he seemed to need to have sex going on in his head even when his body didn't seem to want it."

She suggested that maybe he'd been diabetic, because he injected himself. "He had these hypodermic needles in his dressing room, and he drank gallons of pop—Pepsi, Coke—he drank Royal Crown Cola that he kept in a big ice box in the trailer."

I took Sylvia back to my apartment and we listened to Profokiev's soundtrack for Sergei Eisenstein's *Alexander Nevsky* while I sucked her toes and she masturbated. Then we drank more vodka and Coke and read Strasberg's lectures, which I'd been transcribing from Actors Studio tapes—a tentative book idea being compiled by John Stix, who'd brought me into the project. I told Burgess Meredith that in my lay opinion, the emphasis was too much on psychoanalysis, and I thought the themes—or the stream of thought running beneath the stuff—seemed to circumvent the real guts of the art, the creative spirit, perhaps, or the kind of spontaneous artistry that I found so inspiring in many actors and artists.

Stix was into analysis every other day at fifty bucks a crack, and he'd often doze "on the couch" straight through the session. But Stix said the shrink told him, it was "very significant." He said that Stix was unconsciously avoiding the analysis and that it was necessary to step up sessions to a daily basis, which Stix did because he had the money, rather than admitting the possibility that he was getting older, or needed to cut down on his smoking, lay off the scotch a little and get a good night's sleep—or maybe just face the fact that he was a short, homely Jewish homosexual nobody was attracted to.

He told me he feared women's breasts, becoming anxious when facing a woman that she'd press herself against him and he'd be pierced by the points of her breasts.

Not to be left out in the head scene, I'd started seeing Lawrence Hatterer, the head psychiatrist at Payne Whitney Clinic of New York Hospital—seeing him free of charge as one subject of a book he was writing on "the artist in society." Oddly, Hatterer was the shrink Gena had consulted years before when the banshees were sneaking after her. I told Hatterer I was still seeing the actress Burgess Meredith had sent me after, but it was clear she was a sadomasochist. She wanted me to choke her "softly" while having sex, and then sort of went into a fit. I didn't mind the belts she buckled tight around my waist—sometimes so tight I couldn't breathe—but I didn't want to be spanked or whipped. The psychiatrist suggested I back out gracefully.

The scene I'd been working on with Brooke from Ionesco's *Jack or the Submission* was halfway through rehearsals when Brooke broke down shaking and sobbing. Her life was falling apart—she was getting a divorce, she said, and she hated acting and hated herself. Things had been bad for a spell, her husband sneaking into the classes to catch Brooke and I kissing during the scene—or not during the scene. She said he was convinced we were having an affair. He'd gone as far, she believed, as hiring a detective.

Problems intensified to the point where Brooke finally told me she couldn't continue working on the scene. She suggested her friend Jane Fonda take her place since she was interested in getting into the Studio. Because we were doing a directed scene, chances were outstanding for both of us. Brooke took me to Jane's—actually to Henry Fonda's apartment, where Jane was staying since returning from an art-school stint in Paris.

I liked Jane's blonde pony tail and long neck, and by the second rehearsal we were on the bed together. She'd shaved her pubic hair deep into the V-shaped crevice of her crotch—more like a pie-patch than a natural blend of her body from belly to thighs.

Something was missing from the relationship, and I didn't know what it was. There was always the feeling that wherever she knew she had to be next, most of her was actually already *there*. Left behind was the tense, fretful shell of a pretty girl whose top front teeth were a little big for her mouth. It took energy to pull Jane into the moment at hand—energy that drained from the work—and the strain called for more relaxation, more candles and pillows with the scent of perfume and cosmetics, and the smell of her body. That long, willowy body was luscious, but there didn't seem to be a point to lovemaking, unless it was to blow off a little steam.

Was I really looking for a relationship, and did I think maybe I could concoct one with Jane Fonda who was running through a whole slew of friends, including an affair with James Franciscas, the lead in the half-hour *Naked City* series? I appeared in two of the shows myself, both directed by Stuart Rosenberg, a solid craftsman with whom I'd soon do quite a bit of work in Hollywood.

I never got a chance to speak with Franciscas the first time around, but the during the second *Naked City* show we had a couple of scenes together, and between takes we talked about Jane. I didn't realize that he seriously believed he had a monogamous relationship with her—as though she'd lie awake dreaming only of him. He said, "I know she's very much in love with me, but I'm not sure if I want that sort of clinging involvement . . ." He said *he* was holding the "puppet strings," and hadn't decided whether or not *he'd* continue the relationship.

I had something to eat at Jane's after the show, never mentioning Franciscas. She cooked macaroni and some sort of meat, and we sat on cushions on the floor, Jane sitting on my foot, agitated and preoccupied at the same time. I was leaving for France as soon as Howard received my expenses from producer Manny Tiedman, and Jane gave me names of people to say hello to in Paris. Because of the television work I was doing, and Jane's modeling and running around, and with the film pending, the Actors Studio scene was pushed to the back burner, though we were still going to give it try.

We went for a drink at Jim Downey's restaurant one night, and Jane was fluttering around with a couple of friends. Brooke showed up with someone else, and I ran into Sal Mineo in the men's room.

I was washing my hands when I looked up into the mirror and Sal was standing to my side. He said, "Hi." I said hello. He said, "I know you, you know . . ." He was wearing yellow-tinted aviator glasses and apologized that he couldn't remember my name "at the moment," but said, "You were the friend of Jimmy's . . . I'd like to talk to you," and his face got red. I remembered a time on the Warners lot when Sal was walking ahead of Jimmy and me, all of us heading to the commissary, and Jimmy snuck up behind Sal and pinched him on the butt. Sal had jumped, flustered, then grinned with that same red in his face as now, in Downey's men's room.

His hair was very black, and tousled in a Tony Curtis waterfall style nobody wore anymore. He had on a big or roll-collar sport shirt and a huge knot in his red tie. After *Rebel*, Sal had gotten the big-gun send up toward stardom from Warners, but somehow it was falling flat. Pinching his ass like that had been about the only time Jimmy had made any sort of direct contact with him outside of shooting a scene. With Nick Adams it had been the same way, even with Natalie Wood—Jimmy avoided them. Once off the set, he went out of his way to go in the opposite direction.

Sal seemed a lot taller than he'd been back then. I asked him what he was doing in New York, and he said, "Hiding." I didn't ask him what he was hiding from, and again he said he wanted to talk to me. I said, "I haven't talked about Jimmy to people. We just don't talk about him."

He said he understood that, and then started to say something about Jimmy—he said he remembered "it" very well, though I didn't know what "it" was. "I can't talk about it in here," he said and asked if he could give me a call sometime. I gave him my phone number, and he thanked me and left the men's room. Though I expected him to call, it would be many, many years before we'd make contact again.

Jane and I grabbed another drink in Downey's, then a taxi to my apartment on 73rd near Central Park West. She said nothing in the taxi, but remained slumped back, staring out the window. I remember thinking how pretty she was and how much I was drawn to something about her, and she'd later tell me it had been "self-recognition." She said we were so alike in some ways it was "almost like incest," "burning up at both ends . . ."

Tennessee Williams once told me, "These people are all mad, you understand. All mad to get into each other's bread baskets, but leaving nothing for the mice. It's as though there's nothing more to life, and perhaps there isn't . . ." I'd met Williams through Joanne Woodward, while Paul Newman was doing *Sweet Bird of Youth* on Broadway. Joanne was pregnant, and I accompanied her as her "date" to the premiere of Faulkner's *The Sound and the Fury*. She wore a loose maternity dress, and I had on a black shirt, flowered tie and sneakers.

Williams drank Jack Daniels on the rocks in Downey's, and liked to buy drinks for me and talk about the people he hated in New York and Florida. I didn't know why he told me about the people he hated in Florida, because I'd never been to Florida. He said he didn't hate anyone in Hollywood at the moment, because "at this present time," he said, I don't think Hollywood exists—except as a long urinal you can piss in from right here, and it's all downhill from here to there . . ."

After the taxi reached my building on 73rd, Jane and I got out, surprised to see a young woman down on her rump against the iron gate to my basement apartment. Though her hands were covering her face, I could tell it was Gena. She wore a turquoise suede skirt and jacket and high spiked heels, a mask of makeup, blotched and streaked, and her eyes were wild. She was having a nervous breakdown, she said, and knew it was wrong to come to me, but there was nowhere else to go.

Jane helped me get her into the apartment, but said that Gena should go to a hospital instead. She couldn't stop shaking. I had some valium, gave Gena one and put the rest in my pocket. Gena said she'd be okay—just needed somewhere to sit, get a grip and make a couple of phone calls. She was shaking so bad she couldn't hold the receiver, and then couldn't remember who she was calling.

"She needs to see a doctor," Jane kept saying. I told her I didn't want Gena there, but knew she was in trouble. Jane said I should stay with her, and that she would leave. I didn't want Jane to go. I looked to see if there was anything Gena might use to kill herself, but figured if she'd wanted to do it, she could have done it before getting to my place—that is, unless I was supposed to play some essential part in the act.

Right when I left Hollywood for New York, Gena had taken her daughter—five then—to an adoption center in the south part of L.A., to be farmed out to foster homes. I didn't know exactly when the little girl had been retrieved—by Gena's father, who took the child to live with him while Gena ran on the fast track.

Making sure Gena was settled with the valium kicking in, I walked Jane to Central Park West and waved down a cab. I said, "I'm sorry . . ." I really wanted to spend time with Jane. She said Gena was still my wife, wasn't she? I said legally, yes, but that it had zeroed out two years before. Jane said, "Unless you're divorced, she's still your *wife*, and I'd get her to a hospital. She looks like she's going to explode . . ."

We kissed goodnight in the dark in front of the small cathedral. I said, "I really could love you . . ." It was a lingering kiss, with almost desperate, tentative probes pulled back and held in check. The cabby gunned the motor and said, "You goin' or what?" I opened the door and Jane got in. She pulled it shut as the taxi drove off.

Going to Paris was a big break, as well as a kissing away of the friendship with Jane and her search for an ideal situation. Anyway, I had no room to gripe, with the thirty or so girls I'd been seeing that year. Damn! While having these exciting little flings, I was pretty much playing with people, though I hadn't planned it that way. I'd been called a *roué*—a Don Juan, who thought I had the magic touch to turn almost any female to jelly in a couple of minutes. But ultimately I was alone, "alone on a wide, wide sea . . ."

That's what I'd been seeing Lawrence Hatterer about—"sexual addiction," he called it. There had been times when I'd picked up a few different different girls on the same day. I told myself it was all a kind of game: albeit a serious one. I opened myself up to possibilities, believing that if that *right* one somehow clicked, we'd join like Ying and Yang and then I'd move her in as I'd done with Gena.

A few more years would go by with me thinking I was still married, when I wasn't. I'd never been able to pin her down for the divorce, even though our Connecticut marriage proved to have been illegal, despite the blood tests, judge and witnesses. Connecticut wouldn't recognize Gena's Mexican divorce from her former husband and so, knowingly or not, she'd become a bigamist by marrying me.

Later that night after showing up on my doorstep in turquoise suede, she told me she'd become a call girl, working a regular Madison Avenue book. But she'd almost been murdered that day by one of the johns, who had tried to suffocate her with a pillow while fucking her. He'd said he wanted her to die. She was going back to the shrink at Payne Whitney Clinic—Hatterer, she said—to try to shake off the dope and sex and pull her life together. I sensed she was hinting at another stab with me.

She stayed in my apartment to rest up while I spent the weekend at Gore Vidal's in the country, waiting for a flight date. After the airline ticket arrived, I hung out a couple of days in the Village with Myra Tamarkin, a girl I'd worked with in Stix's class—some good work, on scenes from Williams' *Orpheus Descending*. Myra was short and black-haired like Gena, with a lovely little body. She was like a young Italian starlet with sweet, white skin. I loved her skin, and her body, and we'd spend hours talking and having coffee, after which we'd head back to the Village and I'd pull down her panties all over again.

Jane was notches above some of the others, but part of it was high-risk chemistry, romantic notions of having somewhere to go once you get off the bed. I kept thinking about her long blonde thighs on my shoulders and her pained look—quietly gasping, keeping the secret. I'd picture her quivering and panting, those high breasts rising and falling with her rib cage.

But I felt I was probably yesterday's news as soon as I'd left for the airport. I wasn't looking back. Instead, I was eager to meet Jean Seberg. But at that time, in Paris, it would not be Jean Seberg I'd meet, but the "international sex-kitten," Brigitte Bardot.

SEARCHING FOR RIMBAUD

I THOUGHT THE PLANE WAS GOING TO CRASH into the Atlantic. Some sort of pocket or vacuum dropped the Air France carrier down at such a pitch that things slid in the aisles, and the passengers lurched or fell.

It didn't last long, but it gave me a charge, like sticking my thumb in a light socket, and I thought about dying. JONATHAN GILMORE KILLED IN AIRPLANE CRASH EN ROUTE TO PARIS, the headline might read, somewhere in the back pages, down at the bottom maybe. I thought about Jimmy Dean's fatal crash—his body twisted, broken, though not yet dead when Bill Hickman climbed onto the crushed Porsche to pull him out. Hickman said Jimmy had moved—made noises—but that he could also hear the air escaping from his lungs. Jimmy had talked about Paris, but he'd never made it out of the country except to Tijuana to see the bulls.

I wondered if John Hodiak had died without much pain. I missed those people. They were very different, but in some ways alike—both mavericks, both hurting, though John hurt more than Jimmy. And John was scared, failing as he did. He was frightened to death. I wrote in my notebook that I felt a strong need to talk to Hodiak.

Ida Lupino told me about her discussions with Errol Flynn on the subject of psychic vibrations and extrasensory phenomena. Flynn swore he'd reach back from the "the other side" to Ida. She'd be ready for it whenever Flynn "decided to make it happen." "Frankly," she said, "I don't think it's going to be that far into the future. He's not in the best of shape."

I hadn't been able to keep up drinking with Flynn at the Garden of Allah pool, where he'd rented a bungalow and was writing his memoirs. I'd fake swallows and slush the stuff around, spilling it out of the glass while we watched his frisky teenage girlfriend Beverly romp around the pool, her legs, back and stomach as golden as honey on pancakes. He'd start drinking around eleven in the morning, and soon he'd be well into his second fifth of vodka.

When the Air France took its nose-dive, I'd been dozing with my ballpoint and notebook on top of the movie script. The story was a post-Korean-conflict *La Boheme* with a few soap opera twists and pages of bad dialogue, that they said would improve in translation. George Litto at William Morris said, "It's an awful script, but a supporting lead." I was an ex-GI, filling the Rodolfo role borrowed from Puccini, and Jean Seberg would be Mimi, only she didn't die in the movie. My friend— the Marcello character—would do the dying. Litto said a young actor named Bruce Dern was doing the Marcello role, but that Dern would only be in Paris three days, and two weeks into the schedule.

"Five more hours to Paris . . ." I wrote. My black turtleneck sweater still smelled of Jane Fonda's perfume, and I started to write her an in-flight letter but threw it away. I smoked and tried to get some sleep, but scenes from *Lifeboat* and *Desert Fury,* and even pieces of the Indian movies Hodiak used to play, ran through my head. While in and out of this, I wondered if Dennis Hopper would ever seriously think about killing himself. I kept thinking of the small oil painting with the ugly, misshapen mouth Vincent Price had given him.

After two hours at the Paris airport, I was paged to the phone. I was fearful it would be complicated French and I wouldn't understand what they were saying. But it was an American named Brian Russell, associate producer to Manny Tiedman. He suggested I taxi into Paris to the production office, and we'd have lunch before getting settled. He sounded like somebody on the verge of a breakdown.

I paid the driver American currency, which I didn't think he was supposed to take, but it was double what he would get for the fare in francs. He talked about Hitler as we drove up the Champs Elysees, and said he'd been standing on the street when Hitler and his brass were at the Arc de Triomphe. Not a dry eye in Paris, the driver said. His brother had been a teacher, married to a Jewish girl, and had lost his wife and children. They'd already been dead for months while his brother, unaware of their cremations, was attempting to find a way to have them freed. Nazi intermediaries, had taken what he had left, promising to get word from his dead wife and children.

The driver said he'd personally been as close to Hitler as an umbrella he pointed out on the sidewalk, and if it'd been a gun he could have changed world history.

I asked him what had happened to his brother, and he said he had gone to work for the Resistance. When he learned the truth about his family, his own life meant nothing to him, and now he too, the driver said, was free. After the war he was decorated, a year later he committed suicide because of grief over his children. If there had been more Nazis to kill, the driver said, his brother might have lived on. Killing had kept him alive. "When we stopped the war," he said, "the past came back . . ."

I got out of the taxi by the Opera, quickly found the building I was looking for and rang from the downstairs phone for the production office. Brian Russell said he'd be right down, but it was twenty minutes before he stepped out of the elevator cage. He was tall and thin, with a beard and watery eyes. He shook my hand warmly, had the consignor take my bag and went to hail another taxi.

He was giving me a little tour as we headed for lunch—before he got around to breaking the bad news about the production delays. Over wine, he said, "We weren't expecting you this soon. Manny had to go to Rome where the schedule's being juggled around a bit . . ."

Russell spoke quickly, evasively, and seemed to circumvent or qualify almost everything. Oh, I was on salary, he assured me, except I'd be reimbursed the per diem at the end of the week when Manny had forwarded funds from Rome. "That's where the pocketbook is," Russell said, "and unfortunately neither Manny nor I have our hands on the purse strings."

"Who does?" I asked. "The Italians," he replied, "at this point." In fact, he had not known I was arriving in Paris until early that morning. "If you won't mind," he said, "I'm putting you up at a private place this weekend, and Monday we'll have your hotel straightened out." He said I should have been arriving the following week, but Manny had managed a deal on the one-way ticket with the open-ended return as yet unvouched for.

I noticed a dog in the restaurant, and Russell said they were permitted. Then, sighing, he said, "Saint Joan," meaning Jean Seberg, was no longer in the picture. A young Italian actress had the role instead. "An exciting talent," he said, "with a large European following . . ." I asked about the movie's American release and the consequences of having no stateside names attached, and he agreed that the "root problem" they were facing was with the distribution deal Manny had spent a year putting together based on Seberg's participation.

He spoke rapidly in French to the waiter, then sketched a map to help me find the apartment in the Montmarte. I said, "Do you know any of the places where Arthur Rimbaud lived?" "Who?" he asked. I said, "Rimbaud—the poet." He said no, he didn't know. But the address for the apartment was easy to locate, he said, on Place Blanche almost opposite the Moulin Rouge. Taking a key off his own ring, he gave it to me, saying it was in case "the lady" was to let me in was out. He then spoke to the maitre d' and signed the check in Tiedman's company name.

I felt nervous, worried, yet at the same time—once I was back near the Opera—excited to be on my own. After walking a long way, my concerns over the movie situation faded as it gradually dawned on me that these were the streets of Paris beneath my feet. But I had trouble telling whether I was walking east or west, and soon I was lost. The city was so much larger than I'd imagined it would be from the movies. Uncertain of where I was heading, I ambled a mile or more north and came to a place once-called Le Bateau-Lavoir, "the laundry boat," a dilapidated building where Picasso and Braque, Von Dongen and Modigliani had painted.

I hung around this hallowed ground until my head started to spin. In the nearest little cafe, I drank some wine and coffee and wrote in a letter that I'd become a kid actor not by my own volition. In fact, I'd always wanted to be an artist—a painter. I saw myself as a silly American actor, an absurd role I'd foisted upon myself out of weakness and fear. It was only ego, skin, and if I stayed deaf and blind to that artist calling woven somewhere into all my cells and nerves, I'd lose any chance at that "one glorious hour."

I needed to get drunk. Anyone could understand that.

It wasn't Russell's apartment I entered, but one owned by an

139

attractive Latvian woman around forty, Maija, a designer and dress-maker who showed me her inscribed photographs of Marcel Marceau, Jean Louis Barrault, Edith Piaf, Jean Cocteau and Josephine Baker. The rooms occupied a second floor on Place Blanche across from the old windmill of the Moulin Rouge. I used the key to get into the building, climbed the narrow stairs and heard music. I rang the bell and Maija opened the door, laughing and talking on a red telephone. There were several rooms, one after the other like a New York railroad flat, the first with a long cutting table, sewing machines, rows of garments on pipe racks, and some showgirl costumes with big feathered headdress-es. The second room was a living room occupied by a life-sized plas-ter statue of Maurice Chevalier. The actor had signed his name on one leg when he'd given her the statue. A very ornate, beaded hat with plumes perched on the statue's head.

I told her my grandmother had won a plaster bust of Basil Rathbone as Sherlock Holmes in a raffle for a Los Angeles Irish-American organization raising money for those who'd been bombed-out in Britain during the war. I'd sung and danced on the small stage a few times at those get-togethers, where Rathbone often played his vio-lin. Maija said she'd lived in L.A. during the war, married to an American soldier who'd been shipped overseas. She'd worked in a para-chute factory, and at one point she'd been a fire warden, knocking on doors during the blackouts to warn people not to leak any light.

My grandmother used to boil black dye and cotton sheets in big vats on the stove—blackout curtains for those who couldn't afford them. We'd never any enemy planes, though, I told Maija, although I could remember the skies filled with American bombers and fighters. An older cousin flew a P-38 and never came back. I remember his salute the last time I saw him—his thumb and first finger fixed in an OK sign. When his plane was reported missing, I stepped up the squashing and saving of tin cans and foil from cigarette and gum wrap-pers, as though that would somehow help the efforts to locate him.

After the bombing of Pearl Harbor, I'd watched L.A.'s Japanese loaded into trucks and trains at Union Station, then hauled away to camps in the desert. One boy my age, my playmate and friend, put his hands against the glass from inside the train window. I'd wanted to reach up, but I was too short and the military guards were keeping back the people who weren't Japanese.

In church, as an acolyte, I'd light the candles on the altar and listen to the bombers flying overhead toward the ocean. I'd pray for the pilots and the bombardiers— and also for the Americans who were Japanese, but I couldn't tell anyone I was doing that.

Maija's soldier husband had been killed during the Normandy invasion, she told me, and after trying to get work in the studios, she had returned to Europe—her parents needed her. "I came back not unpatriotically," she said. "Never that, for I am still an American citizen."

She pinned her hair up in a mound on top of her head and wore cat's-eye glasses with bits of rhinestone or sparkling glass embedded in the heavy black frames. My girlfriend Sherry had worn sunglasses like that at Hollywood High.

We shared a bottle of wine as we talked, then she opened some Napoleon cognac. She wanted to know more about my days as an acolyte, and if I'd ever had "naughty" thoughts in church that I could not help thinking. French songs were coming from a radio installed into an old upright crank-handle phonograph. One wall was jammed with books. She knew James Jones, the writer, then living in Paris, and other expatriates—from Josephine Baker to the American poets on the Left Bank. She knew Jean Seberg and Francoise Sagan, and told me "confidentially" that Seberg had not been signed for the Tiedman movie, though the producer had touted that to his Italian investors. She said, "Russell has even approached Juliet Greco, but that is now a ridiculous notion, with her recent successes . . ."

I said I liked Greco—I'd listened to her records—and Maija said, "She's in Paris, I think. You should meet her . . ." The brandy on top of the wine was stoking us up, and I asked her if there was such a thing as absinthe anymore. "Oh, yes," she said. A couple of companies outside the city were producing it, but it was difficult to obtain in other countries. She said there was one—perhaps two—"holes" that served it, usually with soda water in a separate canister. She said, "Aren't you afraid it will damage your brain?" I said I wasn't worried about my brain. We were both hungry, and I said I was craving an old-fashioned steak I could sink my teeth into. She settled back into the soft sofa and said she was contemplating whether she wanted to have dinner or whether she wanted to have me.

I straightened up a little and said, "What about this guy Russell? He said you're his lady friend."

"We are friendly," she said. "I work for the film companies he's worked with, but our relationship is cordial and professional." Then she did something that reminded me of the scene in *The Big Sleep* where the girl in the bookshop lets her hair down for Bogart, and takes off her glasses.

She did, in fact, undo her hair and it fell shining to her shoulders, Then she removed her glasses. "Russell and I are not lovers," she said. "He would very much like that to be so, but we have never been to bed. He is not my cup of tea," she said. "You are."

It wasn't because I'd been shy, not wanting to tell her the secret thoughts I'd had as an acolyte in the church, she told me, but that I had a "boy quality" that softened the "hard edges" of an otherwise quite masculine nature. She said, "I am very partial to younger, very attractive men . . ."

Later, she said I "fucked beautifully," and that my mouth was "from heaven, although, as Juliet Greco would say, 'it is bound for hell.'" With such images floating around the Latvian's boudoir, I asked her if she knew any places where Rimbaud had lived, or cafes he'd hung around in. She said she was not sure herself whether the buildings still stood—there were so many derelict areas, in shambles, the buildings deteriorated, many gutted and restructured, or demolished and replaced. Some areas, she said, "where nothing has been done, are infested with rats . . ."

But a friend of hers, a former circus clown named Claude, could tell me if such places still existed. The biographer Enid Starkie had talked to Claude about the poet for the writer's remarkable work on Rimbaud. "There is nothing about Paris that Claude does not know," she said. "But I must warn you, he will no doubt be quite interested and taken with you. He is not as attractive as I am. In fact, he looks as old as the city, and perhaps he is . . ."

I told her I would be interested only in seeing the city, and she said in that case she'd be looking forward to my coming back that night.

Claude was indeed old, with a face creased like a pouch. He was completely bald, and stood on spindly, slightly bowed legs that hurried him about brisk and jittery like a chicken, and wore a big coat made of mismatched monkey skins.

After cashing in my American currency for francs, I spent several whirlwind days between Maija's and on a kind of speeded-up hopscotch tour through Paris with the frenzied clown. He knew everybody from Burt Lancaster to Walter Winchell, and people bought him drinks wherever he went—and me as well—at Le Dome, Aux Deux Magots,

Harry's Bar, while eating at Lipp, and a on quick run through the Crazy Horse.

I kept thanking Claude, and he kept saying, "Why are you thanking me? Because I am in love with Maija, I have taken you on board my life today, but this day is no different than the rest of my days . . ."

We were on some little street south of St. Germaine, and the clown stopped me beneath the stuffed head of a horse beneath a butcher's awning. Claude stared up into my face, then pulled up his sleeve and showed me the numbers tattooed on his forearm. "I was in Belsen, you know. Did she tell you that? They worked me like this dirty dead horse. I'm Dutch—and a Jew—a Dutch Jew, but I survived," he said. "All around me they died, and I watched them die like I am now watching myself die, only I'm dying more slowly. They went fast, most of them. I have cancer, and it's spreading through me like rot in the core of an apple. I drink to kill the pain . . . If I stand still, I'm in pain. Life is meaningless. I was a famous performer before the war. I was adulated. I own property—I own the building Maija lives in. Did she tell you that? I am in love with her, but it is hopeless because life contains no intrinsic meaning. Do you have meaning in your life?"

I said I thought I did. He said, "Cling to that as a child clings to its mother's breast. Never let it go. Circumstances have forced me to let the meaning of my life go. I had fame—as you will have one day, with your poet's face and dangerous spirit. Now I only have death at my side . . ." He took my arm, squeezing my muscles and grinning suddenly. "You have nothing to thank me for. Come, we need to drink, and I must show you where Arthur Rimbaud would have nightly sex with strangers. He would lurk in alleys, and he went down into the sewers.

"He had sex with animals, you know? He tore pages from the Holy Bible to wipe his rectum and threw the dirtied pages from the windows. He was homicidal, you know—whether he ever murdered isn't known, and I doubt it, for the one he was murdering was inside of him. In his defiance and anguish for truth he was loved by God—loved by *God,* my friend—and far holier than the masses he despised . . ."

Brigitte Bardot was pregnant and said she felt like her belly button was about to pop out. She feared it would rise outwards like the lid of a spider's trap door. She placed my hand on her stomach so I could feel how she was swelling. She said she had no feeling for the child's father, whom she had not married. Bardot was divorced from the young director Roger Vadim, who was soon to marry Jane Fonda—a situation I had no way of guessing while close to Jane.

What Bardot wanted to know from me was, if James Dean had been a girl, would he have had an abortion—that is, pursued his career—or would he have had the baby and married its father? We were in a hallway on the top floor of a building somewhere off the Rue de la Paix, not far from the Opera, and sitting on some steep iron steps that led to the roof. Filling the hallway were voices and sounds of the party down the hall. Brigitte had told me she could not talk in the crowded room, but what she had to say to me was a "matter of life and death . . ."

As Bardot led me out of the main room, she told a woman in a fedora-style hat and a long suede jacket to "stand in" for her and "chatter like a parrot." It took several minutes to get into the hall, because people kept stopping Bardot, talking effusively and reaching for her hands. Her lovely face was fixed in a glowing smile, and she introduced me as "Jonathan, the close friend of the dead," by which she meant James Dean.

I was intensely aware of her, and she kept smiling and playing me like a yo-yo. She wore black, except for some sort of cotton trousers or jodhpurs, beneath a baggy skirt. There was something so incredibly perfect about her, like a religious icon. I quickly got the notion that her pregnancy, and especially the marriage to the young French actor she had no feelings for, was most unsettling to Bardot at that point in her life—a perplexing disruption of her career. I could see something in her that was strange and foreign from the moment we met, something that kept showing as though threaded through the pieces of what she was saying. The bouncing, saucy international sexpot she played on the screen seemed a cover for her lack of feeling for humanity in general. She said she experienced an intense empathy for animals, "for the littlest dog on the street," because it carried in its spirit an "unpoisoned pureness" that she could spontaneously relate to. "Bardot the animal"— that's where it came from.

When I told her, "I believe man is the only true disease in nature," she lit up and said I knew exactly what she was talking about. "It is the same thing that James Dean understood inside of his person," she said, "that could never be observed through the roles he played." So, she asked, taking my hand and squeezing it, would Jimmy go ahead and have the baby, marrying the father, or would he place his professional or personal needs above the customary sense of morality?

I was afraid to answer her question honestly. She seemed so vulnerable in her sincerity. Even while trying to appear more philosophical than she actually was, those eyes hid nothing of what she felt, and the attraction we shared right then was electric, like an arc flashing between two poles, buzzing at moments like a current. Little did I know that I'd be facing the same question myself a couple of years later with the Hungarian freedom fighter I'd eventually marry, and that I'd understand Bardot far better in retrospect.

She was divorced from Vadim and said that the pregnancy represented the kind of change that takes one to a different plateau. It would no longer be just a matter of deliberating which part to play or not to play, or who to know or who not to know. She knew in her heart that she did not want to make the change.

If Jimmy had been a girl, I said, it would have largely depended on the importance of the unborn's father in his immediate life. I could maybe see Jimmy bypassing a movie to have the baby, but I couldn't in all honesty see a long-term engagement with parenthood. I told Bardot that I was the product of a broken home, and whether I'd been with one parent or the other, I had survived, and been granted a life that I now led as *I* decided.

I offered her two convincing, yet opposed sides to the question. Jimmy might have dumped the fetus in a second the first chance he got, possibly even as another flipping of a "fuck you" in the face of convention. But I said that he probably would have weighed his choices very carefully, because for Jimmy the child would have represented the same pureness Bardot saw in animals.

The "poisoning" was not something God-given, but layered into the creature's being by convention—by the step-by-step initiation of the innocent's assault on truth, as Franz Kafka put it, or to paraphrase George Orwell, by the imperceptible and gradual destruction of one's ability to recognize what was false.

"Oui!" Bardot said. "Yes—yes." I'd struck a chord, and she leaned forward from the step above to kiss me on the mouth. Her lips seemed to have some searching, independent life of their own—a thankful kiss at first, comradely, even appreciative, but in a moment the two mouths touching, moving over one another, becoming something else. Our eyes were wide open and that high-voltage spark was jumping from hers to mine and back again. In a few minutes, she was up and hurrying down the stairs back to the party, pulling me by the hand, the wetness of her lips still on my mouth.

Several days later I had a conversation about Bardot with Francoise Sagan. We'd been introduced by Brian Russell, who was still claiming to be coaxing Jean Seberg back into the project. I saw right away that Sagan did not like Russell. I told her I had met and talked to Bardot about Dean, though I did not divulge what we'd shared. Sagan said Brigitte had suddenly decided to marry the young actor, Jacques, and that they'd have the baby, though Sagan believed it was much to Bardot's dissatisfaction. She predicted Bardot would become "extinct." "She will be alive," the writer said, "but the person she is will become extinct as things change around us . . ."

It would be almost a quarter of a century before I'd discuss the possibility of an affair with Bardot again, this time in the south of France—a possibility, that is, if I'd been sure a "female James Dean" would have aborted the baby. "Then I would not have gotten married," Bardot might have said, "and we would have had an affair . . ." Still, a time to seize such an opportunity—a kind of obligation to nostalgia— would not escape us completely.

I was temporarily stranded in Paris by Tiedman's company, staying in a good hotel for a week and a half while Russell was trying to hide from the Italian "sensation," the monster beneath the Gina Lolabrigida mask. For two days we read the scenes together through a translator while the spaghetti star swilled quarts of lemonade and pumped me for tidbits about Betty Grable and Marilyn Monroe. Then she checked out and returned to Rome, according to the prop master I met on the only day of any actual filming. Tiedman had set up a French crew and hired actors, but couldn't get the funds released from the Italians, who were at odds with his backers in Algeria. The producer had returned to Rome to try to wrangle the financing exclusively from the Italians. It was possible, the prop master told me, that the entire production would move to Rome, "if it ever gets off the ground." Believing they would be able to get a green light, Russell suggested it was more economical to keep me on tap than fly me back to the States then back again, since with a pay-or-play contract devised by Howard Austin, they would have to pay me off whether or not they shot the movie.

I was lodged in a fifth-floor walk-up in a narrow building on the Left Bank, an attic with a slanted ceiling and skylight, and a door to a little ridge of balcony along the edge of the roof, one large room with a sink, toilet and bidet in the hall at the head of the narrow stairs. A double bed, a chest, a table and one chair served as furnishings, and a few wooden boxes stacked along one wall for shelving. Instead of a closet, there were ornate lion's-head hooks nailed into the wall, layered over with two-hundred years of paint and dirt.

Russell paid a lump sum on the per diem in francs, and I hung out at a cafe down the street from the Beaux Arts, writing letters to New York and Hollywood. I even carried a baguette of bread from the bakery to my garret, drank wine, and ate candy or bread with mustard while awaiting a new shooting schedule from Rome.

Francoise told me Jean Seberg had been warned by the French producer Raoul Levy that financial problems haunted Tiedman and that his deals were erected on the shakiest foundations. Jean had backed off until the company was able to prove it could complete the filming. Raoul told her they couldn't do it.

I told Sagan that they had to pay me one way or another, and she said with a smile, "So here you sit in a Paris garret, adoring our city while you're being paid to suffer . . ."

It was true. I even managed to procure a typewriter from Russell's office and began to set down a novel about a situation not so unlike the one at hand. I wrote to Anais Nin, having talked to her on occasion at filmmaker Curtis Harrington's in Hollywood. For years she'd been shuttling between two different lives, two different men, one in New York, the other in L.A.

My friend the novelist Bernard Wolf, once secretary to Leon Trotsky in Mexico, had recommended Maurice Girodias at Olympia Press in Paris. Bernie had published with Olympia several "apprentice novels," as he called them, and said if they were halfway good, and contained lots of sex scenes, one could always count on a few bucks from Maurice—at least enough to keep hitting the cellar-joint freak shows and "existential gin mills" on the dark side of the City of Lights. Most Americans I met living in Paris seemed to be somehow damaged, although it wasn't always apparant to the eye. They'd gone nuts in the States and drifted off, or sent away to art school or on indefinite "vacations"—as Jane Fonda had been by her father. The Beats were the worst, hanging around a Left Bank hotel scribbling nonsense, or cutting out and pasting up a bunch of scraps, or wasting good paint or boards and canvas—most of the time shooting heroin and staying so wasted they'd flop for days wherever they went on the nod.

William Burroughs was also at the hotel, genuinely in pain—he seemed to shriek with every breath. A sad man, all static like an old radio on the fritz, he'd shot his wife in the head with a gun in Mexico, killed her, though he claimed to have only been showing off his marksmanship. The police were always looking for him. Emaciated and desperate, he was a lecherous spook. Another post-Beat American, Gregory Corso—a loud and obnoxious poet—shouted that he had to keep pulling Burroughs out of public cans, where "he's always on his knees giving blowjobs to anyone who'll whip it out!" Burroughs made him sick, he said, and he'd have "to kill Bill" sooner or later; he'd have to "beat him to death" and turn Burroughs' face into a "flattened mass of burger."

The narrow street, rue Git le Coeur (the Lying Heart), led from rue St. André des Arts to the quay. An American drunk, Bob Gardner, had lived on the top floor of the hotel and was constantly colliding with Gregory Corso. "I hated him," Gardner said. "He was one of the only people I've ever thoroughly hated. I even hated his shoes." Gardner loaned money to Burroughs on several occasions, and Burroughs was always putting the tap on him. "I didn't mind giving Burroughs money," he told me, "even though I figured I probably wouldn't get it back. But I did, you know. Years later I wrote him in New York, and he actually sent me a money order."

The Beat Hotel was surrounded by Chinese restaurants and frame shops, a couple of cafes and an African club. A few times I hung out with Gardner in one of the cafés or shared a bottle with him in his hotel room. From what I observed, these Beats just sat around continually threatening each other and stealing each other's dope. At that time, I also met Harold Norse, an American dancer-artist-writer who was working at the Beat Hotel on a series of small paintings he called "cosmographs." He told me Corso was having a fling with Jean Seberg when she wasn't on a picture, and we talked a little about Monty Clift. He knew Girodias at Olympia Press, and we discussed writing, and Jack Kerouac. One afternoon at the Deux Magots, I told Harold my idea for a novel, and he advised me to write it. "Don't let it fucking run out on you," he said. "The goddamn things'll run out like an unsatisfied lover . . ."

Burroughs knew where to find the best absinthe in a section of Paris he called "the sewer," and I went with him and another poet named Frank Milne, from Hoboken, who wore some sort of turban on his head with a bunch of fake jewels stitched to the front above the eyes. Burroughs kept staring at my crotch and almost obscenely licking his lips, or making strange remarks about "a penis colony in the desert." He drank quickly, painfully, and at one point began sweating and shaking. His eyes rolled up like an epileptic's, and he seemed to go into a kind of fit. I got up and away from him when he started frothing at the mouth and shitting his pants.

Frank Milne's turban fell off as he tried to pull Burroughs back into a sitting position and get him out of the cafe. The turban was dirty inside and I didn't pick it up, but as I followed them out I noticed Frank's bald head had a square scar like a flap on the crown, as though he had a metal plate in his head, or his skull had been operated on.

One gray morning the rain was pounding on my skylight, and the Chinese girl I'd met, a mime in a little cafe theater, was asleep in my bed, curled up like a cat in the blanket against the damp wall. I'd slept in my pants and black leather jacket. The rain was so loud I could barely hear the woman who owned the place knocking on the door. Her apartment was on the fourth floor in the rear, where I was wanted on the telephone.

The production was at a temporary standstill, Russell reported. "These Italians want to take the deal out of France," he said. "They're goddamned pirates!" True or not, funds had been frozen in Rome and the "exciting international star" was doing a "biblical picture" with an American muscle man.

Russell had been instructed by Tiedman to settle with me in lieu of further delays. In the event the financing was released, he said, "We can fly you back and get cracking on the picture whether we shoot it in Rome or half of it here."

The landlady was chopping up a long fish as I talked to Russell, and when I hung up she looked at me and asked if I was writing a book. I said sort of, and she said if I was going to stay in the room her husband could fix a small oven, but I'd have to help carry it up because her husband's back was "no good." I thanked her and said I'd let her know. She nodded. If I had the oven upstairs I could fry some fish, she said.

It was too early to call Maija, who slept until noon, and so I went back upstairs to where the Chinese girl was putting on her yellow rubber shoes. Water pools were spreading on the floor from the leaks in the roof and skylight, and some of my typed pages were soaked. I spread them out on the bed to dry, and the girl and I left and walked along St. Germaine in the gray rain.

An agent named Bullock, close friend of my mentor of the moment Constance Bennett, was inviting William Morris to at least frame a co-representation deal for my appearing in a Broadway play with Jean Seberg—a story called *There Was a Little Girl*, being put together by Josh Logan. Constance Bennett had talked to Logan, and George Litto at the Morris agency was talking to Bullock about splitting the commission if I'd do the play.

Rose Tobias in New York wanted me for a Kaiser Aluminum show, and Stuart Rosenberg, now in Hollywood, had MCA call Litto about my availability for a movie. I'd written a long letter to Constance Bennett the day before, telling her I was eager to meet Josh Logan. Maybe the play with Jean Seberg was destined to come off, I told him, since the Paris movie was dangling, but I'd have to wait to see what they were going to do, because the pay-or-play clause structured by Howard left no room to walk out on Tiedman. I'd mailed the letter on St. Germaine shortly before meeting the Chinese mime.

Li Fon was unusual because her hair was more red than black, but she said as far as she knew her lineage reached back into ancient China "through and through Mandarin," she said.

We had coffee and croissants, then browsed the booksellers along the Seine. I found a small leather-bound copy of Charles Baudelaire's *Les Fleurs du Mal* and, at another stall, an old copy of Rimbaud's poems and letters. Li Fon bought an exquisite small print of the green apple by Cezanne, saying she had a larger one but wanted to carry a smaller print with her at all times. I said I felt that way about a couple of Rimbaud's poems.

After walking part of the way across Pont St. Michel, we stopped to stare at Notre Dame and smoke a cigarette. At night the cathedral was like a giant, living thing, with the buttresses sticking out like legs. But although everything about it had to do with the "human touch," in that drizzle it seemed somehow forlorn and beyond reach.

I could stay in Paris or, probably, leave on the next Air France to New York. I stood there on the bridge, kissing Li Fon—my eyes closed, but I was seeing Bardot. Li Fon's mouth was inviting, she had lovely breasts, and my right hand was inside her shirt as we kissed. We then walked for a long while and grabbed something to eat in a little cafe by the Eiffel Tower. I recalled the long talk I'd had with Franchot Tone in Gore Vidal's apartment as we shared a bottle of Gore's good scotch. We had talked about Franchot's movie *The Man on the Eiffel Tower*, and about murder, and Tone had told me how he'd met the Black Dahlia in the Formosa Cafe by Goldwyn Studios. He'd felt sorry for her, he said, but she was so lovely, with "that raven black hair and white, white skin like a geisha girl." He'd been drawn to her "almost irresistibly." "A femme fatale," he'd said, who turned out to be "a cold tomato, as far as the smooching goes . . ."

I called Maija from the cafe and told her about Russell's call. She said she knew Tiedman had lost the deal. "Take what you can get," she advised, "while there's still something on the table." I'd have trouble getting anything once it was gone. "He has many lawsuits against him," she said. "You'd have to get in line to sue him . . ." She asked if I was coming to see her, and I said probably—but first I had to deal with Russell. She said, "If you are leaving Paris, I want you to go knowing that you are welcome back."

After another quick call, I took Li Fon to the Metro, got her a first class ticket and kissed her again, then hurried to the cafe at the Opera, where Russell had said he'd meet me.

The check was less than the contract called for, and made out on a Swiss bank and signed by Russell acting for Tiedman. He also gave me an envelope with two-thousand francs, the additional per diem as agreed, and an open Air France ticket to New York, which voided the initial return ticket. As soon as we finished shaking hands, I telephoned Maija, asking about the Swiss check.

Something had to be done, she said. When I mentioned the francs, she said, "My god, they must be as guilty as sin." She said she'd call Claude and asked me to phone back. When I reached her again she suggested meeting in front of the Hotel Lancaster in thirty minutes. My check would be cashed, though the rate would be somewhat steep due to the fast exchange into francs against the Swiss bank, then back into U.S. dollars. "Not even a ten-franc piece will be mine," she said. "I am doing this for *amour* . . ."

By two o'clock I had the money in my black sealskin passport case, along with two small photos: Li Fon in an arcade, sticking her tongue out, and one of Maija's passport pictures. Maija said, "Speaking of sin, you are obligated to me now, because payment on that check would have been stopped the minute you boarded that airplane. So I have saved you." She said I would have to see the can-can before leaving.

"As corny as it may sound, there is magic in the Moulin Rouge at midnight that is nowhere else on earth . . ."

For two days I wrestled with the idea of staying longer in Paris. I talked to Harold Norse, who urged me to stay on and write the novel for Girodias. He said, "As long as it's dirty, Maurice will buy it. You can stay in Paris . . ." He talked about when he'd been a ballet dancer in New York, and about Burroughs and Kerouac, and spoke of his own writing. We drank wine and watched the rain beating on the St. Germaine sidewalk. I thought he was brilliant.

When the rain let up, I stood on the narrow ridge of the balcony of his little attic apartment and gazed at Paris, a wonder impossible to describe. It had to be experienced, felt, smelled and recognized in some inner part of oneself that had nothing to do with words. It was hard to believe that I was somewhere so far away when it seemed like such a *right* place to be. Yet I didn't know which part of me wanted to stay. It wasn't the actor. He wanted to get on the road, and to hell with everyone and everything. Harold said, "You know, you're like Pinocchio . . ." I didn't know what he meant until later.

I'd written my mother, and she'd answered with a strange letter mentioning a visit Jimmy Dean had payed her four years before, and conversations I'd never known about. He'd asked her a number of personal and penetrating questions having to do with her own inability to provide a home for me during most of my life. He'd wanted to know how that had affected her feelings for me, and if she felt that I had been able to come to terms with my own feelings, and if not, how that could have caused some of the lack of affection between mother and son.

It took me a day to get through to her in L.A., and by the time she was on the phone it was late and I could tell she'd been drinking. "Why don't you stay in Paris since you've got the money to do it?" she said. "Write the book you're talking about and sell it to that character. Maybe get more money to stay longer. Hell, I'll trade places with you!"

I spent the morning in bed with Maija. That afternoon, I went with Li Fon to see Baudelaire's grave in the Montparnasse cemetery. It reminded me of when I was a kid and used to wrap dolls like mummies. Baudelaire's cenotaph was huge, and stretched lengthwise on the stone slab was a statue of the poet wrapped like a mummy, except for his face, open to the sky for the rest of time.

I wanted to see Modigliani's grave, but instead we wound up at

Cafe Flore drinking wine and eating bread and mustard. Li Fon's French was perfect, and that evening she read Baudelaire's poems and Rimbaud's *A Season in Hell* by candlelight while we drank a pint of absinthe Maija had smuggled to me as a joke.

Cut it with the soda, it still tasted strange-but-good, though it made Li Fon sick. She threw up several times, saying something about an allergic reaction to the wormwood. Then she slept naked, moaning, tossing and turning the rest of the night.

By the next day I'd made up my mind to catch the plane to New York. Li Fon wanted the room, so I told the old lady that I'd be gone for a while and that the Chinese girl would be taking care of things for me. I didn't call Maija—figured I'd write her a long letter. I was afraid she would talk me out of leaving. She'd have said the actor in me had won over the other spirit—"the true one," she'd called it. As I taxied to the airport, I kept thinking about what Harold Norse had said, and about that line from Pinocchio came to me, where the fox and the cat are leading the wooden boy away, singing promises of fame and fortune.

HANGING AROUND THE GARDEN OF ALLAH

THEY HAD RIGGED 24-HOUR SPOTLIGHTS on the walls of the Garden of
Allah to keep the bums out of the bushes. A chain-link cyclone fence
prohibited whores from turning tricks behind the buildings, so they
headed through the front door instead. Wine and beer bottles, cigarette
butts, tampons, used rubbers and crumpled paper sacks were piled
against the peeling sides of the bungalows. Cops had fished a stiff from
the weeds behind the swimming pool—he'd been dead a few days. The
management then hired a couple of Filipinos to pour cement along the
back wall and stud it with broken glass to discourage climbers.

One garage door was nailed shut. A woman had been strangled and
found with a branch pushed into her vagina. Identification later showed
arrests for prostitution, and although the L.A. County Sheriff's detective said there were no leads, he advised locking the garages. "They'll
solicit in your rumble seat," he said, "if you don't keep your head on
backwards and padlock the door . . ."

Other hookers paced the lobby, the hallways and the restaurant
bar, hustling watered-down drinks or pretending to use the telephone.
Meanwhile, a pair of pimps jobbed them out of a broom closet. A Negro
pickpocket named Simms had a scam going in the men's room, where

he faked the role of porter with a whisk broom.

The world-famous Garden of Allah on Sunset had somehow died overnight, and all that was going on was the scavenging of its remains. The maintenance and cleaning help had been laid off, and word spread to Schwab's that change was laying around the floor of the cocktail lounge because nobody vacuumed anymore. A few unemployed actors snuck into the lounge to feel around beneath the tables and circular booths, wedging their fingers into the seams of the seats to pry out loose change. It was always so dark no one could see what they were doing in there.

Leonard Kantor, out from New York to write *The Untouchables* for television, also a feature for producer Joe Shaftell, stayed at the Garden before moving down the Strip to the Park Sunset. But he wanted to live at the beach, he said, "to look out sometimes and see nothing but ocean." I spent a couple of days at the Garden pool with Leonard after returning from New York. I'd let go of my 73rd Street apartment, urging Gena to take the place, at least until she'd figured out what she was going to do.

The afternoon I got back from Paris, I found her sitting in bed reading the funny papers and eating raisin-and-cinnamon toast. A squeaky bisexual actor from the Actors Studio was camping out in Jane Fonda's apartment, and the invisible wall between Jane and me was like a skid of bricks.

With the collapse of Tiedman's movie, I quickly answered Stuart Rosenberg's call on the possibility of working in Tennessee Williams' *Night of the Iguana*, then in the planning stages. Stuart had relocated to Hollywood, and one afternoon he and his wife were visiting Patricia Medina at the Garden—one of the last celebrity tenants, along with Errol Flynn, whose life was like a leaking ship caught on the rocks. Stuart invited me to lunch, and Patricia Medina said Flynn was on a non-stop drunk. She believed he was in "very poor shape . . ."

Despite the rumors of improvement, Flynn now drank mornings instead of eating. His eyelids were puffed into slits, and blood was having trouble finding its way to his hands and feet. He was obsessed with "death's close touch," as he put it, and parried daily with the idea of dying. In a last-ditch attempt to grab onto life, he dallied desperately with teenage sex. He wanted young girls—juveniles, he said—to give him oral sex while he watched the action in a long mirror fixed to a closet door.

He called Ida Lupino one morning and said he thought he was dying because he couldn't get out of bed. His "limbs," he said, had "petrified in the dark." His neck wouldn't turn, he told her, and he'd lay facing the mirror, watching for the "grim reaper's shadow to fall across the bed." But then his teenage girlfriend Beverly would come to sit on his face for a while, and soon Flynn would be back in the saddle, twisting open another fifth of vodka. According to Ida, he said, "False alarm, dear, but do not fear. You've got my word I'll call you the minute I've reached the other side . . ." How was he going to call? He only laughed and said, "That's for me to know and you to discover!" At the moment, he told her, "There's a party going on next door and I am the honored guest."

Out-of-town Shriners stayed at the Garden, and nobody cared how much noise they made. But the police were always there as though in and out of a revolving door. Some butchers attending a Hollywood convention tried to skewer and roast a lamb in a room and caught their bungalow on fire. Several fire trucks showed up to douse the blaze, and when it was out, the management boarded up the bungalow, stuffing rags in the cracks to keep the ashes out of the pool.

Stuart Rosenberg's wife got sick from a Swiss-cheese sandwich, and Patricia Medina was crying because the Garden was going to be torn down—the entire north end of the block on Sunset was slated to be leveled for a new bank building.

Kantor and I were eating steaks in the Fog Cutter when I told him I'd been invited to the big last bash at the Garden—a "demolition party." I told him about John Darrow's suggestion that we lease a two-bedroom beach house in Malibu. It was an older two-story place stuck out over the water on pilings. Darrow said he could get me an option to buy at the expiration of a one-year lease. Since Kantor and I were both pretty much shuttling between coasts, I felt the house might make a good investment.

I asked about the young actress from Malibu, and John said he no longer represented her because he couldn't get her any work. "In this town," he said, "a girl with a wooden snatch is like a boy without a prick." She was a good person, a good actress, no matter what John said. He could have been sounding off about anyone—it was just the ugly side of him, the side that had been hammered into shape by Hollywood.

I bought a bronze '57 T-Bird from an ex-fighter, a used-car sales-man friend of Paul Newman's, and drove Kantor to Malibu to see Darrow's real estate pal.

When I met Darrow later at his office on the Strip, he tried to sell me on the success he was having with his agency. What caught my eye most in the lavish office was a photograph of John Hodiak standing alone on a bare Broadway stage. "That was from the first play he did," Darrow said, adding that I could take the picture if I wanted it. "The only way you can sell a dead man is to an undertaker." Then he said, "But if you're in the market for an agent, I'm here, Jonathan. Just pick up the phone, pick it up anyway, even if you *don't* want an new agent. We can have a drink or dinner . . ."

But I already had a new agent. Since landing in L.A., I'd been guest starring or featured in a number of television roles. A show Stuart Rosenberg directed kicked them off, with the lead in a segment of *Lineup.*

Raymond Burr was responsible for linking me up with his agent, Lester Salkow, whose brother was with the *Perry Mason* series. I'd met Burr through Constance Bennett in New York following the Tiedman fiasco. When George Litto left William Morris to think about his own agency, Burr recommended me to Salkow and his associate, Mark Levin.

Blonde, pretty Susan Oliver from the Broadway production of *Look Back in Anger* co-starred with me in *Lineup.* As actors, the rapport between Susan and me was instantaneous. Dean Stanton—now *Harry Dean*—had a part in the show, as did Johnny Seven, later a regular on *Perry Mason.*

Susan was staying at the Montecito Hotel north of Hollywood Boulevard, but looking for an apartment. During our first script rehearsal—in Stuart's hotel room at the Hollywood Plaza, before his wife arrived from New York—something clicked between us and we quickly started a relationship. She called me her "young lion," though we didn't have sex during the week of filming at California Studios across the street from RKO.

We *played* at sex, and that was part of the energy between us. We were lovers in the show, married even, but in real life we were actors playing at sex even when we weren't in front of a camera. On loca-tion in San Francisco, Stuart, Susan and I had separate rooms at the St. Francis Hotel. My own room was high up over Union Square, with a grand view of the city, but I spent only one night there. The rest of the time I slept with Susan.

That one night apart was due to a drinking contest that Stuart and a regular on the show, a young guy named Skip Ward, challenged me to at the Purple Onion. Stuart and I talked about the absurd melodrama of the *Lineup* script, though it was fun to shoot, and we talked about French women, and about his wife—a German—and about the difference between French women and German women. We talked about Manny Tiedman, who'd twice tried to hook Stuart into directing, the first time while Stuart was filming the *Big Story* TV series. "A lot of hand-held camera work which I did myself," Stuart said, "and running shots, damn near jumping shots—there wasn't the time or money to even lay tracks for a dolly."

We got into Jimmy Dean and the time Stuart had hired him for a show. "I used him because I thought he *was* this character, right out of the script. He acted it out from the second he walked in the office. I never realized he wasn't that particular character until after he'd done the job. It was like he became the kid in the show from the first meeting. He'd eat and sleep it and be that person until we'd shoot the last shot." Stuart said the "on the run" shooting of early television, which was what Tiedman was after because he was a cheapskate, was what the French were now kneading into their "nouvelle vague."

Stuart wanted to present the San Francisco episode as having "visual quality" at least. His insistence on intricate angles led to awkward positions that took hours to set-up—the opposite of "on the run" shooting—and he quickly ran the show three days over schedule, an almost unheard of occurrence in commercial television. He said he didn't "give a fuck" about the schedule because he'd made the best episode that series would see.

Although that episode broke the camel's back—CBS canceled *Lineup* six segments in—it aired with much success. CBS's Hunt Stromberg Jr. was so excited he called me into his office to announce that he was co-starring me in a new series. *The Aquanauts* was another underwater venture by Ivan Tors of ZIV Productions, home of Lloyd Bridges' *Sea Hunt*. They would proceed with an immediate publicity campaign boosting me as a CBS' "special new discovery," using the *Lineup* episode as a springboard.

Ronnie Haran was a small, beautiful young woman with well-developed breasts. We'd meet in Tops Coffee Shop, and she was spending time with me while I lived at the Park Sunset. It was a real pleasure to sit around the poolside and just look at her in a bikini. I took quite a few pictures of her at the pool, and we'd often take drives into the hills or to the beach. Once we drove to Laguna and stayed at the old Laguna Hotel, and the next morning I took shots of Ronnie posing nude on the big rocks at the beach.

My agent, Mark Levin, steered her into work on *Dobie Gillis*, but I never felt that she was interested in acting. She told me, "I'd rather be an agent. I'd rather be producing a movie than walking around in front of the camera."

We really liked each other, but before long she seemed to be heading in some other direction. She later said her shift had been prompted by an "old flame" she had been thinking of seeing again.

It would be some time before we'd run into one another again, and by then she'd be managing the Whisky a Go Go on the Strip and hooked up with a young rocker named Jim Morrison, and a brand new group called the Doors.

Diane Varsi walked out on her 20th-Century Fox contract. She didn't want to be a star—she didn't even want to be a part of the movie business. "It's destructive to me," she said. "I can't give you a clear-cut reason, but has to do with something deep, something I can't explain because I don't even know myself . . ."

Vampira got a big kick out of Diane's desertion of her stardom, and out of the projected underwater series I was supposed to star in. I'd be running around without a shirt, and she said if I wasn't swinging in the trees with my old girl friend, Sheena of the Jungle, she would "mentally transpose" a big red cross on my chest and back (in her mind, the mark of a traitor).

Hindsight suggests that the new ZIV show might have been my only shot at success. But I didn't want to do a television series. I wanted one-shot showcases—anthologies, featured or guest-starring spots, as I'd been doing on *Bonanza*, *Alfred Hitchcock*, *The Untouchables*, *Ripcord*, *Lawman*—an arm's length of shows leading to bigger and better parts. I hoped this would lead to feature films and the occasional play in New York, rather than entrapment in an empty series—a spin-off to boot— with nowhere to go but into cancellation. Vampira's stamp on me— "that goon in a scuba suit, grinning at the ladies"—would stick to me. But by turning down CBS, I got a different label than the one suggested by Vampira. "Arrogant troublemaker" was the word on me.

I was still debating the point one afternoon when I ran into Schwab's drugstore to make a call and saw Jean Seberg at the counter. I told her we hadn't met, but that I'd thought we'd been set to do a picture in Paris. She said she knew I'd been in Paris—Francoise Sagan had told her—and Jean was very sorry I'd had to "experience the problems with that project." She said, "It was doomed from the start, and I was advised not to get involved. The producer actually went around telling everybody I'd signed to do the darned thing, while he was trying to finagle more money, I'm sure." She said she liked Brian Russell. He had seemed a sincere fellow, though sort of "ridden under" by the producer.

I'd never met Tiedman, I told her, and she said he was a dreadful little man who wore crepe-soled shoes and a serge suit, and who'd "probably sell his mother's heart for a blue-plate special . . ."

Jean was very frank and outgoing, cheerful and even funny. Her hair was still as short as Joan of Arc's, and she wore a small gold identification bracelet. She was eating one half of a tuna sandwich and said if I was hungry I could have the other half. "It's awful to waste good food," she said. "I can't order half a sandwich, and it always makes me feel so guilty, or wasteful—one of the two, I don't know which it is . . . maybe both wasteful *and* guilty . . ."

We talked about Josh Logan and Paris, and about *There Was a Little Girl*. I knew Jane Fonda was up for the role, though Jean had initially been involved, and they now wanted me for a part opposite Jane. "I'd certainly take it if I were you," Jean said. I told her I was up for an underwater series that could conflict, and she said I was in my rights to refuse it in favor of more serious work. She said, "One should turn down something if it's not right—if it's no good, you know."

She said it wasn't an unprofessional attitude, in fact quite the opposite. It was more like "self-preservation for one's career. You have a lot of serious thinking to do . . ." I said a part of me wanted to go back to New York, and I couldn't shake it; nor could I shake the other part that was a "native son of Hollywood." I said I knew she was a long way from home, meaning Iowa, but she said, "Even farther, you know . . . Paris is the only place I call home now. What's in Iowa belongs to my family. It doesn't belong to me."

I talked about Jean to producer Paul Levitt, who ran the Players Ring Theater, and later the three of us met at the Raincheck Room on Santa Monica Boulevard. We drank, and Jean had a small salad and talked to Paul about people at Columbia Pictures.

I wanted to go to Chez Paulette, but Jean didn't, so we went to Cyrano's instead. Steve McQueen's Ferrari was almost blocking the front door. He'd park there so people would have to walk around it, so they'd know he was there.

We maneuvered around the Ferrari and took a small table by the curved wall. I was surprised to see Warren Oates and with a Swiss girl I'd met at the beach once. I talked to Warren and the Swiss girl a little, although she kept looking at Jean.

McQueen spotted Jean as well, but he didn't come over—he didn't want to talk to me. Even when I'd bump into him with Kantor, he'd avoid eye contact with me. He'd always ask Leonard, "How's your birdie?" and Kantor would say, "It's fine, Steve," but McQueen wouldn't look at me. But he stared at the back of Jean's head as if burning holes into her brain.

She seemed uneasy when we left and walked down Holloway to get off the Strip. When we came back for the car in Cyrano's lot, McQueen's Ferrari was gone. Jean put her head back on the seat and turned her face toward me. I said, "I'd like it if you'd come down to my place for a nightcap or something." She said she wanted to go to sleep. I asked if she wanted to go down to the beach, thinking the ocean air would wake her up. I said, "You can sleep down at my place." She just said okay.

Someone, I don't know who, honked as we drove west on Sunset, and we both waved and laughed—a blind wave at a bunch of headlights. I wanted to eat something else, and Jean said she didn't care.

We drove past my place on Pacific Coast and headed to the Sea Lion. I ate red snapper, and Jean had another salad and part of my fish this time. The windows were all steamed over and covered with fog. She told me her marriage was finished. "He's a nice guy, but a damned greedy opportunist—if one can be bothered with such things." She didn't want to be married, but it wasn't because she wanted to play the field.

Heading back through Malibu, I held her hand, and at the beach house I piled some wood I'd gathered at Zuma into the fireplace. She was cold and sat on the floor in front of the fire, drinking Kahlua. I mixed vodka in with my Kahlua, and we listened to music on the radio. The windows were wet with perspiration, running like rain, and the waves crashed against the pilings beneath the house.

We just sat on the floor looking at the fire until she started sniffing at her hands. She wanted to wash them, she said, as well as her face, because something from the Sea Lion or Cyrano's was smelling on her hands and she'd touched her face with her fingers.

When she came out of the bathroom, she said it must have been grease or smoke from those places. She asked if I had a new toothbrush and something she could wear to sleep in. I gave her a new toothbrush and a black cotton turtleneck pullover.

On the bed, she showed me the marks on her stomach from where she'd been burned at the stake in *Saint Joan*. "It was an accident," she said. "but I *did* almost burn, and I couldn't get out of the chains."

Though it had been an accidental fire, she said she'd often wondered if "Otto" hadn't tried to "pull something funny." She thought her stomach was scarred, but I said I could hardly see the marks. I told her she had a beautiful stomach, and I kissed her wherever she claimed there were scars.

Her mouth was lovely and warm and sweet —but also very passionate. I kissed every part of her body. She pulled up the turtleneck and pulled down her panties, getting one leg out and then pulling them back up high on the other leg so that her clothing never quite left her body, but only bared that had been flesh being brought into play. The moon was very bright and appeared to be moving in and out of the sky. Reflections were shifting with the motion of the water.

"Do you believe in divine intervention?" she asked, and I said I didn't know.

"Do you think one can be chosen to fulfill a particular destiny?" she asked, and I said I wasn't sure.

"Do you believe in God?" she asked.

"Well . . ." I replied, "Maybe I do. I'd like to think we're not the center of the universe. Maybe that's religion."

"I'd like this to be religious," she said. "Just between you and me."

I said okay.

She was afraid of Otto Preminger. She didn't want to go to the Park Sunset or Tops Restaurant because Preminger's office was in the building. She didn't want to see him, she said. He'd just try to talk her into something. Preminger believed he had some kind of power over her, she told me, and if one thinks such a thing about a person, that person can usually exercise *some* control over the other person.

It was like Jean had two different people inside her, quite divorced from one another—two different voices, pulling from opposite sides. She moved through the world without being a part of it, as though this awkward mixture of selves in opposition kept her insulated from the life swirling around her, self-contained, detached, but also a prisoner. Marilyn Monroe was like this, as had been Jimmy Dean, but with Jean there was an odd difference—perhaps she really was crazy back then.

She said her "devils" kept her from being free. We were on the beach in a little cafe called La Mer where Jimmy and I had cheeseburgers once, our motorcycles parked on the sand off Pacific Coast Highway. We'd ridden at well over eighty, and at one point we'd reached out and touched fingers above the racing asphalt. He'd said you could feel the vibrations of the pistons and the unevenness of the highway that way. Leaving La Mer, I had told him I was freezing my ass off and he had given me his jacket. He'd had on a white sweat shirt and said he couldn't get cold because "a superstar is insulated against mortal coldness . . ."

Jean told me she could never be that free. "The devils will stop that sort of stuff in a second," she said. "They ride right here . . ." She touched her collar bones with her fingers. "Sitting here, and here. There's one on each side."

I said, "You mean like a devil on one shoulder and an angel on the other?"

She said, "No, these are both unfriendly influences." I asked her how she knew that, and she said they simply told her so. What else did they say, I asked? "They tell me to run my car into other cars," she said, "or drive straight off a cliff. They say I can't present myself as I desire—can't act, can't do it in writing, though they want me to write because if I get sidetracked into that, then I will fail in other things . . ." She said she would fail in writing, and at being a person. When I asked her what she thought the devils might look like, she said, "Oh, like me. They both look like little dolls of myself."

"No horns or tails," I said. "That's imaginative of them."

"Yes, it is!" she said, and laughed. Her face was like sunshine, but I didn't think her brightness was the whole story. What *hurt*, she said, would never show through, it just seemed to swell up inside of her. She said usually she knew how to keep the lid on the pot.

Recollections fail to pinpoint anyone who could actually reach Jean through her mosaic of shields. There were gaps here and there, like small holes one could find if one looked hard enough, chance moments that offered a glimpse into Jean—like a dip or some other motion in a dance, revealing the faces of those devil replicas of herself—but far too brief to really grasp at anything. Those parts of herself would remain untapped and out of reach. She swore that no one could help her out of this.

She was so sparkling bright at times, and that wasn't a mask as others have hinted. I remember having dinner at Frascati, and Dennis Hopper, who was studying acting in Jean's class at Columbia, was having an argument with someone, but even they calmed down when Jean turned on her lights. She was, at times, a joy, and I was infatuated with her notoriety, and with her sexuality. But I would not or could not feel love for her. That wasn't part of our relationship. She was married, and the guy was in France but supposedly on his way to L.A. I was neurotic and self-absorbed, and Jean, while appearing far less neurotic, was actually the lost soul.

I believed that to know the women I worked with, I had to take something of them inside of myself. Jean would pass her saliva into my mouth, and I would want more of it, and more, but the brief relationship was burdened with strange emotions from the start. Like many such affairs, ours was touched with a kind of holiness. I'd thought of having a child with Jane Fonda, but it had never gone further than a spontaneous picture in my head. Jean talked about marriage, though we didn't really know one another, and she was already married—but separated, she said, once and for all. She said she wanted to feel a child moving inside her, and to feed the father of the child the milk from her breast.

I cared for Jean more than I was capable of knowing at the time. Pieces of feelings have survived the years, the movies and books, marriages, divorces and children, and careers and travels. Emotions appear like the tendrils of some slow-growing plant from a seed set down so long ago you don't even remember the planting.

But back then I couldn't reach her. Otto Preminger would tell me confidentially that he could only get at a *part* of her, and that this was all he'd needed, "a smaller part of the overall whole of Jean's personality," he said. "Her psyche, if you will. But it was only that one small part that I was able to single out and isolate and develop, the rest of her which people did not see, was in absolute chaos . . ." The rest of her, he said, had been "paradoxically provoked by the international acceptance of that fragment of her," and once it had come and gone out into the world, any hope for internal reconciliation had been lost.

"That is the Jean that lives in turmoil, in a black hole." Preminger said that some form of self-inflicted injury was inevitable. Had she been smart, he said, Jean would have taken the money and run home "as fast as her two little feet could've carried her." But the lure of fame, as he put it, "held her in bondage. You see, there is no focus to the thing. It is in those that must destroy their lives . . ."

Jean encouraged me in turning down ZIV's underwater series. She was on the bed in Malibu, cracking walnuts with a pair of pliers when she suggested that if I came to Paris we'd make a movie after all. I could work there, and in Rome, but if I got stuck in Hollywood I'd be finished. "You'll be doing the same episodes over and over," she warned. I remembered Jimmy Dean saying that when Hollywood had you, they'd use you until there was nothing left.

Jean said, "Do the play instead . . ."

Josh Logan had optioned the film rights to *Parrish* and thought about Jean in the lead, but decided he wanted Jane Fonda and instead tested her in New York. He also wanted another unknown, Warren Beatty, but abandoned the project to begin working instead on *Tall Story*, a movie for which he'd tested Brooke Heyward as a "family obligation," although Logan later said that Brooke had been "completely unmalleable." In other words, she couldn't act.

I said no thanks to CBS, but while I was flying to New York to meet with Logan for the play, the image of Jimmy—bare-chested in scuba pants—kept sneaking into my head. He wouldn't have turned it down, I thought. He'd have given the town the best damned "aquanaut" they'd ever seen. He'd have done it in a monkey suit. He was the real actor, and I was the rebel.

Jane Fonda was set to play in *There Was a Little Girl* under exclusive contract to Logan. I was staying at the Warrick Hotel when I heard, without registering much surprise, the news that Margaret Sullivan and Leland Heyward's daughter had committed suicide. I was sure it was Brooke. I thought "Wow, so she did it after all." Then I learned that it hadn't been Brooke, but her younger sister, Bridget—the beautiful one, the talented one, the artist whose future was gone before she'd gotten her feet wet in the present. That kind of shocked me.

The play was terrible, a dud, and I turned it down. I told Geoffrey Barr to let Jane do it. Barr said I was crazy and that maybe Hollywood was the only place for someone like me. I said it probably was. He said I'd made a fool of Constance Bennett, and that she was very upset. I said I'd talk to her—she'd understand. I knew she would.

I just couldn't figure out what was happening to me or why I was being such a "knucklehead"—some sort of scarecrow dancing up on a fence and then back down again.

Along with Tony Perkins, I was up for a part in *Tall Story* through Howard Austin, though Logan again wanted Warner Brothers to take on Warren Beatty. Beatty's sister, Shirley MacLaine, let her considerable influence be felt, but the studio needed some kind of "name" and Tony got the part.

Meanwhile, Delmar Daves picked up the option on *Parrish*, wrote a script and was set to direct it for Warners. I returned from New York to test for that picture. Troy Donahue was in it and later told me the reason I hadn't got the co-lead was because Warners had me "blackballed" as a troublemaker. The front office had vetoed Delmar Daves argument that I should be signed for the picture under an exclusive Warners contract.

Delmar took me to lunch and apologized for the fact that he hadn't been able to "buck the big wigs." He didn't exactly say I'd been blackballed, only that they were using existing contract players. He did mention a particular executive who'd suggested I might prove "unpredictable—another Dean, or a Dennis Hopper headache . . ."

Instead of *Parrish*, I did a pilot for Barbara Stanwyck called *Big Jake*. It starred Andy Devine as a grumbly detective, and I played a cub newspaper reporter dogging his heels. We had fun shooting the pilot, which was featured on an anthology show Barbara Stanwyck hosted. She told me about her work with Robert Ryan in *Clash By Night*, in which Marilyn Monroe had had a small but good part. Barbara told me, "Now there's nothing else but television, unless you can create your own damned medicine show somehow. The son of a bitch has blown a hole straight through the fuckin' motion picture business." "I like you," she told me. "I hope the series gets picked up and you stick around for a while."

While Devine and I waited for the green light on the series, Logan's play opened and closed in New York almost overnight. Almost as quickly, Jane went over to the Warners lot to make *Tall Story* with Tony Perkins. I ran into them in the commissary, and Jane seemed very uninterested in talking to me. Her nose was high up in the air. She kept speaking over the top of anything I happened to say. A young actor named Sean Garrison had taken the role I'd turned down, and he was out in Hollywood putting around on a motorscooter in an attempt to appear eccentric. I kept looking at Jane and thinking back to how her half-closed eyes used to glaze over at times.

Tony was very nervous, and stuttering because he knew Howard had expressed his concern over the moviehouse and toilet cruising. He'd kept clean on the legal tangles, thanks to Howard. In the commissary he kept looking away and making stammering jokes that Jane thought were hilarious. She'd throw her head back, laughing loudly, and I could look right down into her pink throat.

The casting director I was seeing on the lot stared at me and said, "*You're* Jonathan Gilmore! Brother, what they've said about you!"

"What've they said?"

"That you're nasty—chips on both your shoulders the size of watermelons—and they say you're headed for trouble. You're uncooperative and hostile. Shall I go on?"

"Who said that?" I asked.

"Hell," he said, "it's the *line* on you. Everybody's got a line, pal."

"So I'm wasting my time with you," I said with an edge.

He laughed a little and said, "But no! Hell, Miss Stanwyck says you're okay, and boy, I gotta tell you, that's a red ribbon in my book any day. So I'm going to give you a run and stick you in *Law Man*, and sort of twaddle that in their noses a little. You reading me?"

"Yeah."

"Good part for you, Jonathan—a disgruntled, arrogant neurotic. A destructive son tracks down his father to kill him. He's so neurotic he thinks his old man caused the death of his mother. A misguided avenger. Sound good to you?"

"I can hardly wait," I said.

Richard Arlen played my father. We worked well together, except for the time I took a swing at him once in the bar—it was called for in the script—and clipped him a little. He said, "I know it's not intentional but I probably deserved it any way."

He told me about the old days at MGM, my mom and Mervyn Leroy and Howard Hughes. He said my mother had been very pretty, but that he remembered she'd been somewhat hard to get along with. He recalled her as being divorced, and that she'd been seen with Howard Hughes a couple of times. But he hadn't pried into anyone's business. "Not when you're working for Hughes." He talked about John Darrow and making *Wings*, and one morning as we were drinking coffee and waiting for a setup, Arlen said he'd seen *Joan of Arc* again. We talked about Jean Seberg, and he knew about her "bouncing back and forth between here and the French," and said he felt sorry for her. She'd inflated too fast, blown up more air than she could hold, and that could "get a person gutted, like you take a deer down . . ." He said he'd be surprised if she found another movie with as much going for her as the one Preminger had "taken out of her."

Arlen's words stuck with me, for when the episode with Jean became so intense as to hint at a loss of control—or a sacrifice of the roles we were playing—the relationship deflated as though it were a balloon that had been popped. We'd say hello and talk a little; we even planned to make a movie together—one I was writing and seeking financing for. But I did not pursue Jean. I was selfish, satisfied that I'd had her, and to know we couldn't go any farther than we'd gone.

Following the Hollywood course may have been in conflict with the ideals of a serious actor, but wanting to be a serious actor, may have been, in a way, my big mistake. As a native L.A. son—a Hollywood kid—I should have known that movies like *Casablanca* and *For Whom the Bell Tolls* and *Double Indemnity* weren't being made anymore. The town was different. It was changing from the outside in, and what I wanted—what was riding me down—was something that had taken hold during the war and peaked around 1947, something I would never get, something that wasn't out there anymore. It was kind of like being in exile.

I saw Ronnie Haran—we were going to drive down to Tijuana and buy boots. We got a hamburger first and decided we had other things to do. She told me, "You're an outlaw. You don't rob liquor stores or stick up gas stations. You're an *art* outlaw. . . An apostate, I guess it's called, or a renegade of some kind. You're not with the flock, you know. You'll always be out there in the frozen land."

During the brief time I hung around with Jean Seberg, she was going to acting classes at Columbia Studios. The old coach I knew from the contract stable had been replaced by a younger "serious" guy who had the power to influence Jean's devils. "Turn down anything that isn't art," he told her. And she, in turn, influenced me. Soon most of the casting people had me branded as a troublemaker, the same as Columbia had branded Jean's coach—then booted him out.

I met him at Jean's apartment south of Hollywood, and he told me, no, he wasn't instructing actors on how to cut their throats with one swipe. "But I'm trying to look at what we're doing and where it's going to lead us . . ."

For Jean, as for so many others, it would lead to psychiatric hospitals and suicide, and for Dennis Hopper, also in Jean's class, it would lead to dope addiction, alcoholism and near-insanity—to "lurching through psychiatric wards" as a kind of grotesque testimony to his own failings.

But most of us had a lot of hell to kick around before the headstones were laid in place.

BREAKING AWAY

EVERYONE'S STAR WAS COMING UP over the mountain except Dennis Hopper's. Even Sally Kellerman had bloomed into a big gorgeous gal working *Outer Limits* and the bit parts in courtroom shows. By the following year, Jean Seberg had star billing in France and had launched the Jean Seberg Film Festival. She was a kind of international oddball, discovered on the rebound by the French and now a "star of the continent." She sent me a postcard saying her search was for "individual values" and Hollywood was governed by "a pack mentality . . . What a horror it is!" Get out of it, she wrote. "Save your hide."

We'd seriously talked about her appearing in the film I'd scripted and was directing, *Blues for Benny*. We were in production on an annex stage of California Studios, and had the use of RKO props and sets. But Jean was abroad and prospering—some perverse French penchant for pranks had made her a Parisian fixture, and our "American new wave movie," along the line of Jean Luc Godard's *Breathless*, would have to sink or swim without Jean.

Brooke Heyward's acting career would go belly up with a misery called *Mad Dog Coll*. "A movie best forgotten" was how it would be remembered. Then, on the loose in Hollywood with wads of family money, Brooke again hooked up with Dennis Hopper. Since cash and couches and draperies as community property might prove a solace against the studio doors being shut so tightly in his face, Dennis married Brooke.

Out of work, Dennis made a stab at being "a real artist," a painter. He rented a cheap studio in the old Central Casting building at Hollywood and Western. While boozing and smoking dope, he splashed and smeared around the paints without purpose or direction, always the true believer breaking beyond convention.

Across the street on the northeast corner was a drugstore with a lunch counter and booths where I'd sometimes run into Dennis. We'd grab coffee while he'd curse the studios for refusing to see the talents he believed he possessed. "His opinion is solely his own," said Lee Wallace, then head of casting at 20th-Century Fox. "Hopper is a boring and shallow person—not a pretty boy but a runt, though maybe if he drives himself crazy enough some spark will fly so at least he'll *appear* interesting, until he burns up. Not only is he a boring actor and a boring person, he is devoid of any screen personality. Without that, you have no commercial appeal—the *only* unforgivable sin in this town. When he's older he might make an interesting character actor, but right now he is what we call 'dead meat' . . ."

By striking the pose of a visual artist, Dennis felt somehow beyond the "clutches" of "the bitch goddess" Warren Oates had harped about, or at least beyond the damaging reach of her representatives, "people like Lee Wallace." He now gave thanks to the heavens that he was done with that "phase" of his life. One afternoon he stared at me and quoted the Bible about being a man and "putting away childish things. "Acting is for kids," he said. "It's fine for kids, but, man, you gotta grow up . . ." Actually, he was parroting Brando.

But the once-promising boy from out of town lacked the resolve to sever himself completely from what he'd narrow down to detail as the "bitch's tit." Secretly he kept hunting after movie roles, hungrily nagging agents and independents and anyone he could corner or had ever worked with.

He got the starring role in Curtis Harrington's first full-length feature, *Night Tide*, which Curtis filmed while on vacation from Jerry Wald, who was quite upset that his associate had done such a thing behind his back. But even *Night Tide* failed to put Dennis over the top or cause any reconsideration of his talent.

Since I'd also wanted to be a painter once, even more than I'd wanted to be an actor, Dennis and I were able to talk a little more earnestly for a change. His frantic desire to paint opened up a channel between us. Despite periods of troubled thinking, he understood in some oblique sense the creative impulse. What kept getting in his way was a fetish for self-flagellation. This was played out via his fascination for underdogs and freaks. In this and other respects, he was not unlike Steve McQueen, yet Dennis' various obsessions were all the more deeply unsettling now that his fame—hardly ever marginal at best— could no longer get in the way.

He asked me about Jimmy Dean and the girl with one leg. A few years had slipped past since *Rebel Without a Cause* and the story of the one-legged girl who'd written about Jimmy kissing her stump, but she was still on Dennis' mind. He'd developed an interest in amputees, cut out pages from a Georg Grosz art book and a medical prosthetics catalog. He showed me photographs of a young woman without any arms. The background setting appeared to be Dennis' studio across the street, with the paint-smeared canvases stacked facing a wall.

He had closeups of her hollowed shoulder-sockets, of her stomach, of her navel, and several shots showed her tucking into her mouth a spoon held between the toes of one foot. He told me he'd met her on the corner of Santa Monica and Western, where she'd been selling newspapers. He said it was the strangest experience to be handed his change by her toes. She was now going to model for a painting—his black and white studies showed her with the toe-held spoon in her mouth. It sounded like something from Tod Browning's *Freaks*. I'd seen a girl like that in the Ringling Brothers sideshow, playing a zither then threading a needle, her face like a young school teacher, with a trace of cosmetics along the ridge of her lips. She'd been with the Alligator Boy, his skin red and ridged, the Man With Two Faces who wore a plastic mask over a jawless skull, the Human Pin Cushion, the Monkey Girl, and a big black man with elephantiasis of the legs.

I sensed that Dennis saw himself up on the platform with these creatures—Dennis the Menace alongside the Alligator Boy and the Red Man With Three Legs.

He showed me the photographs while we were drinking, and at one smashed point he said that "in some way" his painting of the deformed girl would bring to the surface his feelings about the "bitch goddess" he'd raved about, how she was unable to clasp him to her bosom because she had no arms and no hands with which to press his face to her breast. With eyes flashing wildly, he indicated it was the "milk" he sought in his "holy grail." "Seek *hell*," he said. "That I need to live, to breathe, to exist . . ."

It didn't have anything to do with "starring in a fucking movie," he said. "It's why I'm fucking painting and running up against walls—listening to fucking things telling me shit in my head—to get at the *flow*, man, the wellspring of what the fuck I'm doing even being alive!"

He didn't talk about Brooke, because he still thought Brooke and I had been sleeping together in New York when I'd introduced them, and then he'd gone ahead and actually married her. None of the other girls Dennis and I had shared—even the really wild black dancer Marlon Brando sent over because he felt guilty about sleeping with Gena—had been invited around a second time. So the subject of his marriage and their "picket fence" troubles was starting to ricochet like gun-fire.

He seemed to ignite with interest when I mentioned an actress I knew who was an exhibitionist. I'd introduced her to Stuart Rosenberg a couple years earlier. I told Dennis she had a freakish clit, more than an inch in length, and that she got a charge out of baring her bottom. She'd show her ass and wiggle it around and keep looking at you to see how you were enjoying it. I'd seen her recently, I told Dennis, working the box-office of the Hawaii Theater.

Dennis wanted to know if Rosenberg had had her, and I said that, in a manner of speaking, I thought he probably had. One night at Cyrano's, back when Stuart and I were talking about the Tennessee Williams movie, we'd decided to run down to Tijuana in my T-Bird to check out some whorehouses. Stuart wanted to see them, he told me, and maybe talk to a couple of the girls. He said he wanted to watch a girl take off her clothes—not by peeking through a window, but up close, undressing for him. I'd told him about a particular bar called Tres Caballos, where a dancing girl got into a solitary show of such intense self-indulgence that not a word would be said in the place; even the band would stop playing, and everyone would stare at her as she lay on the floor with a beer bottle between her legs, gasping in orgasm. I told Stuart the whole scene was one of the strangest things I'd seen—all those faces and nobody moving a muscle.

"It's all in the eye," Stuart said, as I drove south at a hundred miles an hour to get across the border to the whorehouses before "the mountain devil closes his wings around himself . . ." Stuart said he was probably a voyeur, as nothing seemed to satisfy him quite as much as watching. "Viewing," he said, "holding in the eye and mind the sight of a woman's nakedness, which she's showing you piece by piece and enjoying it . . ."

Sometime after our Tijuana expedition, I brought Sharon, the exhibitionist, over to the Park Sunset to meet Stuart. I told her a little about the director I wanted to do a good turn for—a nice-looking, neat guy who'd get a bang out of her "down and dirty, nobody can love me like me" act. I told her Stuart was a family kind of guy. "If he likes you and has your name in his book of people he's cast with or wants to use, you can almost count on working sometime with Stuart . . ."

I told Dennis she'd said she was just filling in at the box-office while trying to get extra work in television or films, or some work modeling. I'd asked her what sort of modeling, and she'd said, grinning, "Whatcha got?"

Perhaps Dennis had hung around the Hawaii Theater box office waiting for Sharon and offered to pay her for posing in his studio. She'd really been pretty in those days. But I found out she was arrested for shoplifting in the Hollywood Broadway a couple of months later. She did thirty days downtown, was released, but got busted again for prostitution and sent back to jail. It wasn't until two years later, after my friendship with the young Janis Joplin, having returned to L.A. from San Francisco, that I ran into Sharon on the Boulevard. She was on reds and hanging around with a drag-queen named Cootch. She'd become a queer, she said, laughing, and I noticed her teeth had turned yellow. She said it had something to do with the water up in the desert where she'd done a year and two months in the can.

"Sure, I remember Dennis Hopper," she told me. She said he'd wanted her to piss in a coffee jar and then take pictures of her peeing and sitting on the toilet. They wound up fucking, she said. He'd pleaded on his hands and knees, wanting her to smack him with a belt. She said she'd hit him a couple of times, but he'd said "No, no, and asked her to hit him with the "buckle end." Then he'd wanted to whip her, and she'd said she didn't mind—she liked it. "I said just don't hit *me* with the fucking buckle end!"

I believed what she said, because Dennis and I had both known a young starlet named Vikki who'd had similar desires. Sharon said Dennis spent a lot of time blowing grass and talking about "disorienting his senses . . . busting the fucking limits," in order to get out of himself and "make some kind of statement like *art* or something . . ."

She said, "I told him fuck art—art's just bullshit—it's for faggots and drag queens. I said get a *piece* and go out and blow some fucker away."

He said, "Yeah, yeah," he could do that. Inside, she said, he was like a mad dog. The "creative turmoil" he suffered was a nightmare, and only by breaking through like "Alice goes through the mirror" could the mad dog be unleashed. She said, "That's what he kept saying, and asking me to piss more, giving me more and more water to drink out of some fucking milk bottle, so I could pee a lot and he'd get it all photographed, holding his camera with one hand and jerking himself off with the other . . ."

Was she joking? Had she taken any of it seriously? She said she'd been bombed out on whatever he'd been torching, and her memories were "sort of tangled up like grey string," but that "he'd made a lot of sense," she said. "You know, like Jean Genet the writer-outlaw—the great writer doing weird things and getting thrown in prison, like down into one of those holes full of snakes. I know what Dennis was saying about Alice and the looking glass. You aren't who you are, you know? Is Jean Genet a crook and a fag and a thief and a jailbird—or is he a great French writer, a fucking great *world* writer? Or is he both, you know?

"Like Jean Genet," Sharon said, "that's what I think's got Dennis Hopper. He's wounded like an animal you shoot and don't kill, and he's in a bush somewhere, figuring out which way to go with it, but sure as shit can't take it to the PTA or into Miss Tweedle-dum's parlor . . ." With a knowing nod, she said, "Dennis needs to go to jail for a while and maybe see his mad dog won't eat him up from the inside out but like they say, can be man's best friend too, you know?"

Dennis was a goat in Miss Tweedle-dum's parlor, suffocating. No one seemed to take seriously anything he was doing, not even his pregnant wife, Brooke. Soon after her marriage, she no doubt realized that life with Dennis in Hollywood was like living in a Whirlpool washing machine—only nobody was going to come out clean. For both of them, suicide was like an unwanted house guest in the back room, who could always be called out when the going got bad.

And so it would.

Several days into shooting my cheap art film, *Blues for Benny,* I was running cast and crew on twelve-hour shifts, and even as a fledgling director, earning a reputation for treating people like dogs. The gaffer said he'd worked a shoot with Ed Wood—shot the film in four days, so I wasn't doing so bad running two shifts instead of "going nonstop."

Starring in *Blues* was a young actor named Don Quine who'd married an ex-girlfriend. Don had run around a little with me in the Village back east while he'd lived with a photographer. The girl had moved into my apartment uptown, but hadn't been keen on another one staying with us—as a threesome. Our relationship petered out, and Quine, eager to be free of the "clutches" of the photographer, as he put it, quickly—overnight—convinced my ex-girlfriend that he was the boy for her. The daughter of an East Coast millionaire, she had a trust fund fall into her lap, and became pregnant immediately. Marriage followed and, much like Brooke and Dennis' marriage, they fit the bill perfectly—starving actor meets girl with trust fund. When Quine was finished with her, and still desperately wanting to be an actor, he'd moved on over to producer Burt Balaban's daughter— getting her pregnant and making himself a fixture at the Balaban house.

But apart from Eastern Seaboard money, Quine successfully raised independent financing for my film from a group of dentists. Yet the money was almost too tight for him to operate, and when the picture was completed, the company was broke.

I cut the prints, tracks, and negatives myself at a lab on Santa Monica and Vine, and the consensus was that some of the performances were extraordinary, as was a lot of the downtown footage—scenes on old Bunker Hill, up and down Angels Flight, and a kind of documentary on the Long Beach Pike. But while artistically successful, the film was a financial flop. I sent a stack of stills to Jean Seberg in Paris and she said, "I'm sorry I didn't do the picture . . ."

I was broke again, but I wasn't alone. Cecilia, a young Hungarian dancer and Freedom Fighter, was living with me in an apartment on Beachwood, above *Gunsmoke*'s James Arness, whose marriage had just busted apart. Jim was jumping girls downstairs while loudly playing the "Hawaiian War Chant." The girls were not the quiet Miss Kitty types, and their cries went on half the night. It didn't bother Cecilia, who was pregnant with my child—she'd sleep through the noise while I'd lay there wondering where my pending parenthood on a shoestring budget would lead.

After I directed *Blues*, Cecilia and I moved down to the Hollywood Towers, into the second-level penthouse that had been Dick Powell's old one-bedroom apartment. I took acting jobs as they came. I wasn't dropping in and I wasn't dropping out, but busy writing a script for a possible deal with Curtis Harrington, based on a San Francisco beatnik story I'd published the year before.

At first, Cecilia thought about getting an abortion—she was seventeen years old. When she admitted to being afraid, I said, "Let's just have the baby." I thought I wanted an end to the "war chant" living— we'd get married and have the baby as soon as legalities were settled with Gena. I didn't know then that Gena and I had never been legally married as far as the state of Connecticut was concerned.

Cecilia, the girl Freedom Fighter, a Madach related to the writer Imre Madach, the Hungarian Shakespeare, gave birth to our baby under Screen Actors Guild medical coverage on the exact delivery date predicted, for which we won a long run of diaper service and two loads of milk bottles every other morning.

Ursula Maura Gilmore came into the world red-faced and squalling, with a mountain of lovely hair on her perfect head.

I didn't know what kind of a life I intended for my daughter or her mother. I'd sold a script to the hour-long *Naked City* series and spent two weeks in New Orleans on the Curtis Harrington movie, having changed the setting from San Francisco to the French Quarter. I'd sold a couple of stories to Seymour Krim and to another magazine, and I was researching Hollywood's famous unsolved homicide—the Black Dahlia murder case—for a possible script. The 1947 slaying of the young, beautiful would-be actress Elizabeth Short, known as the Black Dahlia, was one of the most grisly murders in the annals of modern crime. The project, called *Who Killed the Black Dahlia?,* was being kicked off by actor Tom Neal, a hell-raiser from World War II movies.

Tom had "brushed shoulders," as he put it, with a couple of Hollywood con men running a scam to raise financing for a movie on the murder. They claimed to have gathered secret information from the cops. With a tidy sum, they ran to Vegas, blew the money, and were arrested.

While not claiming to possess any secret information, Tom had discovered a private dick who'd independently tracked a suspect at the request of the victim's family in Massachusetts. Tom also knew a retired police captain who'd worked the case, as part of the initial task force my own father—an LAPD cop since 1942—had been pooled into. My father had logged many days and a fair share of shoe leather on the early stages of the Black Dahlia investigation, then conducted periodic forays into the case for more than a dozen years.

Tom was on the phone with me almost daily to "get pages piled," as he'd put it, to sew up a deal with the Palm Springs money he claimed to have on tap as co-producer. It was Tom's plan to co-star in the movie as a tough L.A. detective who falls in love with the dead girl—his co-star—but unlike the movie *Laura,* this murdered girl doesn't come back from the grave.

Aided by Jack Webb, who was tight with a few LAPD hotshots thanks to *Dragnet,* I got my feet wet to the knees in the case. I'd never worked with Webb, although he'd interviewed me a couple times for parts in his show and he knew my father.

Though the apples seemed to be sitting in Tom's basket, he still hadn't secured the financing. I didn't know it at the time, but the trouble was Tom's failing career and a subsequent warping of his personality—which added up to a widespread mistrust of Tom's various schemes. Even armed with files from my father, as well as with information from my inside contacts with LAPD's Homicide Bureau and from my acquaintances on the other side of the fence—shadow people that found talking to me easy—Tom couldn't convince the Palm Springs people to release the front money needed to get the movie rolling. Another potential investor, an associate of the Palm Springs people named Gene Harris, was a rich eccentric living in the banquet space of an old Barstow hotel in the desert. A meeting was arranged, and I rode the big red car all the way into San Bernardino, and from there a bus north to Barstow.

The desert heat was stifling, and there were a lot of flies in Harris' banquet room, a large space stuffed with furniture and antique lamps and sinks. The halls still had World War II posters taped to the wallpaper. Though Harris wore glasses as thick as the bottoms of Seltzer bottles, he used a magnifying glass to study the photographs of the dead girl's naked body, severed in half and laid out in a vacant lot south of Hollywood.

He wanted to know if I'd personally seen the body, and I told him I'd been eleven years old at the time and hadn't been invited to crime scenes, though my father had already been a veteran of the force five years by then. But several times, I said, I'd been to the vacant lot with my dad and walked around in the weeds where the body had been found. Right across from there on Crenshaw Boulevard was Rudy's, an Italian restaurant where I'd go with my father and family, after which we'd swing over to the block and park on the street to snoop around.

Harris asked if I'd touched the ground. I said, "I stood on it," and he said no, had I *touched* it with my hand. I had to think back—maybe I'd reached down, pulled at some weeds. I could remember finding used flashbulbs long after the case had dropped from the news. Maybe I'd touched the ground, I said.

"The exact place where the body was?" he asked. I said it had probably been the same area—even the most remote detail about that site had been measured and photographed again and again by the cops. I said the location was almost certainly exact. He said, "Let me see your hand."

My hand? He wanted to look at it. I reminded him that fifteen or so years had passed since then. "I realize that," he said, "but it is still a direct contact between that part of you and the place where her body was lying . . . As well as the bottoms of your feet," he added. I told him I would have been wearing shoes.

Placing his fingers on the palm side of my hand, he rubbed them back and forth several times as though smoothing out a surface. He sat back sighing loudly, looking strangely distant. Suddenly he began to weep. I'd been warned he was eccentric but at this point I thought he was nuts.

Distractedly, he excused himself and suggested I go down to the coffee shop and eat some bacon and eggs. He said he'd join me momentarily, and as soon as I was leaving the room he was already dialing a number on the phone.

Since it was evening, I didn't want bacon and eggs but had chicken-fried steak and a bottle of beer. Harris came down, having changed his clothes and put on a hat. He drank coffee and spoke in a dry, business-like tone. "The problem with all of this has to do with Tom Neal," he said. "You, on the other hand—your father being an actual policeman, and you doing the work you're doing—you're a credible asset to such a project. But Tom Neal is not . . ."

I said Tom had brought the project together. "Only as a vehicle for himself," Harris said, "and frankly, we feel he isn't right for the part. By 'right,' I mean proper, acceptable. It hardly matters what Tom has brought together. You're the one writing the story, basically, from police and private and public information. I personally have interest in this case, and I see no need to divert my interests or funnel them through a blowhard like Tom Neal. He's reckless and impulsive and will ruin whatever he gets his hands on. Producers are a dime a dozen. An actor of Neal's standing and reputation can be had for less than that. Basically," Harris said, "someone will have to come up with a more imaginative business proposition than what has been presented by Tom Neal and his cohorts. By that time, of course, if not sooner, we might all be dead."

He gave me a fifty-dollar bill as reimbursement for my travel expenses and said he'd have me flown back to Hollywood. Another guy working at the Barstow hotel was a pilot and flew me to Burbank in a Piper Cub as soon as I'd finished my chicken-fried steak. Soon I'd see it wasn't the Barstow eccentric running loose at the leash, but Tom Neal himself. It would be very clear one beautiful day to come, when Tom would sneak up on his pretty, new Palm Springs wife as she lay on their sofa and shoot a .45 bullet through her head.

BACK IN THE SADDLE AGAIN

DURING THE MONTHS IN SAN FRANCISCO, I'd written some paperbacks for a couple of Hollywood publishers. One had gone to press, but hadn't paid me a dime. Through a lawyer pal of Gena's father, I got in touch with a buddy of Mickey Cohen and asked if a call could be placed on my behalf—that is, on my lady's and the baby's behalf.

"That won't be no problem," he said, and a check showed up at my door within the week, the first of several to arrive on a regular basis. The Hungarian, the baby and I stayed at the Mark Twain Hotel in Hollywood before moving into an apartment off Sunset a block west of Vine.

Justifiably cited as one of the worst film-makers in history, Ed Wood Jr. was also in the business of writing dirty books. When I met him he was wearing a bright Hawaiian shirt with a pair of bilious neon-yellow pants that sort of shimmered under the fluorescent tubes in Lou Kimzey's office at International Publications. The tub in one of the bathrooms was used as a storage dump for the books they published under the "France" imprint: "your guarantee of exciting and entertaining reading."

Ed Wood often wrote under his own name, as opposed to using a pseudonym, and he'd been writing a little longer than I. But Lou Kimzey's operation wasn't giving Ed the edge he needed—meaning money paid on the barrelhead. Their excuse was always that the book was still at the lawyer's, still in "editing," still being read, and so on and so forth. Ed Wood couldn't wait through the run of Kimzey's lame-brain excuses as to why he hadn't coughed up the hard-earned dough when due, so eventually he went to another publisher, then another, writing book after book at a pace like dribbling a basketball.

Gena's father was also writing for "France," and warned me, "You have to go in there and yell. You have to scream and pound on the desk before he'll pay you. If you call on the phone, you'll never get paid. They're all thieves. Rotten fucking thieves. Go in threatening that you won't leave until he pays you. They're scared of the law, so they won't call the cops to haul you off. He'll pay you something—part of it, all of it—*something* to get your ass out of there."

Ed wasn't screaming or pounding the furniture. He told me, "I know the fucker and I'm afraid of him, because I'll fucking work myself sick and have to fight like a son of a bitch to get the money." For a man who had written and directed movies for a grand a crack, he was looking at easy cash with Kimzey. Collecting it was the trick. Kimzey would hit someone low for maybe three-fifty a book, maybe four-hundred if the writer spilled the beans that he had something hot. Kimzey would get the hungry ones. For the others he'd slug out half a grand to seven-hundred. A few months later, he was paying close to a grand a book—which Ed had made elsewhere. Some a few bucks less, others a little more.

The law was hard and fast: no dirty words, no "cock" or "cunt," you couldn't directly mention the sexual organs, and even pubic hair was taboo. Sex scenes had to result from relationships—couldn't be promiscuous or they would be considered pornography. The books had to have a moral. Good had to shine through in the end. They couldn't even *smell* dirty.

I wrote *Brutal Baby* in nine days and followed it with *Dark Obsession*, another nine-day novel. Then came *Strange Fire*, inspired by a black chick I knew in the Village, and a bunch of bikers. *Lesbos in Panama* was next, another midnight express.

"I've read *Brutal Baby*," Ed told me. "Maybe there's a picture in it. Don't let Kimzey have any rights except First North American. No one's ever asked him for that, so he'll think you're a hot shot."

Ed and I met a couple of times when he was wearing a woman's rayon blouse, which had a sort of metallic sheen except where he'd sweated through the armpits. He looked disheveled and stoned, talking about getting a few grand together to a get a picture on the board. I thought maybe it was pills—he had a pill-head's agitation over things that rubbed him wrong, and he smelled bad. It was fish he reeked of, and he said he'd just been to San Pedro goosing a tuna merchant to invest in a movie. I'd just finished a real gem with Curtis Harrington called *Meat House*. Ed loved the script—humans being canned for sale as food, and a detective-spy sort of cop who's called in to straighten things out but gets an arm chopped off instead, which then goes into one of the cans.

Ed said the same idea could be used in *Brutal Baby*. "In face of fact," he said, it was the very heart of the idea. "That's what's so brutal about it!" Ed had an extraordinary ability for jamming together bunches of disparate material, which he could somehow present with a kind of coherence. Two or more totally unrelated stories could be crammed into the middle, the beginning or end of another story, and somehow it would seem intended—and if the continuity was flawed, at least it was *consistently* flawed from start to finish.

Unconcerned with the bumps and patches, he rushed to get the stuff released. I felt he wanted to pay attention to the glaring faults in what he was doing, but the world he operated in—the insane nine-day novel-writing and ten-day movie-making world—never allowed him a moment of reflection.

He was plagued with nightmares, he told me. He'd plunge into their weird midst, he said, yet somehow couldn't bring their "true horror" into his work. So, he said, he had to "skim the surface as a dreamer, a man possibly dangerous to himself . : ." He always made me think of the worst possible scenario—about what could and would go wrong—and it was all uphill from there.

At this time, Gena told her father that she was out in the desert with some artist painting rocks—not to sell, but to decorate the "desolate" landscape. She told him that "desolation" was the enemy of insight. Next week, he told me, "she could be in Hackensack or Veracruz for all I know." As he patted baby Ursula's head, he clued me in to the fact that my marriage to Gena hadn't been legal.

The Hungarian and I were married a few days later downtown by a judge who recognized me from a television show. When I told him

183

I was working at 20th with Lauren Bacall, he jokingly asked if I could "arrange a date." I laughed and said I'd see what I could do. He would have been an actor, he said, if he'd been able to get enough work to feed a family. If it was the forties again, he said, he'd quit what he was doing right now and go back to the movies, with or without a steady paycheck.

Lauren Bacall was hanging around with Jason Robards Jr., another old alumnus, from Hollywood High who was in and out her sets. She didn't talk about Bogart when Robards was around. Roddy MacDowall was in the movie, and he told Bacall that he had heard I'd run around with James Dean. I told Bacall that Jimmy had told me that Bogart never missed, that he always hit the target no matter what he hunted.

She said Bogey had told her he thought Dean had the "cleanest talent" he'd seen in a decade. Dean's death was doubly sad, he'd said, since it cut his making the Graziano story—which Bogey had been interested in. Bogey said Dean wasn't anything like Brando, "though he mimics him in that first picture a little." Bacall added, "Not many young actors don't." Bogey thought Dean's range was like an accordion, while Brando "was a limited actor" like himself. Dean was the boy in the American living room, "a *good* boy," Bogey had said, faced with problems heaped on him by a previous generation's screwups. Brando was "antisocial" and most successful playing rebel characters outside the law or the mainstream. He wasn't "everyone's son," Bogey had said. Brando just didn't have the range, not like "young Dean."

Who the hell cares about the guy's private life? And what'd he do anyway? Bogey had asked. "At twenty-four, what the hell kind of private life's developed? If he wants to go around with an unzipped fly, what the hell's the difference as long as he delivers the goods? He's a *kid*. Wait'll his pictures get as old as me, then judge what he's done and wonder what the hell his fly had to do with it."

The characters Dean played were familiar because "as Americans we *know* these people, as our sons, or as the kid next door," Bacall said, "or going off to college, or in the living room, or outside tinkering around with his car . . ." Not so with Brando, Bogey said. "You can sympathize with the emotions he presents, but it's hard to sympathize with the guy he's playing."

Bogart had been dead half a dozen years by the time we made *Shock Treatment*. The picture starred Stuart Whitman—Hollywood High again—and featured Roddy MacDowall and Carol Lynley, and Timothy

184

Carey from *East of Eden.*

I'd met Roddy earlier during a terrible dubbing session at Universal for an episode of *Ripcord.* I'd recommended looping just anyone's voice in the long shots, since nobody would know the difference in such a dumb show. Roddy later said, "I saw all these red lights blinking—warning lights—and knew such an unprofessional attitude was going to head you right into trouble." These were the sorts of actions, he said, that had cost Dennis Hopper his Warners contract. We talked about Dennis and Brooke and Jane Fonda over dinner at Ernie's on La Cienega. Roddy then came back to my small house off La Cienega, and we talked mostly about Jane and about Dean, though I avoided mentioning my physical stake in these relationships. My turning down the Broadway play with Josh Logan had been "foolish and undermining," Roddy said, no matter if the play had run only one night. "There is no 'right part' for a professional actor," he said. "There is only work, and one is thankful for it—if one eats and pays rent." My attitude "could very well invite some disastrous results . . ."

Dean was emotionally *needy,* Roddy said, a beggar with rice bowl in hand. "But as an actor," he said, "Dean wouldn't have cared what he did if he'd been applauded and it had answered his needs . . ." But those needs were peculiar to Dean, and nobody else. Riding shotgun with Dean's rebel side had made me no more than one of the screwballs trying to act the same, unless I had had some hidden motive for going along with it.

I told Roddy that I wanted to play roles like Monty Clift's in *Red River* or the character of Donal in Sean O'Casey's *Shadow of a Gunman.* I wanted to do musicals. Those were the things I needed to do as an actor, and they had nothing to do with Dean—dead or alive. But those things were not in front of me, and somehow I couldn't take the things that were, whether it meant "jam on the bread or not . . ."

Roddy put his arms around me, hugging me. I could tell he wanted to kiss me. "There's this shadow hanging over you," he said, "and I do sense it's something not intrinsic to your nature. Something that's been adopted—perhaps involuntarily, and not of your own making." He said, "I feel that I can be of help to you, and possibly I can . . ."

In turning down Roddy's gentle invitation to hit the hay, I couldn't help feeling I was nipping the bud of a worthwhile friendship. Roddy was a prince, but it was like Cloris Leachman would tell me about "the awful tyranny of being beautiful," how it "runs your life. You're always chasing it with your will and with your real self trapped beneath the beauty, struggling to breathe, fighting to be free. You're like the tail end of something. Under the skin is an invisible person always trying to get out!"

Roddy and I were drinking coffee on the *Shock Treatment* set when he again asked if I'd slept with Jimmy. I told him he'd asked me that at Ernie's, and I'd said I couldn't tell him then, and I wasn't telling him now. He said, "So that leaves room for speculation . . ."

He could speculate all he wanted; it was a subject I wasn't talking about. Roddy said, "You were as young and miserable as Dean back then—younger, even, and no doubt sidled to his notions like a Siamese twin. But are you sure they belong to *you,* Jonathan? Perhaps that's the specter. There's nothing holy about sleeping with people. It can be caring, or it can be just plain fun, my friend . . ."

"Once a cocksucker," Dennis Hopper said when I told him about the propositions, "always a cocksucker." Everyone had a line, and although Roddy was a clever fellow, his subtle moves led us no nearer to the romance he might have envisioned. He probably construed the evasions as further proof of my self-destructiveness.

My eye was on Carol Lynley and I gave her a record album for which she'd modeled the cover before gaining a name as a actress. We talked about Nancy Bolles—the young blonde living with her mother on Bedford Mews in the Village while I'd been sharing Norman's 17th Street apartment.

Nancy, Carol Lynley, and Tuesday Weld had been a close-knit trio of teeny golden-haired Manhattan kid models with fame-hungry mothers. Carol had always been the moody and changeable one—sometimes she appeared animated, and I soon realized these were the moments when she felt most secure. Then she'd seem to go into a trance, a sort of melting down of her spirit until she'd be sitting there lifeless as a lump of clay. She lacked the snap and brightness of Tuesday, and even of Nancy—I missed that beautiful blonde young body naked and trembling in bed. But I was now a family man, with child and a legitimate wife. Though faithfulness had fallen away, I wanted to hold the marriage together for my daughter's sake—and as an attempt to somehow set right the bum situation with my own mother.

I'd worked in two 20th movies with Barbara Eden and was flirting with the idea of separating my sex affairs from my marriage. Timothy Carey, also in *Shock Treatment*, said, "It is possible to love many women at the same time and have them love you back, if you give them only the body and the mind—not the spirit." Another time he said, "Give pretty Carol an orange with a cherry in the heart of it!" Most everyone in Hollywood thought Carey was crazy, and they were afraid of him. A tall, powerful, sinewy man with a big long head, he was really a mellow neurotic with enormous talent that remained somehow bottled up. He had some brilliant moments during rehearsals that never found their way to film. Terry Sanders, directing *Shock Treatment*, was unable to capture the gems that Stuart Rosenberg would have singled out. Yet before hitting the big time, Sanders and his brother Dennis had made a superb low-budget picture called *War Hunt* starring John Saxon, another old friend and ex-client of Henry Willson. Saxon was a talented, solid guy, yet never able to break beyond stereotyped, straightjacketing—roles straightjacketed around him—except in low-budget quickies like the Sanders movie.

Shock Treatment was big-studio, and contained enough ambiguities to make it a flop. So many different writers had hammered away at the script, each carrying it farther from its premise. Bernie Wolf, now with several books to his credit and the lead fiction writer for *Playboy*, had been hired to write a version of the story, and later asked to read my copy of the script to see if anything he'd written remained. There was nothing, he said. It was a completely different script—and a far worse story than he remembered.

Bernie had also been hired to write a version of Henry Miller's *Tropic of Capricorn* for Warners. Like most studio-developed projects, none of Bernie's scripts would make it to production. Out from New York to become a hotshot screenwriter, he said, "You use two fingers to write a movie script. For a book you've got to use all ten." He made some big bucks writing these scripts that were never filmed, bought a Richard Neutra house in the hills and married Dolores Michaels, a former actress from Fox undergoing emotional problems. Straight to the rescue, Bernie had her commuting to a high-priced shrink while he kept grinding out stories for Hugh Hefner—turning them into books while secretly believing his well would soon run dry.

A small-time producer named Robert Levy hit the jackpot with a short film of *Fanny Hill*—a fluke at best, though Levy saw it as the door to his future. His wife skipped out on him, and Levy began envisioning success as a wheeler-dealer movie producer. He cobbled together notions for a feature film and got Brando's sidekick, Carlo Fiori, to write a script, which Levy then paid Bernie Wolf to appraise.

"You're in trouble," Bernie told him. "You'd better find a writer who can write." Practically dysfunctional from so many seasons on drugs, Fiori had hodge-podged together an orange crate of literary junk.

Bernie met me for breakfast at Schwab's and said he'd pointed Levy in my direction. "I charged him a grand to tell him Carlo's script stinks—it's hopeless," Bernie said, "I told him to give you a call, that you might be interested in working on it." I said I'd be glad to take a look and see if I could get it on its feet. Bernie said, "Get as much as you can out of these jokers for as little work as possible. These guys never make a movie—they're just jerking themselves off, and everybody else they pull in. Grab what you can and throw the rest to the dogs."

The script was called *Xena,* and I told Levy it was a rotten title. He said it was a modern-day "female Christ" saga. I asked why he was doing such a story, since he said he'd become an orthodox Jew after his wife ran off. He said it would be a "hot" idea—"Christ is hot," and because of *Fanny Hill,* he'd done a study of female movie goers. If the "right ingredients" came together, we'd have a winner. But *Xena* was nothing more than a clutter of ideas. This female Christ did everything; nothing was out of her reach—from parachuting and scuba diving, to running a newspaper, producing and acting in movies, and even racing sports cars. Every man wanted her. Every *woman* wanted her. Politicians and astrologers wanted her. Riddled with every conceivable flaw—a series of dumb situations that will never gel into a story, but which half-assed producers always feel challenged to try, even when logistics plainly show it can't be done—the whole project was ready for the dogs.

Talking to Fiori was pointless. According to Brando and Sam Gilman, Carlo was on dope again, and anyone could see it by looking at him. He was on the outs with Marlon and blamed *Xena* for his condition, claiming the script had almost bought him a nervous breakdown. Dumping the "Jesus bitch" on my doorstep, he told Gilman, was his road to salvation.

In the midst of this, I wrote another quickie for Curtis Harrington, who'd landed another fly-by-night producer. I hammered out a script about a James Bond kind of spy. The fast-traveling producer wound up with an Arab directing the film, having wrenched Curtis out of the deal. The Arab would do it cheaper.

But the quick deal and working briefly with the Arab set me up for another fast one in the planning stage—an Egyptian producer flew me to Alexandria, where I was met by his nephew, a lush. We drank for two days in a ritzy beachside joint—and even in the catacombs—that figured into the script. Then up the Nile we travelled, to Cairo, along a straight highway running through the desert southward along the river.

I stayed in a downtown Cairo hotel for several days listening to long, heated arguments over the new Aswan Dam and the tearing down of Abu Simbel—the holiest of holy places. The producer was a thin, hatchet-faced Egyptian in black silk, with legs as skinny as stovepipes. He kept me hopping on brunches and lunches at the Nile Hilton and other temple-like hotels. His radicalized student son translated the producer's "intense visions," which I believed to be completely unworkable in the case of this moderately low-budget picture. The son confessed that all he really cared about were the catacombs and Abu Simbel.

Hanging around Cairo and the cafes got me working on the script, and the Egyptian wanted to know if I could write it in fourteen days—as the Arab from L.A. had suggested to them—beginning on the first of the month.

I assured them I could do it. The son took me to an Egyptian bank, where a retainer got me started. I sent money back to Hollywood for my wife and daughter, then spent a few days going over ideas with the radical son. We drove and talked, talked and sat in cafes. One cafe was off an alley, its decor surrealistic, everything painted white, with stuffed animals and ostrich eggs, impressive old busts of obscure people, and odd objects such as a human skeleton with copper wires wrapped around the bones. There was a bronze urinal and rows of phallic jars from Greece, mirrors everywhere, of every conceivable size. Seated about the patio at the little round tables were people out of a fairy tale of the Casbah or *Casablanca*—black Africans in ornate hats, decadent intellectuals sipping mint tea, and garish women, one of them festooned with silver and gold watches.

A few times at night we drove out to the pyramids and the Sphinx, and sat in the desert. During daylight, the Egyptian camel drivers fought for the tourist trade—snapshots on shaggy animals with a pyramid in the background. We had drinks at the nearby Mena House, where the son introduced me to Djamila, an Egyptian actress hooked up in some way to play in the movie. She wore a black bikini the day I met her, with a gold chain around her waist and some kind of red stone set in her navel. She said she had been waiting almost two years for the movie which I was writing to get into production. "Enough of politics," she'd say, "it is boring. There is too much to do to allow these politics to destroy us . . ."

The son kept saying, "Tomorrow, if God wills," as we roamed the hot spots of the United Arab Republic. Everywhere we faced giant blown-up portraits of President Gamal Nasser, and the son spat at each one we passed.

Several others had already been asked to write scripts or bring what the son called his father's "misanthropic" ideas to fruition. His mother was dead, and the "old man" had married an American who cheated on him and took his money, making a sorrowful fool of the dignified Egyptian. He said they'd avoided bringing an American into the project until now.

The last guy had been a Brit named Peter Morgan. Morgan was attacked one night by one of the alley cats near the hotel. The son showed me where it had happened, and proceeded to tell me about the rats that preyed upon the children in the city, and how, due to this "diet," they had mutated into giant rats, and how, in order to compensate for the size of the rats, the alley cats had also increased enormously in size. It was one of these massive cats that had leaped onto the Englishman's leg, sinking teeth and claws into skin and muscle, and clung there until two Egyptian boys and one old man with a stick had forced the cat off the man's leg.

"Peter went into shock," the son said. "He had to be hospitalized. My father wants to interweave such a scene into the movie, a catastrophe that befalls the American husband . . ."

Djamila's contribution to the project was never more clear than the night she belly-danced at a club called Night Life Strip. My spending the night with the twenty-one-year-old actress wasn't part of the producer's plan, but instead a sort of show of sincerity by Djamila.

One of my last days there, she drove me along the edge of the Sahara through a Bedreshem village to see the colossal statue of Ramses II and the alabaster sphinx. We drove to the Necropolis of Saqqara to visit the tombs of Apis and others. The son joined us and said it was the dead who now ruled the country, and the actress laughed. She said it was money that ruled the country and money that would get the movie made for her to star in.

Back in Hollywood, I was working on the Egyptian script until something went haywire and the deal was put on hold. A letter from the Alexandrian nephew almost two months later informed me that his uncle had suffered a heart attack, and that his cousin—the son—had been arrested. He was in a "political camp," as he called it. Djamila wrote that he was being tortured, that they were breaking the bones in his feet. She was packing up for Paris.

Shortly after her letter, the nephew contacted me again and mentioned that the motion picture project was being abandoned. His cousin had died from pneumonia, and all rights to any writing I had completed were reverting to me.

Henry Robbins, editing at Dial Press, enthusiastically suggested I do a novel on the Egyptian theme. It was a long-range plan, and in the middle of this another film deal lurched forward—another quickie, this one out of Sherman Grinberg's vault of stock-footage operations. An associate named Roberts had produced a picture and developed it at the Vine Street lab where I'd cut *Blues*. He told me that money from Marion Davies' family had been sunk into the project via Arthur Lake— better known as Dagwood Bumpstead from the old *Blondie* movies. "Second money" was expected from Technicolor. They wanted a surf- ing movie—the "real thing," Roberts said, "no honeymoon or beach dancing shit . . ." A young guy named David Lee had shot some surfing footage and made a bundle around the world showing the reels to the music of the Ventures and the Beach Boys. Lee was in Hawaii waiting for the big wave to break. They wanted a script written around the footage—a semi-documentary drama. Roberts asked, "How soon can you leave for Hawaii?"

Again, a warning from Bernie Wolf. "Go cautious," he said. "You're going to be running yourself into nowhere with these charac- ters if they aren't paying you big bucks up front. They're taking you for a ride."

But I had a wife and kid to support. I wasn't on Hugh Hefner's payroll, so on the plane above the Pacific I scribbled notes about the bullfighter in the photo Jimmy Dean had been so nuts about—the tore- ador isolated in the midst of thousands of yelling people, like some odd- ball surfer bobbing on a sea of bodies. But the surfers were crazier than the matadors because nobody was paying them to break their necks. The challenge sprang from deep inside, that old sense of "discoveries to be made" that Jimmy had harped about. The matador with the bull and the moment of truth, or naked and "Solo Suzuki" down the side of a crashing mountain of ocean. These guys weren't hotdoggers or beach show-offs, but loners that hung back, waiting for the "dragon"—the big wave of Waiamea Bay.

David Lee picked me up at the Honolulu airport. We'd gone to Hollywood High the same semester, but we'd hung out with different crowds. Blond, blue-eyed, six-two, still a shining Hollywood High face, even with a decade or so of dust tacked on. He asked me if I could talk Frankie Avalon into the deal—at least get him some of the footage to take a look at. I'd worked with Avalon in a picture, but we weren't that chummy. "What about Barbara Eden?" I said.

With David was his wife Ann, who looked vaguely familiar to me. A blonde Swedish girl was also along for the ride. Going down the ramp, I collided with Peter O'Toole, who'd been staring back at the blonde. "Oh, I didn't see you!" he said to me, his eyes rolling hazily. "I'm terrible sorry—"

"No, it was my fault," I said. We shook hands.

"It's been nice chatting," he said and climbed the gangplank into the airplane.

We got coffee in Coffee Dan's, the same chain as on Hollywood Boulevard, and David sketched out the deal. Dagwood's son, Arthur Lake Jr., was in his twenties and would play a small role in the movie, which David didn't mind because Arthur had a big supply of dope on the island. His father, however, kept stressing the danger of drugs creeping into America "from that dirty Chinese world." Dagwood wanted to make a "good" film—he wasn't sure what that meant, but felt like he had an opportunity to give a free hand to some creative aspects. "Being Dagwood all these years has kept me from using my imagination in other ways," he said, then fell down drunk in the hallway of the Royal Hawaiian.

We were immediately in tune when I told David how I'd like to focus the story through the adventures of a big wave rider—a *cinema verité* approach, using an interview technique, weaving a reporter in and out. I'd get Greg Muleavy—a struggling actor friend I'd met at Dick Powell's apartment when he came to the door selling encyclope-dias—to play it. (Greg would later have a big run with a lead on the television series *Mary Hartman, Mary Hartman.*) We could build the previously shot footage around a docudrama story.

David said everything was hinging on the waves breaking at

Waiamea. They'd been sitting around for a month waiting for the big wave. "Nothing so far," he told me as we drove from Honolulu through vast pineapple fields, then past Pearl Harbor. My uncle had been a Navy diver and gone down after the Japanese bombing to try to cut through the ships' hulls with a welding torch to get the bodies to the surface, but it had been hopeless.

We drove past Schofield Barracks to the northwest side of the island and to the town of Haleiwa, where we stopped at a small cafe on the highway. David, Anne and the blonde had large salads with cheese dressing, while I had a small dinner salad with French. I wasn't sure who the blonde was or how she fit into the situation.

The cook told us a cockfight was being held in a tent behind some shacks down the road. We left to watch, and after talking to a Filipino, who was the cook's cousin and who'd helped with the camera equipment on shoots, we were let into the tent. Others were suspicious of me, thinking I might be a Hawaii Five-0 cop. Ann stayed in the car, saying she was going to sleep, but was joined almost immediately by the blonde, who had blanched when some chicken blood flew against her leg.

That night all three of them were in and out of the bathroom throwing up. I was the only one who hadn't eaten the cheese dressing.

The long grassy yard of the house in Haleiwa dropped into the surf near Puaena Point—an isolated house on a private dirt road also used by the military. There were several large rooms with sea air blowing through. I slept on a couch in the living room, which was almost barren except for stacks of movie equipment flown in from Hollywood. Hungry before dropping off to sleep, I grabbed some Ritz crackers from an almost empty cabinet, but when I tipped the box a couple of cockroaches ran out and scurried across the counter.

That night, I was half-dreaming about my three-year-old daughter. She was running ahead of me in her red jacket, her dark hair blowing around her head.

Ann had been staring at me all evening. Next day on the beach, while David was shooting the "pipeline," she said, "You don't remember me, do you?" I said no, but there *was* something familiar about her. "We went on a blind date," she said. "I was going to Burbank High. I didn't remember it right away, but I looked in my diary last night, and it's there—the blind date, and it was you."

She said I'd had a green two-door Ford and we'd gone to Bob's

Big Boy Drive-in and "ate fries and a frozen malt we had to spoon out of that metal goblet . . ." "With the cherry on top," I said. She said, "I thought you were so good-looking, and I wanted you to kiss me but you didn't."

Then I remembered. She'd had terrible breath. I hadn't kissed her or dated her again. I told her I remembered the date, and that I'd had a fever—I'd been coming down with a bug and hadn't wanted to pass it on. I said I hadn't told her that because I'd really wanted to date her again and was afraid that if she thought she might catch the flu she wouldn't go out with me. She looked really cute now, grown up and in a bikini, and she didn't have bad breath any longer. I'd made up the excuse about the fever because I sensed something desperate about her. "I'm really depressed," she sighed, almost inviting advances.

Though David and I had gone to Hollywood High, I barely remembered him. He looked different. Ann told me that when he wasn't filming, he was smoking dope and talking about the Viet Minh. He believed they had agents operating throughout the islands. "He thinks their purpose is to infiltrate the intelligentsia," she said, "by doctoring the dope with a chemical that'll induce some kind of preliminary brainwashing."

I said I found that really strange. She said, "I don't use dope. As you see, I don't even smoke cigarettes. Last night he said he thought *you'd* put something in what we ate, like the Viet Minh put in the dope. He said, 'He's not sick, is he?' I'm just warning you," she said, "in case he says some weird things you might not understand." She said he'd been under a lot of pressure and that the marriage was falling apart. It was crumbling right before their eyes, and neither one of them, could do anything about it.

I asked who the blonde girl was, and she replied, "We met her at the airport a week ago, and he invited her to come and stay with us. She's occupying the room you were supposed to have. So I'm sorry about the couch situation, too. I want her to take off. She says she's waiting to meet some friends in Honolulu."

Once or twice a day, the Haleiwa house would rumble and shake as tanks and armored trucks passed the kitchen window, climbing down the dirt into the jungles for army war games as they were called. It had also occurred to David while he was stoned that if I was a spy, I was in a strategic area and the "notes" I kept writing could be "coded material relating to the war games."

He was okay when he wasn't stoned. But the bum marriage and

the wait for the big wave at Waiamea Bay about four miles north was twisting him into a pretzel. He wasn't alone—for two months a dozen big-wave surfers had waited on the beach in sleeping in bags or cardboard boxes. David said, "You never know for sure when they're going to go nuts. A while back there was a bad stabbing—two guys checked out. You could say they're overdue now—it's been almost a month and a half. Nobody can figure why the wave doesn't break. Hawaiians have some magic mumbo-jumbo to bring the ocean in so that it hits that shelf out there. That's what makes the wave so big—the water folding up on itself. But so far even their magic's done nothing."

Meanwhile, my meetings with Dagwood at the Royal Hawaiian at Wakiki dragged on. We'd sit on his beach-level terrace drinking gin and tonics and watch the sun sink into the ocean. There was a kind of greenish glow or flash for an instant when the sun went down behind the horizon. "It happens every day," Lake said, "this time of year." He had little in mind for a movie—only that Arthur Jr., wanted to try a little acting. "He doesn't know what else to do except get into trouble," Lake said.

While talking about some projects I'd written, we got into the Black Dahlia deal Tom Neal had been trying to promote. Lake had met Neal, and told me, "People in the business were afraid of his uncontrollable rages. They said he was liable to blow up at any time . . . The awful beating he gave Franchot Tone over that trollop Barbara Payton caused Hollywood to turn its back on Neal. We moved in very different circles, you understand."

Tom's problems had now capped themselves with the murder of his wife. He was found guilty of "involuntary manslaughter" and sentenced to prison. Lake said the feeling was that they should throw away the key. The Black Dahlia murder situation Neal had tried to "whip up for personal gain," Lake said, had been a sore spot for William Randolph Hearst for years, "for reasons best left unexplained . . ."

Lake spent days ruminating over the past while pouring gin into himself. He talked about the Westerns he'd made in the 1920s, and about working with Gloria Swanson. His wife, Patty, supposedly the niece of Marion Davies, spoke of Lake's vaudeville childhood as son of an actress mother and an acrobat father. "He joined the act on stage when he was only three years old," she said.

Whether or not Lake's wife, formerly Patricia Van Cleve, was Marion Davies' illegitimate daughter by Hearst, as rumored, Lake's friendship with Hearst Jr. stretched back before his marriage to Patty, who co-starred with him in a '50s television series. That he had landed the role of Dagwood through Marion Davies and Hearst was not a secret.

When Dagwood did come up with some "angles" for the movie, they seemed hopelessly rooted to his light-comedy stints. He'd catch himself saying something silly, and it was as though he'd clap an invisible hand across his mouth. While dismissing Tom Neal and the Dahlia case, Lake said there'd been another murder "just before that Black Dahlia got it," and that "she was a high-class kid." He made some connection between the other one's family and the Hearst newspapers, and then said, "They even looked alike, you know." I asked him who, and he said the two dead girls. He said, "Oh, the other one was a cutie, too. You know how they'd get around the Hollywood Canteen during the war . . ."

We were alone on the Royal Hawaiian terrace when he said that, and a look of fear flashed in his eyes. He stared at me sort of blankly for moments, then raised his glass and kept it glued to his lips. When he'd emptied it and brought it down, he said, "Just as long as we get a couple of shots in the movie of these little picaninny Hawaiians on those long home-grown boards . . ." He stared out at the Waikiki surf and said, "You can see a couple of them around here on Saturdays."

A few mornings later, the house in Haleiwa shook on its foundation as though the army tanks were coming through the walls. David was running through the rooms gathering camera equipment, shouting, "The waves are breaking at Waiamea!"

We stationed ourselves on the tip of a little peninsula where the waves thundered into the bay. A quarter mile from the beach, the waves took full force and the surfers plunged in, climbing up onto the crest. The face of each wave was a perpendicular three-story wall of rushing water with surfers poised on it, their boards poking out, poking into the air, like little sticks.

One surfer, Billy, had dolphins tattooed on his feet and bore like a medal a wide scar down his back where he'd been ripped open once by a flying board. He wore a small silver crucifix on a tight leather thong around his neck, but told me he wasn't a Christian. He said, "If I'm anything, man, I'm a Buddhist." I asked him why he was wearing a cross with Jesus on it, and he said, "Because He's the one that's with me when I ride the wave."

Tin Can, another surfer, wiped out on a wave that morning and washed up on the beach minutes later, still alive, but he'd broken an ankle and dislocated his shoulder. After they taped his ankle and wrapped adhesive bandaging around his shoulder and chest, he said he was going back for another wave. But he couldn't carry the board. He asked Billy to take it—and Dogger, and Pig, and Orville—but no one would help him—a kind of custom they had of backing out of another's suicide.

"You got to walk a fine line," Billy said. "Like you don't do anything all year except wait for the big wave. I mean you ride—you hitch and ride waves all over the States, but there's no waves like these. And it's over with fast. But while you're here, you're responsible for no one else's thing. If you go down, man, you go down on your *own*, and if you don't go down, you're going for the greatest high you'll ever know. It's just you and the wave. There's no room for spreading anything into anyone's else's karma . . ."

I looked at the little crucifix again and I said, "But you're not really alone out there, as you say."

He smiled. "I look alone to life's eyes," he said, "and on this film it'll look like I'm alone up there, because as far as I know no one's photographed a *real* spirit . . ."

Did he think of himself as religious? He said the only religion was the ride. "You live for the wave. Before and after the wave, you're just waiting for the wave. Only out here, right now, does it come together—man, God, life and it doesn't come together without death standing right in there with you. The wave's my religion. It's just now—there's no other time," he said, and hurried back to the jagged peninsula.

From where David was filming, the giant waves roared past and you could almost see them in profile. You looked up against the sun to see the surfers poised on their boards—toothpicks balancing miraculously on the edge of that enormous wall of water.

With only two surfers hospitalized, they celebrated that night with a beach bonfire of deadwood and pineapple crates. Tin Can and Pig and the others were drunk and stoned, and the Filipino skewered half a pig and buried piles of potatoes under the coals with a couple dozen wieners in tinfoil. Gallons of wine were passed back and forth, along with a metal lunch box of pot. Surfers jumped around telling tales of broken bones and board-fractured skulls, and of the impending mysteries of mammoth waves off Australia and South Africa—if only they could get the money to get there. A portable radio was playing the Beatles, and someone was strumming a guitar. I kept watching Billy, who sat off by himself, smoking dope and staring into the inky depths of the ocean, the surface glittering with stars and the reflection of the flames.

David hurried back and forth from the house to the beach, bringing wine and rolling joints while I sat in the sand near the fire with Ann. Eating a roasted wiener, she talked about wanting a child like my daughter, but said it wasn't "going to work out" with David. She said, "I'll never get pregnant in this marriage."

She stared at me, the light of the fire dancing on her face. Behind her, on the other side of the fire, I saw David squatting beside a blonde girl, his back facing us. The lunch box was tucked under one arm as he braced himself in the sand with his other hand to lean over and kiss the girl on the mouth. I quickly looked to the fire when he glanced around, pulling the blonde to her feet. Both headed up the slope to the house, while Ann watched a twisted branch crackle and burn. She said to me, "I want to get pregnant . . ."

FROM BIG WAVE TO MURDER

DOG SHIT WAS DRIED HARD on the rugs in the halls of Marion Davies' Santa Monica beach mansion. The wall by the kitchen phone was scrawled with black crayoned numbers and names, some smudged to dirty smears and doodles. When David Lee and I entered through the kitchen, a fat, sweaty man sucking a cigar was on his knees hammering at pipes sticking out of a wall.

In the main room facing the private beach, Dagwood and Patty Lake sat slumped on a long bamboo sofa, sipping drinks and waiting for David to convince them of the relevance of the script. Dagwood had accused the story of glorifying the "great unwashed" instead of showing the "cute Hawaiian picaninnies" and their "humorous antics . . ."

Behind the Lakes stood an old grand piano draped with silver-threaded shawls and a clutter of gold-framed portraits of Marion Davies, of Hearst and Lake and Patty, plus group shots of Lake and Hearst's sons and Lake with their arms hanging over each other's shoulders. The picture-frame glass seemed sticky with some kind of tartar or grease.

Dennis Hopper was set to play the lead in the surfing film. A young actress I'd met through Ed Wood named Pat Barringer was in the film, along with Luana Anders, who'd appeared in Curtis Harrington's *Night Tide* with Dennis. We were going into pre-production, keeping a tight rein on the budget, with me directing the picture. David L. Wolper Productions was investing if Lake would pledge the completion bond through Technicolor and release his claim on the Hawaiian footage.

But Dagwood's deal with Technicolor had been shaky at best, and David, now producing, had gone directly to Wolper for release and backing. He could not free the footage shot in Hawaii that Lake had financed—for an amount Wolper said was "ridiculously demanding" and as "overblown as a Dagwood sandwich." Lake was fudging on any further investments into a project he claimed was now "distasteful and politically offensive." "This Gilmore," he'd told David, "is some kind of anarchist."

Before more deals could be made, Lake insisted I'd have to rewrite the script to his satisfaction. The story, he said, was a "treatise on nihilism," "populated with Marxists and bums," and he asked David, "What is this Gilmore guy—some kind of commie, for God's sake? This sort of crap can *never* be associated with the Hearst family . . ." What he wanted, he told me, was "some of the old-fashioned humor of the Blondie movies." He then fell into a stupor while Patty kept pushing him upright on the sofa. Smiling oddly, her face looking somehow unreal—perhaps it was the strange lighting from the gilded pineapple-shaped wall lights that gave her that shadowy, flattened look.

Discouraged, David decided to seek independent financing from San Diego, which would allow him to control the Hawaiian footage, circumventing Lake's participation. Meanwhile, we'd cast the picture out of Wolper's offices and plan pre-production as soon as David made the deal.

I'd brought Andy Janczak from *Blues* in to film the surfing movie. The soundman was from California Studios, and nervous about committing because he was set for two skin-horror shoots as soon as *they* had their bucks on board. We met at Musso & Frank's on Hollywood Boulevard a couple of times to talk it over. Pat Barringer was fretting over a quickie called *Ghouls and Dolls,* in which she played a double role—one almost naked as a dancing blonde who gets turned into gold à la James Bond's *Goldfinger* dish. She was also anxious about something Ed Wood was piecing together from six or seven other cheap tit-and-horror flicks.

Meanwhile, Dennis had trailed Martin Luther King Jr.'s Freedom March in the South and shot stacks of striking black and white photographs, which he showed me one afternoon in Hollywood after we'd left Wolper's. He said he wanted to get a showing or a book published out of it, and I suggested two New York people I knew who could possibly connect him with an agent. One was Diane Arbus—a true artist who'd broken from the mainstream as a photographer and was shooting freaks and rejects.

While waiting for the green light on the movie, I got a call about Barbara Payton from the editor at a North Hollywood paperback publisher I'd written potboilers for. At first I thought he was suggesting Barbara for the movie. I'd never met Barbara nor talked to her, but she'd written an autobiography, which they were publishing. She'd been trying to contact me—something personal, she'd told the editor, that had to do with Tom Neal, then in prison.

The editor gave my number to Barbara, and in a matter of minutes she was on the phone. She'd been in touch with Tom, she said, and he'd mentioned the Black Dahlia project. If anything should come of it, he'd like to try to get some money for further appeals. I said not much was happening with the project, and Barbara said she believed she knew about "an involvement" between the Black Dahlia—Elizabeth Short—and the actor Barbara had married, Franchot Tone, shortly after "Tom's fistfight with Franchot."

She said, "This information will give you some insight into the way we're all living." She wanted some money for the interview because she was broke, and asked that I not use her name, "unless I suddenly die or something, which isn't so unthinkable the way things're going."

When I mentioned her to Dennis, he said, "Barbara *Payton!* She was getting to be a big star, man. I don't think anybody knows she's still alive."

She'd hit the skids. "I'm a drunk," she said, "drinking wine all day and writing poetry." She was turning cheap tricks to stay afloat—boulevard creeps and jokers on Main Street. She was shooting smack but denied she was a junky, though she'd been busted twice on Sunset by a Sheriff's detective I knew from when we were acolytes. He'd been working narco when he busted Barbara, "with the smack and a load already under her skin," he said. "We weren't interested in the two-bit tricks she was turning in that motel room—that was Vice. We were on her for junk, trying to nail her connection. It was kept out of the papers because a guy at the *Hollywood Citizen-News* felt sorry for her—with a lot of damn good reason . . . She was a sad, sad case.

201

A talented beauty who turned into a fat, pathetic slob . . ."

Discovered by James Cagney, who made her his protégé, Barbara starred in movies opposite Cagney and Gregory Peck, but her personal life was a mess—a disaster running neck-and-neck with her success.

"She thought her shit didn't stink," said one producer who'd known Barbara. "She was a pig's ear Cagney had the hots for, and everyone tried to turn her into silk. She was a pig with a pig's attitude about life and herself."

Drunkenness, brawls, and then out of work—theft, prostitution, soliciting an undercover cop—drugs, blackouts, spiraling downward . . .

"I thought she'd be dead in a real short time," the detective said, "like Lenny Bruce, who I'd also busted for dope. I figured Barbara'd be dead a lot sooner than it actually took."

The producer said she was sex crazy. "A whore that'd fuck your dog if it humped her leg," he said. "But she didn't like it—she didn't enjoy it, there was never any love. Yet she couldn't say no. She even tried it with other girls. She was an easy score—she went out of her way for it. Some jerk comes along and says 'Hey baby, I'm going to lay you,' and pulls her into a car and drives off. Screws her in the car and dumps her off when he's done. She just goes along. That was more important to her than being an actress, than being a professional. She had the kiss of death stamped on her head like you get a rubber stamp on your hand at the fair. No good fairy's kiss on that kid, and getting involved with Tom Neal was another sign of her need to wreck her life . . ."

Barbara looked fat and bleached-out, a walking mess with sores on her face and the backs of her hands, which she'd tried to hide with pancake makeup that didn't match the color of her skin. We met in the little lunch counter of the drugstore at Santa Monica and Western. As bad as she looked, there was something about her eyes—the girl James Cagney had been so taken with, shining out of her face, the bright blonde starlet trapped somewhere inside the dilapidated slob that was only thirty-seven years old.

I looked at the small scabs on her arms as she spread a sheath of poems she'd written. "I'd appreciate your reading these," she said, "and letting me know what you think. I'd like to sell them. Some are about Hollywood." She said she was "living just around the corner" and needed money, "now that I'm getting evicted—again."

With me was an old Hollywood High friend, Jim Davidson, who

told Barbara he'd been raised by his father two doors down on Santa Monica. His dad had been a studio strike-breaker. He said it had always been an unfriendly neighborhood, good for winos and tin-horns and guys that fix shoes. Barbara said, "And queers and cheap whores and poets . . ."

Barbara had written Tom again, but hadn't heard back. "I'm afraid to see him," she said. "And if he gets out, I'd be afraid of him coming after me. That's how it always was. I'd try to get myself straightened up a little, and he could sweet-talk better than he could breathe, and he'd go all night at having sex. He was like a sex maniac—there was something wrong with him. I'm sure he's corn-holing half the guys in prison, knowing Tom. Some people can get their kicks by themselves, but he can't do that. He always had to get his kicks at someone else's expense, no matter what the hell it was . . . Like shooting his wife— she was a cute kid, a good-looking girl. Shooting her in the fucking head! You see why I say I'm scared of him. I shouldn't have written him at all . . ."

What she had to tell me was confidential. She didn't mind my taping our conversation and said she wasn't pulling any punches. "I'll talk straight out, and if it helps with my book, then that's so much the better. But what I'm telling you isn't pretty, and I wouldn't be sitting here blabbing it out if I didn't need money."

After the brawl over Barbara between Tom and Franchot that sent Franchot to the hospital with a concussion and "never talking the same way again," Barbara said, she married Franchot just to spite Tom. "But it was a very short marriage," she told me. "Franchot was a sweet man but had a bad masochistic streak in his personality. He wanted something beautiful for its own sake, not for what it did for him." Barbara was gorgeous and young and fit the bill. "He wanted me to be what I was— so he said at the start." But with Tom, there had been chemistry. They couldn't stay out of bed. It was simmering and "cooking," all the time. She was quick to see in Franchot's nature "that purist's obsession for a thing of beauty, and sometimes just *parts* of a woman could satisfy him—legs, breasts, your hind end," she said. "It didn't matter, and it could change depending on his state of mind."

At times Franchot seemed to need only a "kind of humbling of himself before these things," Barbara said, "like my asshole in cut-up black silk underwear . . ."

After she married Tone, she said, they'd visited Miami for the opening of a movie she was starring in. "The mayor of Miami gave me the key to the city." She said, "This event was in the newspapers, and we were having a ball. Franchot was drinking heavily, and there were stories in the papers about the Black Dahlia murder in Los Angeles . . . about the victim having tried to get in movies, and how she'd lived in Miami sometimes. The reporter writing about me and Franchot talked about the murder and asked us if we'd like to see where she'd lived. Franchot was keen to do this, though I didn't think much about it. What was the difference whether she lived in Miami or Siam? She was dead. But Franchot had this natural curiosity.

"The reporter drove us a ways to this little court, a small bunch of bungalows in a horseshoe, with a sidewalk going around the front. There was grass in the middle that was long or had weeds—and nobody was taking care of anything. Maybe no one was living there. The whole place was run down.

"Where the murder victim had lived was a little room with a small bedroom. A kind of wooden sideboard or serving board in the wall with a mirror in it, a small place, with a fancy overhead light in the living room—it had a lot of points sticking out of it, like stars laid over one another. Plaster walls, sort of chipping or wrinkling, chipped stuff on them. I said to Franchot, 'So what's the deal?' He was just staring around at the place.

"Then the guy took us to a hamburger place just down the street and said she'd worked there during the war, slinging hash on and off, and hung around with a lot of service guys. The jerk that ran the place was a German, and the reporter asked us if we wanted to meet him. Franchot said he did, but I didn't see the point. The reporter said the guy'd had a lot of trouble because of being German during the war, though he was an American and going blind—something to do with a chemical explosion . . ."

It wasn't until Barbara and Tone returned to L.A. that Franchot told her he'd met the Black Dahlia before, in Hollywood. "It was when he was thinking about making *The Lady From Shanghai,* before he lost the option to Orson Welles. Franchot said he'd been in a bad state over that deal when he ran into the Dahlia girl in the Formosa Cafe across from the Goldwyn Studios. He'd been drinking, and said he'd embarrassed her and hurt her feelings because of his callous attitude. He said he told her he felt like he was a real shit. He kept telling her he wasn't worth a shit, and the girl kept insisting that he was a valuable person . . .

"As he was telling me this incident," Barbara said, "he started sobbing and was on the floor clawing at my knees, saying how he deserved everything rotten and wanted to be defecated on. He had told her he would be fitting for him to be shit on. Just like that. He promised to put the girl in a movie if she'd accommodate him and put an end to his foolishness, truly put him in his place . . .

"If she'd been any sort of stand-up gal, I'm sure she'd have put him in his place by walking out of it, though Franchot had a way of pleading and working on a person—like talking a turkey out of Thanksgiving. Only once, when he was out of his head like I've just described, did he ask me to do that to him—to shit on him. I refused. It made me sick—not the idea of what he wanted, but Franchot's idea of allowing himself to be in situations like a living toilet. I know being busted up by Tom in that fight was something Franchot really wanted—actually *wanted* . . ."

When we'd finished talking about Franchot and the dead girl, Barbara said she believed with the publication of her book (which had nothing to do with the Black Dahlia in it) there might be the possibility of a comeback. She said, "This town takes your body away from you, but they also want the soul. Until they get the soul *with* the body, you're skating on thin ice. When you give up the soul, you give life. What happens then is, you're the walking dead. They just haven't put you in the ground yet."

Dennis said he wanted to meet Barbara, and when I talked to her again I told her what he'd said, and that maybe he'd take some pictures for her book. She said it wasn't a bad idea, and I gave her Dennis' message service and said she could make her own contacts with him. Later Dennis said they had made contact, and that she'd given him head in a bar booth downtown.

Speaking about Jim Davidson, she said, "That friend of yours, Jim, is a pretty nice-looking guy, and he's *smart*, too, not like some fucking phonies I know."

I said, "I'll tell you something that should be confidential, but he didn't say *not* to tell you, so what the shit . . ." I told her Davidson had said he'd been very attracted to her, and that a couple of her poems had hit him in the gut.

Like Carol Burnett and David Lee, Jim Davidson had graduated Hollywood High with promise, but like Barbara Payton, he'd wound up in a hole. Along with another mutual friend, kid Golden Gloves champ Manny Samon, and a "Mexican" named Carlos Castaneda, the three had sort of stumbled into a dumpy guest house behind some apartments near L.A. City College. Samon was sort of suffering a breakdown from imagining he'd raped and murdered a campus girl, while Carlos—in love with moonbeams—wrote poems to a female college teacher who'd said he showed promise. Davidson was studying some kind of useless philosophy, and all three of them were always looking and hoping to get laid. Samon was the first to hook up, driving off with a big black cleaning lady after trying to hang himself in the shower. He tied the rope to the fixture, but being chunky and thickboned, he only managed to pull the pipes from the wall.

With no shower, Jim and Carlos moved into a front apartment managed by another friend, Frank, a would-be writer working at the VA crazy house. Sharing the cramped quarters throughout the year, the two had little space for furniture. "Carlos would sit around on these tatami mats," Jim said, "with those big chubby legs crossed, trying to look like a Buddha. We'd hang around a little all-night restaurant up in Hollywood, or go to the Million Dollar Theater downtown on Broadway to see Luis Buñuel films in Spanish, no subtitles. There'd be kids screaming and climbing over the seats.

"Carlos liked to tell tall tales all the time," Davidson said, "personal things, making things up. He was a creative guy with a vivid imagination, but made up these ridiculous stories, and I'd call him on it, but he said it made him feel important. He made up a story about some Indian like Tonto, only this guy was a medicine man. He'd tell a couple of girls we talked to about this Tonto character, like he had this close friend who was weird and important. None of the girls were impressed enough to do anything with Carlos . . .

"This medicine-man Tonto was just like some imaginary playmate you make up when you're little," Jim recalled. "When we started at UCLA, it was Tonto who was sharing his secrets with Carlos. We'd sit around in this little apartment on Madison while he wrote his thesis about this Indian character. We had another friend with a doctorate in literature who accused Carlos of being a liar and a phony, and found himself in agreement with the anthropology department, which became furious when they found out Carlos' tale seemed to be nothing more than a piece of fiction.

"One girl really liked Carlos, but she was like a chinless Olive Oyl.

He was trying to call her one night when some guy got mad at him for hogging the phone and pulled Carlos off it and slapped him.

"Carlos came back and sat on the tatami mat crying, sitting on pillows without his pants on. His short, bare legs were chubby and brown, and he looked at them, poking at his legs, and said he was a nothing. 'I'm nothing,' he said. 'I'm just a little brown man.'

"After that is when he started talking about Fernando Pessoa, the Portuguese poet who wrote under many different names, and that he, Carlos, was descended from that superior man. He said that he was related to Pessoa by some blood connection, and about how he, too, was a superior man in the Portuguese tradition, not just a little brown man that someone could slap in the face.

People who told the truth were fools, Carlos said. He believed lying was more creative than telling the truth. There was never any such person as Don Juan," said Jim. Even the name was Carlos' joke about his inability to get laid. The whole Indian thing was just his imaginative wanderings—like he'd wander at night, never sleeping much. He'd just sit around making up stories to get people to think of him as an intelligent and important person.

"After he got that stuff published, he got some fat checks and moved to Malibu, had a big security system set up, and you couldn't even see the house. He said, '*Nobody* is going to slap Carlos Castaneda . . .' He told me he didn't care that UCLA thought he was a fake, or that *anyone* thought he was a fake. He was going to keep on lying because a superior man never tells the truth—he tells what he *wants* to be the truth."

Drugs? Mushrooms? Dope? "Not Carlos," said Jim. "Never touched the stuff. When he got some money, he wore elegant dark suits and kept his shoes perfectly shined. He always kept his shoes shined. Carlos said, 'When a person gets fame, then he has shiny shoes.' To have shoes that were very shiny was important to him."

"There was no depth to Carlos," said another friend, a Ph.D. "He wouldn't go out on lecture circuits because he was afraid of being challenged. His theory of the superior man who lies was okay as an individual position behind a security wall at Malibu Beach, but on the podium he feared those who could dig into his lies. When UCLA found out there was no medicine man, they kicked him out. It was all fake . . ."

Like Castaneda's fabrications about the medicine man, Dennis Hopper was equally busy conjuring up sexual fantasies that didn't gel with his day-to-day world. Afraid of the James Dean subject, and afraid to talk about it with me because his agent, Bob Raison, had hinted at some homosexual tomfoolery, Dennis avoided the subject for fear it might shift the same light to him. Instead, he chuckled about sex scenes with girls he invented in his head. In a drunken moment, he confessed he was a habitual if not compulsive masturbator, and that after concocting the fantasies, he'd try to pawn them off as real occurrences, as part of his ritual "self-abuse."

He seemed genuinely depressed when the surfing movie went belly up after David Lee's failure to nab the San Diego financing. Dagwood sat on the Marion Davies money like a fat kid on a pile of gumballs.

Pat Barringer was working in the "Astra-Vision and Sexicolor" movie Ed Wood had scripted—he was also acting as assistant director. He'd talked about the possibility of doing a project with some money coming from Lou Kimzey's sexy paperback publishing business. (Lou would later get into biker magazines out of Malibu). But money was tight, and when Bernie Wolf hooked *Playboy* into an advance to cover what was going to prove "a sensational murder trial in Tucson" and asked me to work with him on it for cash in hand, I jumped at the chance.

The bait he'd used to land *Playboy* money was that the alleged killer, charged with polishing off three pretty young girls and dumping their bodies in the desert, was an Elvis-emulating former state gymnastics champ considered a "Lothario" by the media. Bernie said, "Hugh Hefner's a sap and loves a Lothario, no matter what he's guilty of. Just a little greasing about these blonde cuties who chased after this guy, and I could see Hefner's mouth watering."

Pocketing a big share of the profits while someone else—namely me—did the work. Bernie arranged our flights to Tucson. He said he'd already talked to *Fugitive* television star David Janssen about movie potential, and if Janssen got the money for a picture, I'd be working on a script with Bernie.

We had a fast breakfast meeting in Beverly Hills with Janssen, who intended to star in the film as a lawyer in the murder case. The guy, Charles Schmid, was being tried for two of the murders, although the cause of death of the two victims had not been determined. According to the prosecutor, the motive was to cover up for the previous murder, a third girl, whose body had never been recovered. Nor had the accused—Schmid, or "Smitty," as he was called—been indicted for that other murder. Janssen had talked to the County Attorney in Tucson, and believed the case would set some precedents in American law. "From my view," Janssen said, "it's about how fucked up the law gets. Is it even *legal* to try a guy in such a manner?"

Apart from myself, Janssen would prove to be the only other person to express concern about the accused's being presumed guilty previous to any trial being held. Another aspect of the case had Janssen even more mystified. Teenagers hanging around Tucson's "kid dance joints" knew about the murders months before Smitty was arrested. "It had become a kind of 'What's new?' sort of thing," Janssen said, "and 'Oh, yeah, I heard about Smitty killing the girls,' and 'so what else is new?' This is an American tragedy," Janssen said, "a phenomenon." And Bernie agreed with him.

By noon we had landed at Tucson. I'd been going over the clippings Bernie had gathered,along with Janssen's notes, trying to decidewhether or not there was actually any evidence against the accused.

Meanwhile, Hugh Hefner was having second thoughts about publishing an article on "such a morbid situation." He said, "Murder is an unpleasant topic—what're we going to do with *murder?* This Arizona guy's a sociopath or something. I mean, he's *killed* girls. Our readers aren't interested in killing girls. That's for detective enthusiasts. Lovely females are playthings—they're for joy and sensuality. This is the view of the American male. This is what they pay for."

But Bernie had the dough, and Hefner was going to have to give some serious thought to the prospective article—either offending his readers or eating the loss, since Wolf was already blowing the money he laughingly called a "kill fee."

We checked into a one-bedroom suite at the Pioneer Hotel, a short walk to the courthouse and newspaper office. *The Tucson Citizen* and the *Arizona Daily Star,* two separate newspapers, shared the same building. Dave Briniger, editor of the *Star,* loaned us clippings and photographs out of the morgue.

Another day, he called me into his office for a cup of coffee and asked, "Where's Mr. Wolf?" I said he was still asleep at the hotel, and Briniger checked his watch. He smiled and said, "If by chance you happen to come up with an article on your own that's not headed for Wolf's magazine, I'd like to take a look at it. Maybe a feature about runaways—we've got them scrambling out of here as though some-one's yelled 'Fire!' Once they get past the town limits they seem to vanish. I'm talking about something like an *Observer* article, with a lit-tle different angle than we're used to." When I finished my coffee, he said, "This is between you and me, you understand. I'm not talking about Wolf or *Playboy*. We're not interested in that cream-puff nonsense, and personally, I don't like Mr. Wolf. You understand, that's just my personal feeling."

The editor would later tell me, "I wanted to see how far you'd go, given a little old-time newspaper incentive. You were like a young reporter being hoodwinked by these wire-service hotshots and Hollywood characters into fronting for them. You'd be making the inroads with Smitty's pals and the kids, getting behind the scenes while these character sat in their air-conditioned suites yakking up war stories . . ."

Not only had the major U.S. magazines come to Tucson for the trial, but scores of reporters were arriving from as far away as Paris and Japan. A stringer from Holland was gathering clippings and racing around with a photographer named Lawrence Schiller, who'd checked into the Ramada Inn to get an exclusive on "the killer," but Smitty's attorney had blocked all avenues to the accused. And everyone else was looking in the wrong places—like at the backs of each other's heads.

Schmid was claiming innocent. He'd been framed, the defense said, by his closest pal, Richie Bruns, who'd allegedly helped Smitty bury two of the bodies. Bruns had worried himself sick over his own involve-ment, and to avoid getting in dutch, he'd ratted on Smitty, offering himself as the state's star witness even as Smitty was fingering *him* for the murders. Even a few kids were on Smitty's side.

Another Tucson paper, *The American*, a twice-weekly focusing on local news, dug into the "human interest" angle. *American* reporter Lois Hudson, a retired major from Army Intelligence, was writing "the other side of the story—anything the other papers were afraid to print," such as: "Is Schmid Telling the Truth?" Smitty's teeny-bopper wife, Diane, claimed he was "completely innocent."

Through Lois I met Smitty's wife, who'd married him three months prior to his arrest—three months after the two murders for which bodies had been ID'd. Very few others seemed to know Diane even existed. Short and thin, she wore her dyed-black hair high in a bouffant that was taller than her head. Her fair, almost delicate face was covered with makeup that was too light and had a chalky, opaque quality. In short order, she'd lead me to Smitty's foster parents, who ran a nursing home. They were being accused of spoiling their "adopted murderer son" rotten, to the point where he believed he was beyond "the laws others must live by . . ."

The Schmids did not like their son's young wife, and Diane was quick to relate to me their criticisms of her—one of them being the makeup she wore. When I asked why she wore it, she told me Smitty wanted her to; he insisted and on the particular shade, and on the powdery pancake base. From what I learned later, blonde Gretchen Fritz, his ex-girlfriend and one of the murder victims, always wore the same sort of makeup, although on Gretchen it hadn't seem so bleached out. What it did on Diane, however, was make her look more like Gretchen. He'd wanted Diane to dye her hair as black as his own, yet at the same time recapture the face of Gretchen, the girl he was accused of strangling.

The first day of the trial, Smitty looked over with an Elvis smile and nodded to me. I nodded back. We exchanged a kind of smile that said, "Well . . . here we go."

During a recess, I leaned forward and told Smitty I wanted to write a level, unbiased story about this case. Diane had told him she was talking to me, a friend of Lois Hudson, who Smitty believed was on their side. He said, "I'm not testifying. My attorney doesn't want me to get up there, so there's no way for me to present my side. I can't talk to anyone. Maybe through something you're writing . . . " He stopped talking and stared straight ahead as his attorney hurried to the table.

A couple of days later, Bernie broke off with David Janssen, claiming the actor had lost his objectivity. "He's more concerned about this fucking murder trial than with getting a movie deal." He warned me not to lose my objectivity, saying, "All this in-depth investigating is a waste of time. You're coming up with stuff like the wife angle and all this love life crap with a murderer. It's not what I'm looking for." He'd talked to Hefner, he said, who was "very disappointed." What Bernie couldn't use for Hefner, he suggested I use for my own research. "*You* write a book on your own," he said. "You're doing a lot of work, and I'm personally not as involved in any of this as you've become. We're operating on different wave-lengths."

Janssen called me the next morning from a *Fugitive* location, and said, "Bernie's pooh-poohing the ideas I set forth at the start about this guy getting railroaded. Whether he's guilty or not is beside the point. I think it needs testing in an impartial courtroom. But obviously the state's got an easy task, with Bernie and the rest of the media strapping this kid in the gas chamber even before the testimony's in. What I've been wanting to do is take a look at that side of the situation, whether Bernie's interested or not."

Rather than trying to talk about other approaches, Bernie accused Janssen of manipulating me, then "dismissed" me, saying I should go "sit on the fence with Janssen." Bernie was checking out of the Pioneer Hotel and moving over to the Ramada with the *Life* magazine boys. "We're not barking up the same tree," he said, "so I don't see the need for any further association between us."

But Smitty had found a buddy—the youngest in a gaggle of journalists hungry for the how and why of the murders. The question wasn't *if* Smitty did it, but how he did it, and why. That's what bothered Janssen.

Fired by Bernie, I flew back to L.A., talked to Janssen and then met with Robert Levy. We made a deal over a possible movie on the case—the killer's side of the story—and as quickly as I'd left, was on a plane back to Tucson.

I took a cheap hotel room downtown the night before the verdicts: "Guilty on both counts." Diane was at the hotel the next morning, knocking on my door. "Smitty wants to see you," she said.

Now, behind the greenish-tinted bullet proof glass at Pima County Jail, I saw a different Smitty. This was the one *Life* portrayed as the dreamy-eyed, smooth-talking "Pied Piper of Tucson." No longer slicked down as though ironed flat, his glistening black hair rose high in a pompadour, and the collar of his jail-issue shirt was up against the back of his neck. Cool. As cool as it gets, the blue eyes alive with light and intensity, so pale the pupils seemed as black and penetrating as a snake's. We talked over the telephone. He said he'd already written me over a hundred pages of his story—"the whole case," which he hadn't presented in court. We worked out a deal, an exclusive: I'd tell his story, and no one else would have access to Charles Schmid, found guilty of murdering two girls. He faced two death sentences and still another trial for the murder of the first victim, who had never been found.

When Diane got on the line, Smitty's eyes narrowed and his head rocked slightly from side to side. Whatever he was saying into that carefully cupped mouthpiece seemed to turn the girl's spine to jelly and weaken her knees. With those eyes and that voice, he was reaching right through the glass. In moments, he'd turned her into putty.

He could talk to me, he said, because I was "open." I'd *understand*. And so began the game we'd play. "No corpus delicti," he kept saying, and though he was facing not one, but two trips to the gas chamber, we set about finding a way to beat the upcoming murder trial.

Over the next few weeks we were monitored and screened, our letters photographed, examined and documented by the County Attorney as Smitty poured out a vivid and complex tale. It wasn't the real story, as I'd eventually see, but was lucid and imaginative, with some almost indiscernible pin holes that, in time, would lead me right into the killer's mind.

Death Sentence Jet-Setters

A SMALL CONCRETE BLOCK BUILDING called the "Little House," about the size of a two-car garage, with a long, narrow tin smoke stack, was where the State of Arizona put the condemned to death by lethal gas. After the two murder trials, Smitty was moved to the state prison at Florence, within constant view of the Little House, to await execution.

Not long after his arrival on Death Row, he wanted me to contact the world-famous lawyer Percy Foreman about defending him at the next murder trial. "There's nobody else who can do it," Smitty said, "and if we can beat this one, it'll throw out the convictions for the other two."

I wasn't sure that was the way it would work, but said I'd try my best with Foreman. The lawyer had had an astonishing victory in the Candy Mossler murder trial, another "missing body" case. It was Candy's husband, Jacques, a wealthy older man who she and her lover nephew were accused of deep-sixing. Neither the nephew nor Candy were in jail during the trial. They were guests at the Miami Hilton, with the state footing the expenses—an arrangement wrangled by Foreman. The giant-like, white-maned Texan had told Candy to put up $250,000 in cash, jewels or securities, and he'd walk them out of the

214

courtroom. In over one hundred murder cases, Foreman said he'd lost only one client to the hot seat.

Candy put up the jewels in the lawyer's name, went to trial and was acquitted, along with the nephew—no longer Candy's lover. Rich now, Candy moved to Houston and took up a whirlwind affair with rock'n'roller Chuck Berry, while lawyer Foreman went on to save more murderers.

After spending a few nights in Smitty's small house next to his foster parents' across from the nursing home, I rented an apartment on Speedway near Smitty's old haunts. His house had been locked up since his arrest the previous year, and while the state had described the two girls as having been murdered on the street beside their car, I found out later they'd actually been killed in Smitty's house—one, his girl-friend, strangled in the tiny bedroom, the younger one choked to death in the living room. Unknown to anyone at the time, except for Smitty and whomever he'd blabbed his secret to, he'd had sex with the younger girl's body.

It was Foreman's view that, regardless of Smitty's guilt or inno-cence, "anyone who looks like him and acts like him ought to have a bushel of psychiatric testimony for screwing up like that," Foreman said. "And his lawyer ought to take half the juice." Though fascinated with Smitty's situation, Foreman wasn't keen on entering a case with two verdicts in; besides which, the money wasn't there, and both houses and the nursing home were already in hock. I talked to him a number of times from L.A. and Tucson before he declined. He backed off, rec-ommending instead "a young fellow who's had quite a bit of success named Lee Bailey. He might throw down the gauntlet for this boy in Tucson . . ."

F. Lee Bailey had defended the Boston Strangler, and after a few conversations, he arranged to pilot his own Lear jet to a meeting in Tucson. I'd invited Lois Hudson to meet Bailey, and George Scott of KCUB Radio.

Driving north to the prison, Bailey and I discussed the case while going over the press book I'd gathered. He said, "This is just the stuff we need to bust the case wide open." He told me about a client he knew who was "guilty as hell," but played the innocent game all the way. Bailey said he didn't personally care if someone was guilty or not. "They usually always are," he said. It was the money, the pub-licity, and his own neck that concerned Bailey. He had a case on the books in Florida—a guy named Coppolino who had indeed killed his wife—and Bailey was heading back to defend him against first-degree murder.

At the old territorial prison, Bailey stared up at the small mirrors on the corners of the walls. When Smitty came in, wearing the baggy prison jacket and trousers, Bailey said, "He's really small, isn't he?" Smitty harped on his innocence, and Bailey said the first thing would be to get a lie detector test, which Smitty was in favor of. He'd reportedly asked for sodium pentothal, but Bailey said the lie detector was the ticket. They'd throw the results right in the County Attorney's face, "assuming they're good results," he said. "I've got the top polygraph man in the field. We'll hit them where it hurts."

George Scott wanted to interview Smitty, who'd asked me to handle it. He'd made me his personal manager. He didn't want to jeopardize any legal angles in the works, and I arranged for Scott to come to Death Row and tape the interview, just the three of us. What I witnessed convinced me that Smitty might pass Bailey's polygraph test, but not because he was innocent. He did one of the most stunning acts I'd ever seen, bar none. No actor I'd known could have carried off such a poignant, convincing performance. He went on for an hour, almost non-stop.

I glimpsed the depth of Smitty's ability to manipulate, cajole and convince, and it eventually occurred to me that I, too, was being manipulated, as skillfully as a brain surgeon guides his scalpel through the twists and turns in your head. The carrot for me, of course, was that Smitty had granted me exclusive rights to his life story, trusting me to incite the law and the press to his advantage. I'd trusted him—not exactly *believing*, but maintaining a "middle of the road" position.

Yet something else was happening as we moved into the big time with the hotshot lawyers and the media—a subtle bristling that Smitty provoked in me. Those hypnotic pale eyes stared at me for just a few seconds in the room where Scott was taping the interview, and Smitty saw that I knew he was giving a great performance. He luxuriated in my admiration of his ability to make a tall tale sound as credible as the golden rule, but at the same time he saw that this crack in his veneer might let something spill forth that he had no intention of placing on view. Our game was getting a little dangerous.

Two of the kids from the Johnny's Fat Boy Drive-in crowd for which Smitty used to hold court talked about getting married across the border in Nogales and staging a big party at a Mexican friend's house. I was to meet them at the Matador Hotel. I went because I needed to get out of Tucson for a couple of days. Though the kids didn't show up, I hung out across the border, stoned on tequila, going through a kind of purging of the things in my head. I couldn't hold to the middle-of-the-road any longer, nor could I hold at bay the nagging fact of Smitty's guilt.

The boy Smitty had confided in as to how he'd killed the two girls hit me for urgent traveling expenses. He said Smitty had told him he'd had a hard-on while he strangled them—almost had an orgasm, but instead pissed in his pants the minute he finished them off. He'd had to strangle the younger one twice because he hadn't killed her the first time.

He'd engaged in sex with the younger girl after he killed her, the boy said, because he'd never done anything with her, Smitty had said, though he'd thought about it. He said the body "jumped and moved" as though she were still alive. When he was done, he drove the bodies in the girl's car up in the desert to the "old drinking spot," dumped them on the ground and drove away. He said if the boy breathed a word of what he'd been told, Smitty would cut off his hands and feet and bury him alive in the desert.

The boy blabbed to his pals that Smitty said he'd killed the girls, though he didn't supply any details, fearing that if he mentioned Smitty's hard-on, he'd surely lose his hands and feet, along with his life. I asked the boy why he hadn't told the whole story, and he said, "Oh, I didn't believe all the things he said—he always said crazy stuff. But I did think he'd killed them, because they were gone and only he seemed to know what had happened to them. It made sense. And then Smitty took his friend Richie up to show him the bodies and get Richie to help him to bury them. He drove Richie out to where the first one was buried, the one that's never showed up, and stuck a stick down in the ground to see how she smelled after being down there so long . . .

"I believed him because of the way he threatened me to kill me if I talked about him having a hard-on and pissing. Smitty felt that was worse, probably, than simply having killed them—especially the sex with a dead girl, like he's a vampire or something. That was different. That was far-*out*, man. How he threatened me was something I'd never experienced, and I didn't doubt for a minute that he'd do it if I repeated stuff. He hadn't even told his best friend, Richie, about having sex with the dead girl, the little one . . ."

Richie Bruns endured Schmid's accusations with a grin and a grain of salt. He said, "Smitty's just trying to get even 'cause I ratted on him. It was a hard thing for me to do to him, but it had to be done. It doesn't bother me that he's done that. It bothers me that everyone in town thinks *I'm* some freak . . ."

Believing he could "wax the ass off these local yokels," Bailey took on Smitty's defense in the third murder after he'd been whipped by Florida and lost the Coppolino case. He needed a "boost back up," and without the girl's body, he said, "there's no way they're going to convict him. It's like tearing open a paper doll—that's all they've got—a paper doll. That's their case. By a stroke of fortune, they won hands down on the first trial for the other two murders, using this third—actually the first of the alleged murders—as just motive for the other two. And with no body, those first two convictions can't hold water. If nothing else, the appeals court will throw all this into the garbage can. Smitty will be a free man."

Figuring on a hot movie deal in lieu of a fat retainer for undertaking the case, Bailey overlooked the legalities of the exclusive contracts I held with Smitty and his parents, and the release his wife, Diane, had signed. Having placed himself out on a limb, Bailey cut short his relationship with me and with Schmid's parents, and engaged in the second trial thinking he'd badger Arizona into an acquittal.

But it didn't work that way. William Schaffer III, the prosecuting attorney, was not the "local yokel" Bailey labelled him, but a brilliant lawyer bent on beating Bailey at his own game.

If nobody had been able to find a body, then it didn't exist, Bailey contended. And should the girl turn up alive, after Schmidt had been executed, a worse crime than murder would have been committed in the eyes of God. Everyone had searched the desert for the girl's body, even the two who supposedly knew where she'd been buried. No one was able to find the grave. Their stories, incriminating in the first trial of Schmid, now carried less strength, especialy with one boy now refusing to testify.

The last time I saw Smitty before the trial ended, he said the state was pulling a fast one and Bailey was pulling a fast one, and that he could trust no one—not even his own parents. He said they were working out some sort of deal with Bailey. They wanted Smitty to plead guilty, save himself from a third death sentence and hammer away at the first two convictions on appeals. As long as the body never turned up, there would always be doubt. It would be "inconclusive middle of the road," Smitty said, winking at me.

Sitting across from Smitty, listening to him and watching him, was like looking into the face of a dog, an animal behind bars. It seemed somehow a simple fact: these were not human eyes.

Bailey was able to keep Smitty off the "hot seat," at least for this murder. Persuaded to plead guilty, he got fifty years to life. Bailey said it was not a "loss," since he'd saved the boy's life—that could never be considered a loss. With that, he climbed into his Lear jet and flew out of Tucson.

Believing that Smitty was now all washed up and in a vulnerable position, a skillful probation officer managed over several meetings to talk him into showing the Sheriff where he'd hidden the first body.

I watched from a distance the day Smitty led the law into the desert, then directly to that forlorn spot. He was like a dog who knew the exact location of the bone he'd buried long ago—in this case, the skeleton of a fifteen-year-old girl. With manacled hands, Smitty carefully cradled the girl's skull as the remains were brought up out of the ground.

Kiss Tomorrow Goodbye

BACK IN HOLLYWOOD, BARBARA PAYTON WAS DEAD. Actually, she'd died in the bathroom of her parents' house in San Diego. She'd just turned thirty-nine. It was like Lenny Bruce the year before—slumped down dead by the toilet.

Meanwhile, the life of young Janis Joplin had swung from ground-zero to landing straight-up midnight in one fast season since she'd slithered onto the Monterey Pop Festival stage. In a tight silver-white body-hugging outfit, she'd stomped her foot hard on the boards the same way old Hank had done, shrieked once loud and long, and from that point on no one who knew what rock was about would ever forget who Janis was.

In her ascent, Janis kicked some holes and others climbed through, thickening the swarm of rock groups since the Beatles. In came tall, thin poet-faced Jim Morrison, with John Densmore, a drummer, and two others calling themselves the Doors. They kicked off at the London Fog, a dumping ground for groups near the Whisky on the Strip. Morrison hadn't really played his hand yet—he was still figuring out what it was. He was hanging around, staying stoned, trying to rifle together some repertoire that would hopefully grab somebody by the balls.

His gangling droop-faced charm caught Ronnie Haran; she even housed Morrison, who had been sleeping in doorways and backseats. When the group was dumped by the London Fog, Ronnie managed to bring them to the Whiskey as an opening group—loosening up the crowd for Buffalo Springfield. It was okay when Morrison wasn't too stoned to stand on his feet.

I can still see him, eye to eye—but was he conscious? His own sack of consciousness was half full of dope, snort, and boozed to the gills. Far out. Zonksville. Micro-poet-cum-bong-headed-showman.

He was different, all right, and it took me a little while to get a fix on this potentially super showman—a kind of daredevil Liberace of the hippie circus, minus the candelabra. The real bummer for Morrison was that he was nuts, or at least a part of him was, like some snapped-in-two electrical line, leaping and sparking and jumping wild.

The quasi-poet in him talked the "black ship of death" while he wallowed in dope and booze with a righteous gusto anyone suicide-prone might envy. He talked about blowing the lid. He said the top of the skull goes off like the lid of a Zippo lighter.

Morrison ached to be a star, a top dog. He wouldn't say it that way, but his lack of force—or *heart*, as Janis called it—held him and the Doors back as a kind of a hazy medallion, an out-of-focus Don Quixote. And there, despite the *Three Penny Opera* black ship of death baloney he battered down into his performances, he'd drag the three others in the group—and usually the audience—on a kind of fanciful, kaleidoscopic roller-ride through his own shallow head trips.

Elvis Presley said to me, "The Doors were good as a group . . . The music was pretty good, but it wasn't rock'n'roll. It wasn't rock, and it wasn't blues. The guy on the drums—that Densmore—he was darn good. He was an artist, man. But Morrison had his own thing going, and maybe it was a product of the times and of the mind-trip-pin' hippie symbolism. But it wasn't rock, and it wasn't going to last."

Morrison's true pain didn't shine through the music. He wanted to suffer—"Without pain there can be no art," he said, and cranked up the watts of his life as he cranked up performance watts. The statement was clearly his own. Wrecking one's life—that was Morrison's bottom-dollar gift, and salutes are due. At wrecking lives, Jim Morrison takes the crown for his singular, outrageous effort. He went at it with a vengeance. No one could top him at laying waste a measure of talent and much opportunity. He was no Elvis, no Beatles. Here was the true sneaky-pete boy-wonder wino with an insatiable thirst for his own finale. Unable to fuse the showman, the musical talent, the good voice or the even the consciousness of an era into being the *star*, Morrison's top-banana persona came laced together with death. "*Real* death," Morrison said, "the experience of transcendence . . ." The real trick was getting out of his own skin.

Janis saw him as a kind of Hollywood loser. "A freak," she said. "He's like the guy sticking knives in himself. If you dig the scene, you go in the tent and that's what you're gettin'. You don't go to a fucking hot-dog stand for a candlelight dinner."

I'd been writing the book on Smitty and the Tucson murders, and a few articles for Art Kunkin's *L.A. Free Press*—practically a one-man operation on Melrose Avenue. After a trip to New York to sell the book, I was back in San Francisco and caught two movies starring Barbara Payton—*Kiss Tomorrow Goodbye,* the Cagney picture, and *Bad Blonde.* Janis Joplin went with me and drank a six-pack as we sat through the films. She'd drop the cans to the floor when she was done, and some of them rolled towards the front of the theater, knocking against the metal legs of the seats.

Janis had said to me, "Hey, man, how's the chick with the swollen heart?" I told her the last I'd heard, the speed freak was dead. Janis said, "Well, nobody probably said she was going to be immortal, you know . . ." Janis dressed in bells and feathers, with a pink boa around her head like a gigantic fluffy halo. It wiggled and wagged as she went, with the bells ringing and clinking against the floozy dress, her feet sparkling in gold shoes with fake jewels that glittered when she stepped into daylight. Sometime that year she'd started rouging her cheeks into two bright balls, as vivid as apples. Janis was now famous.

The Porsche Speedster she sped around in was a hand-painted psychedelic mess of Day-Glo spray paint. She'd wham down on the gas, careening recklessly around other cars, or jamming the brakes so suddenly she'd find herself pressed to the wheel, or the person next to her would be thrown forward from the seat.

Boozed up or shot up with high-grade smack, Janis at times seemed to radiate a euphoria others could only pray for. "I never hold back," she told people with a patronizing smile. "I'm always on the outer limits of probability." She looked a little like Phyllis Diller used to look, and she wouldn't believe we hadn't slept together in North Beach those few years back. "Why not?" she asked. "What happened— what'd we do instead?"

"We didn't do anything," I said. "We just hung around." This conversation took place in my high-performance Camaro, driving downtown past the Gate Theater. I glanced to the right and saw long-haired Sam Andrew, a member of her band, walking in the direction we were heading. I said, "There's Sam . . ." Janis said it wasn't him. I said, "Sure it is!" She insisted that it wasn't Sam, though he looked over as we drove past and raised his hand as if to wave or call us to a stop. But Janis turned her back to the passenger side and said again it wasn't Sam. And even if it was, she said, she had no interest in looking at someone who'd burn someone else out of their dope.

"Dope is sweet," she'd said, "dope is right, and when you get the right dope, you can be sitting pretty sweet . . ."

Dope was everything. It was everywhere, and everyone was trying to get higher. I kept my mouth shut. I couldn't hack the dope, but held the position that people were going to do what they wanted to do, and preferably without any feedback from anyone else. I was sure I still had a lot of Owsley acid drifting around somewhere in my nerves like space dust floating in and out, though I'd never had a bum trip— even that last one, boosting for two days or more and just maxing out. The high was like blowing up a balloon to its fullest, maybe stretching it a little beyond the bursting point. There wasn't anywhere else to go. I thought I'd probably never even smoke a joint again if someone offered it.

Janis did, but I said I'd pass. She was smoking pot in a small pipe— it had a weird smell, and I kept my window down. She said I was wasting a hell of a high. I said I was fine, that I'd been half-crocked since getting to the Bay Area two days before the campus riots. Since those earlier post-beat, pre-hippie North Beach days, I'd thought about Janis from time to time, and I'd ask after her, contacting Dick Warren and a couple of the others who'd hung around back then. One of them, who had wanted me to whip out a scenario for some Kerouac kind of story, said he'd been the last to party with her before she headed out for New York. "I'd wanted to screw her, but she was shacking with that spade chick and talking about another chick she was going to ball in the Village, so we got high instead—some sort of mushroom shit she'd scored that I had to have pumped out my stomach."

Dick said he'd stopped by Chip's one night, going in through the back porch, and found them in the sack, "Chip's legs around Janis's neck, and Janis all bunched up and going at her like crazy . . ."

Chip had told him she and Janis were in love. "Then Janis split," Dick said, and we didn't know where she'd gone until she wrote a bunch of letters from New York, all sent at the same time for some reason, like you'd write two or three letters to someone and mail them all in separate envelopes." He believed she'd wound up on the street back East and started "trying the hooker number." Next he heard, Dick said, was she'd gone back to Port Arthur—rescued by her folks. "Off the dope and going straight, and through with the blues."

She'd started seeing a shrink and returned to college in Beaumont, Texas and was even singing in the church. Until the following year, when "that old lonesome whistle" Hank had sung about started blowing again.

Through a hodgepodge of cobbled-together connections, Janis was back in Frisco. Only the blues now were thrown to pitches way beyond what she'd known—amplified music, now jacked up and called "psychedelic rock." "It's what the dropouts listen to," Dick said, "when their heads are opened by the raunchy dope, and John, Paul, George and Ringo . . ."

Not that he was faulting the scene too seriously, he said, "Because there's nothing serious about it. There's nothing new here. It's just dope. The whole movement, as they call it, is just plain bad dope. Tune in and turn on and drop out and get high and suck flowers and everything's *dope*. They're trying to call it something, some counter-cultural bullshit, but the whole thing's dope and scoring and bad fucking music. And no matter how loud Janis is singing now, it all derives from some of yesterday's solid talent. What we've got fucking up the city here is a bunch of howdy-doody airheads pumped up with chicken dope. All it's producing is a bunch of psychopaths. A good fix would kill 'em, and we could get the streets swept off . . ."

The same month Janis hit the big time at the Monterey Pop Festival, a microbus of hippies lost control of their VW, lunged over the curb and onto the sidewalk of Page Street near the Panhandle, running down Dick Warren and a black musician named Kettle, who suffered a broken leg and shoulder. Dick was not as lucky. He was pinned under the bus when the hippie driver got out and knelt down. "Man, I didn't see the street," he said. "Which way is it to the Oakland

Bridge, man?"

Dick's spine was injured, and he lost the use of his legs. The hippie was the son of a Salt Lake City heart surgeon, and while Dick was permanently confined to a wheelchair, he was financially set for the rest of his life. By '69, though, when I was running around town with Janis, Dick had already lost one leg—amputated—and was in the hospital for an operation on the other one. I called and went to see him, but I didn't go in right away. I stayed out in the corridor looking into the ward through the porthole-like glass in the door. I could see Dick in the bed spraying himself with something out of a can he kept shaking, and just staring out the window.

He told me he was off junk, but shooting a lot of morphine. He said "It's legitimate—for the pain." He was having a car custom-built so he could get around, and he was getting married to a Korean woman. He'd become a Buddhist, he said, and he also said there had been a retroactive clause in the insurance settlement from the accident. "As soon as they took off that leg, it was like the joker's on the slot machine. A whole row of even faces—all grinning, man. I'm buying a house in Sausalito." He said if they had to take the other leg, it'd be another jackpot. He said, "I don't need the bread now, but I don't care if they take it off. It's just in the way—won't support the weight of your hat . . . And I'm going to be a father like you," he said. "We're going to have a kid. She's four months pregnant. Nothing wrong in that department."

He talked about Janis—how much money she was making, and about the Japanese doll she'd sent him. "It's about a yard high," he said. Before he got off smack, he was seeing her around, and he said he'd met his wife-to-be through a girl named Peggy, "one of Janis's girlfriends," he said. "Not that my girl's a queer. She was doing some stuff in a shop this Peggy runs in the Haight."

A nurse came in and gave him a shot, and when she walked away he grinned and said, "It's like living on a cloud these days . . ."

The hippie microbus driver? "He aced himself," Dick said, "not even a year after he wrecked me. It wasn't guilt—it wasn't anything related to my problems. I don't think a hippie's got enough sensitivity to understand guilt, or any sort of overview of life. He ate poison. Some of the airheads shacking with him said they thought he was doing acid. Some spirit, or maybe something living underneath the sink, said he should eat the stuff in the box with the little picture of the pirate's flag on it . . ."

He said there were all kinds of holes burned through the kid's upper insides. "It took him three days to die," Dick said, smiling.

Dick had read my articles on Charles Schmid and Tucson, before I'd gotten F. Lee Bailey into the case, and Dick wanted to see if I now thought the guy was worth keeping alive. I said I didn't think he was, and that I had nothing against executing him. He said, "So you're for the hot seat now?"

I said I wasn't sure. Once I'd finished the game with Smitty, I knew I'd never be able to look into those eyes again. I'd learned that Smitty would replay the mental pictures of the murders he'd committed, over and over. Outwardly, he was like some zombie unable to see the humanity in another. Inwardly, Smitty would shift his focus to his imagined worth and power—viewing himself on spiritual plane few could appreciate let alone understand.

I remembered Richie Bruns talking to me in Johnnie's Fat Boy Drive-in not long after Smitty had led the law to the buried girl's skeleton. The sun was setting, and the red light was pouring into the restaurant and across the table where we sat. Richie said, "I don't want you to get the wrong idea about what I think about Smitty. Everything he did was all right with me. I don't fault him for what he did. I just didn't want my personal neck in the same noose. But what Smitty did was okay in my book . . ."

Like Charlie Manson a little later, and his crew of dope-spaced hippies who called themselves the "Family," Smitty would beat the death sentences by a national moratorium imposed on capital punishment. Most of them would enjoy a certain notoriety, even luxuriate in it, contracting for personal comforts, education, redemption by religion, and even marriage with the possibility of eventual freedom.

But Smitty would pay the piper a few years later; he was murdered in prison. Two other convicts took him down for reasons unrelated to his own crimes, stabbing him repeatedly in the body and eye. Tough as he was, it took Smitty several days to die. He'd hang in constant agony, like the kid who had run over Dick, then swallowed the poison.

Not so Charlie Manson, Susan Atkins and the rest of that grungy flock. Another prisoner would attempt to set Manson on fire, but without much success; Charlie would suffer only minimal discomforts.

Low-budget producer Robert Levy, like a quarterback unable to run the touchdown with the ball in his hands and a clear scrimmage ahead, failed to nail down financing for the several movie projects we'd developed. When Manson and Family hit the news, an attorney poker pal advised Levy to get in on the ground floor—sew up a deal with Manson while the handcuffs were still cold, getting a script on the murders of Sharon Tate and the others, and selling the package.

Though Los Angeles held warrants for Manson on the several murders, Charlie was still in custody in the desert town of Independence, north of L.A., being tried for the destruction of County property—charges stemming from his Death Valley hideout days. Levy and I drove to the desert, and while his attorney pal set up a meeting with Charlie, I talked to two of the Family girls not in custody at the time—Lynnette "Squeaky" Fromme and a blonde named Sandra Goode. Both hippie girls were wandering around the little town looking for handouts and "a tent or chicken coop" to shelter the two babies they were hauling around with them. Sandra said the one in her arms was Manson's "own" —by blood, she said. "We're all one with Charlie." These two girls were like voodoo dolls hand-crafted by their hero with Charlie breathing his "infinite spirit" through both of them. The breath, according to Lynnette Fromme, issued directly from Jesus Christ, who was Charlie— as were the Devil, Buddha, Mahatma Gandhi and the souls of their dozen or more victims, including coffee heiress Abigail Folger and the beautiful actress Sharon Tate, wife of director Roman Polanski, the father of the unborn baby son Sharon was carrying to term at the time she was repeatedly stabbed to death.

The one responsible for the frenzied knifing and cutting of Sharon Tate was Manson's self-proclaimed soul-mate—sick, sad, air-head Susan Atkins. But like Smitty's best pal, Richie Bruns, Atkins was also the one who did the ratting—not to save her own neck, as did Richie, but to take credit for the blood bath and to share the "glory" with Charlie and the others who could be convicted of the murders.

It was the same Lawrence Schiller who'd been trying to get something going with Smitty who sold the Susan Atkins story. Schiller's "checkbook journalism," as it was called by the media, never delved too far beyond the gloss—like his half-naked photographs of Marilyn Monroe not long before her death.

"Wild with a kind of sex energy" after plunging the knife in and out of actress Sharon Tate, Susan Atkins said she tasted the victim's blood and wanted to cut the baby from the womb. She wanted to take it to Charlie, to be raised as "a warrior and one of our own." Or the baby could have been sacrificed, Susan later said, skewered and eaten as "warriors eat the hearts of enemies slain in battle . . ." The Mansonites didn't know their victims, but chose at random the houses they would sneak into. They liked to espouse the "enemy" idea since it provided a broader "understanding" of the purposes of the killings, when in fact the core reasons were peculiar to Manson, and Manson alone. He simply had his dope-wasted stragglers and would-be hippies do his dirty work.

Bright-eyed and lust-ignited before finding religion in jail, Atkins confessed a desire to taste the unborn's kidneys and liver, but there had not been time to cut the baby out of the dead mother. "There were still two others we had yet to finish off," Susan explained. "They weren't dead yet, and there wasn't time to open her up and get the baby out, though my intentions had been in line with Charlie's wishes—to drink the blood of the unborn child."

Battle lines had been defined by the Beatles, "right in the *White Album*," said Charlie, and the messages were clear. Once he was brought to L.A. to stand trial for the murders, Levy and I began to gather together Manson's story—directly from Charlie. Strangely, the more time Levy spent with Manson, the more the producer seemed to pull back from chasing the movie possibility. He began to find himself more and more involved—not in believing Charlie's spiel, but in understanding something about the so-called cult leader, and it was this "meeting of minds" that was changing Levy. When then-president Richard Nixon said he believed Manson to be "guilty," prior to the verdicts, Levy went on a bandwagon in a last-ditch attempt to clinch a movie deal—he was on the front pages of the L.A. papers, milking Nixon's blunder for all it was worth. He'd managed to find a trailer for Squeaky Fromme and Sandra Goode, "because of the babies." He said to me, "Those babies are the only innocent ones. God help them."

Matthew Katz, who managed the Jefferson Airplane, was handling the Tucson book for me and negotiating with Doubleday for its publication. He'd been involved with Fred Gorner's book about trying to find where Amelia Earhart's plane went down. Katz was in San Francisco with the Airplane, and we were going to meet at a Russian restaurant. Grace Slick was supposed to catch up with us there.

Janis showed up—she was all tensed up and bunched up, and she didn't like Katz, though, oddly, Katz seemed to feel that she did. We were an odd group, a loose gathering of bodies moving from one watering hole to another.

Grace Slick was interested in some of the songs Charles Schmid was writing, and with the killers' "notoriety," Katz believed some money could be made. Janis only liked one of the songs—about "rattlesnake hearts and candy kisses." She said she'd do the music for it. Later she sang the lyrics cold, making up music as she read, and then she sang it again and the music sounded as though she'd recorded it. She said, "That's how it should be . . ." It was possible, she said, if he didn't get the gas, he'd make a mint on the "rattlesnake heart" song and pay his lawyer to juggle appeals.

Janis liked what I told her about the house slippers Percy Foreman's wife wore, all covered with diamonds and gold. Foreman had told me how clients gave him their diamond engagement and wedding rings—to cover legal expenses—and his wife sewed them all over her house-slippers, in which she shuffled around their Texas mansion. He also took in washing machines and refrigerators, automobiles, and even lawn mowers and table saws.

We had a discussion about Janis's feet, her black toenail polish, and whether we were going to go to bed or not. I looked at her wrists and her hands, then bent my head down and kissed her on the back of one hand. She turned her hand over and I put my lips into her palm, then kissed the palm of her other hand. She shivered.

She asked me if I liked her breasts, and I said I did. She wanted to know if she should make them bigger, "shoot them full of shit and make them stick way out?"

Sex with her was more mental than physical, but draining—and at moments, confusing. She pushed herself through it, and I don't know what she got out of it. There was a wildness and sloppy abandon. Then she dropped right into unconsciousness, her breathing quick and shallow. Once I checked her pulse because I thought she was dead.

The "trance" over, she was ready to go. She had friends in bars across the Bay, and we hung out in these, drinking, shooting pool in one bar and joking about the singer Johnny Ace. She sang pieces of his song "Pledging My Love" and said, "I'm gonna play Johnny Ace," and put her hand to her head, one finger to her temple, thumb cocked like a pistol hammer, "Bang! Bang!"

I said Johnny had only had one bang, and she said, "But he really had only one song, too . . ." She shot up in the restroom of one bar, and was bleeding from the nose when she came out. The next day we ran into a guy she knew named Carlie, and the three of us went back into Frisco for more drinks at a bar near Fort Mason. I think she shot up again in that place—"boosting," Carlie called it. We'd been eating pretzels and those pickled things that are kept in big jars behind the bar, so we went over to Tommy's Joynt for buffalo stew and wine, and from there—at Carlie's invitation—to a showing at a downtown art gallery. Janis put on more rouge, and her face was shining and swollen, and her nose kept bleeding. At one point, a rush of bloody mucus ran from her nostrils. With the rouge, she looked a demented clown.

The art show consisted of tubes of light or neon running at angles, and Janis said loudly, "This is weird. What the shit is this? Looks like someone's fucking plumbing!"

Heading back, she leaned against me and said, "You need a taste, sweetie, to get where I'm goin' . . ." I said no, it was okay, I was stoned enough. She said, "You won't love me any less if I do, will you? Will you promise that? Will you tell me that and make it a promise?"

After a while, when Carlie was gone, Janis just sat glassy-eyed on the bed looking through the Yellow Pages while I made some calls.

Back in Hollywood, Dennis Hopper still had my script, *Breaking Hard,* which he was trying to buy from me in order to direct the picture himself. But he was running into problems because the studio he was after wouldn't involve themselves in footage legally tied to David Lee and Dagwood. After some legal wrangling, Technicolor seemed tied into it somewhere, and yet without that footage coming gratis with the script; the studio wasn't about to finance the project. Dennis said the chances were slim on the surfing script, but what else did I have cooking?

He and Jane Fonda's younger brother, Peter, had a fair shot at a deal, he told me. They'd become partners since working together on *The Trip.* I said we could get together and talk as soon as I'd cleared certain legal disputes concerning a treatment I'd just written for actor George McCready's son, and the title belonged to me. We arranged to meet at a restaurant on La Cienega by a theater. Dennis showed up with a painter friend, and with me was my wife, Cecilia, and my pal and gofer, Ward Bagger.

The treatment for McCready's son was for a feature called *Out Takes,* about two buddies who score big on a cocaine deal and head out for New Orleans on motorcycles—riding abreast on the highways as I'd once ridden with Jimmy Dean. I even had a scene in the story with them touching hands at seventy miles an hour. The two guys in the story get hooked into a lot of freaky action—ideas I'd noted down on my New Orleans expedition. Mirroring what I'd written in *Naked City* a few years before, they encounter a guy with a shotgun. In *Out Takes,* it's Errol Flynn's "grim reaper" that's tracking them, littering the roadways with reminders of death. At the end, the guys lose the bikes outside a whorehouse in the French Quarter, wind up stealing a '59 Cadillac convertible, and chance to cross paths with death on an otherwise deserted highway. Both heroes get blown away by the shotgun blasts of a total stranger.

The original title had been *Hot Wire,* and when George McCready's son lost his backing, the story came back to me. Dennis's brother-in-law Bill Heyward, was also scouting ideas for a possible deal Peter and Dennis might swing through Roger Corman, who had let Dennis direct some second-unit work on *The Trip.*

Dennis thought *Out Takes* was a great idea and agreed to take it to Peter. Together they'd push it with American International Pictures, and if they got a green light, they'd have me do the script and Dennis would direct it. If I didn't do the script, I'd get paid for the story and credited accordingly.

It sounded good. I said sure. Like Jean Seberg, Dennis said, "We'll make a picture together yet . . ."

I didn't hear from him for a while, and only after I went to Brooke to get back the surfing script did Dennis tell me that he couldn't get the deal through AIP and therefore wouldn't be using the biker story. He said they were developing some idea Peter had come up with under the working title *Riding Easy*—a play on my title *Breaking Hard*—about two guys who score big on a cocaine deal and ride bikes across country to New Orleans "in search of America," only to find it in both barrels of a redneck's shot gun. That was my basic story—*Out Takes*—just as I'd outlined it for Dennis, although I hadn't written the part Nicholson would finally play—the juiced-up Southern lawyer. But the story line was there, and I wanted my end of the deal.

They said they couldn't get the financing from AIP, and both Dennis and Brooke claimed the deal was dead. But to lend some credibility to the project— to make it seem like something other than just another low-budget Peter Fonda bike movie, Dennis and Fonda hired in a writer, Terry Southern to whip up a short, revised treatment. They began to shop around for a deal with someone who'd let Dennis direct the picture, as well as star in it with Peter. But nobody seemed willing to let Dennis direct a movie, no matter how low the budget.

Jack Nicholson didn't have a part in any picture at the time. He'd written a movie called *Head,* featuring the Monkees, and desperately wanted to bail out of acting and do some serious screenwriting. I tried to get Jack a job with Levy's Pebble Productions, and although the work looked promising, he took off to play a part in Dennis and Peter's movie once they had finally found the money to make it.

"I didn't know you'd had anything to do with that story in the initial stages of it," Jack later told me. "Reading what you wrote and seeing how the picture came out—well, they owed you. There is no question in my mind." The question was not, it seemed to Jack, how could Dennis have done that—but why?

A red-headed girl who knew Ronnie Haran came to me and said Jim Morrison wanted to talk to me. I asked what about, and she said, "The clothes James Dean was wearing when he got killed in the Porsche."

Again it was James Dean, as if I toted around some talisman that could be stroked by the true devotee. Morrison was now approaching me as if to share some of the secrets all bundled up in his jumbled metaphors and poses. I couldn't get to know him—the brief jump-start occasions were too quick, too explosively engaged, though I didn't think that made much difference, as each moment of Morrison showed the whole of him.

I told him I didn't know what had happened to Dean's clothes. He'd been taken him to a hospital in Paso Robles after the accident, already dead. The body had been claimed by Dean's father and removed for transport to Indiana.

Morrison said he'd been told the clothes, torn and bloody, had not been claimed along with the other effects belonging to Dean. The clothes had been part of the investigation and when it was over, the clothes had been left behind to be destroyed. Morrison said he believed Dean's clothes were removed from the hospital by a technician, then passed to someone at Warner Brothers. From there—who knows?

"The same thing with the wrecked Porsche," Morrison said, alluding to its strange disappearance after being exhibited across the country. He wanted to make a film, and the clothes Dean died in were to play an important part. "There's a question about James Dean's premonitions of an early death," he said, "like he knew it would happen, and when it would happen."

I said I wasn't sure that Dean had really known that. Morrison believed he had. "He tapped a source where all the answers lie," he said. "This source is an almanac, man. You turn to the page you want, and the answer is yours."

I said I'd like to see such an almanac, and he said it wasn't a matter of sight. I said, "You've looked into this yourself?"

"The way the blind man sees," he said. "You know, I won't see thirty. I'll be dead before I'll reach thirty years of age." After our meeting, he told the redhead I'd spooked him. "He says there's death looking out of your eyes," she said. " But he doesn't mean *you're* death, man." Morrison had said he was looking at the death in himself, as if in my eyes there were mirrors into which he saw his own death looking back at him, like it was saying, "You ain't getting away, man. I'm keeping on your ass." She said, "He wants to talk to you, but says he'll have to do it like with a screen between you and him, or he'll use a towel—you know, hold a towel over his face so no ghosts get into you and are looking back at him."

Next time I saw Morrison he was totally wasted. He'd drunk a bottle of scotch, smoked a bowl of grass and dropped enough pills to weight a shark line. But it was the Owsley acid he was after.

I had a stock in the freezer compartment of the pad in Silver Lake, and I'd been dropping acid every day for two months. I'd finished building the bike—a Harley chopper that started with a '52 rigid frame and a '54 transmission. I'd bought a brand new FLH engine and had been getting high and riding. I'd never had a bad trip on the acid. Some did. I'd even boost before coming down, and once I dropped three times past the boost just to see how high I could get.

Some nights I'd cruise the Hollywood Hills, or down to a hotdog stand, where I'd drink coffee and smoke and look at the million lights playing over the chrome and the glistening black enamel. Or ride—being a bird in the wind along Pacific Coast Highway, flying with the moon over the ocean. Three-hundred-million moons moving on the black water. Earlier rides would come through my head. Remembering

Jimmy—a long time in the wind.

I didn't boost on the rides because of the delay in escalation. I'd head north up the grapevine and eat a steak at the top of the hill on the way to Bakersfield. Old Highway 99 held a few dark stretches where I could open the bike and let it roll straight wide open. But sometimes, at close to a hundred miles per hour, the springer front end would start vibrating and jumping, and I'd have to slow down or go airborne. Coasting easy was the best, like Jesus Christ was right behind me on the pillion pad and I could stick out my elbows and feel His knee caps.

I'd gone as high as I could go—never sleeping, never closing my eyes unless I wanted to boogie on the pretty lights. My back had been pressed to the ceiling of how high I could get, and I'd been looking down on a world from something like a satellite, my arms and legs hanging down into infinity. It was a world not like the green earth, but like an eternal spark—like a finger painting by Michelangelo none of this in visual terms, but as sensations in the brain. I had to read them through signals, or like feeling Braille with some sixth sense.

I gave the last of the Owsley stash to the redhead, who I suppose passed it over to Morrison, a substitute for Dean's death clothes. By then the Doors were going big time, but you couldn't pin Morrison to commercial success. He faked not giving a shit, and sang about killing his father and fucking his mother. The real part of him was too weird and strung out and desperate. Suicidal stunts and pranks—ledge walking, body throwing, jumping out of windows and waving his dick around . . . all of it showier than a solitary game of Russian roulette. Jumping out of a window wasn't the way he'd go, he said. He'd seen his time in the almanac. It was a secret, he said.

The thread of his music, Morrison claimed, was an opening of consciousness in the vein of Artaud. But his closeness to Artaud was perhaps the crystallizing of an aspiring imitator via self-crucifixion. It wasn't the music that was making a dent—it was Morrison himself, not the performer or the self-styled poet, but the one who was wrecking his life. His rush of unconventionality led him into center stage for a brief strut in the spotlight.

It wasn't the fame he chased, but the idea of himself as a bullet ricocheting through his own insides, tearing away inside in high profile, breaking himself into many pieces, like blasting open a keg to let the goods blow out. He went into a variable reality in which he saw himself as a forerunner shooting through a universe, daring others to follow. He had a fix on what it was Jimmy Dean had been driven by; and what Rimbaud's craziness was all about. Morrison was chasing that element that made them who they were, and made them know they had to smash themselves apart and let the "other" one out.

BLOODLETTING

FACING CHARLIE MANSON WAS LIKE WATCHING a caged inmate in a nut house. *Watching*, because you didn't really have an exchange with Manson. You were the target, appreciative or otherwise, for a gamut of histrionics that would have dumbfounded Sigmund Freud. Charlie *looked* nuts. Most of what he said sounded nuts. I'd seen the scam before, and for a guy who'd spent most of his life locked up in any number of cages—most of it unwarranted and without provocation on his part—the guy had the shuck down to a first-rate act. Basically, he seemed like an *Amboy Dukes*-type hood off any East Coast street corner, but Manson had given it a twist by turning hippie at a highly opportune time—getting in at a run. Free-love air-head teenyboppers and doped-out girls jumping up and down on anyone who asked for it was the sort of easy challenge Charlie was after, the line of least resistance. As a very short, ugly little man, Charlie wasn't hot on resistance. He said he liked the back-door way of life, and could always get in through a back-door, no matter whose house it was.

Like Smitty before him, Charlie wanted to be a star. He sang and played guitar. He made up songs and dreamed of himself in the spotlight. He talked and talked at these L.A. jail meetings, often stressing what

236

he said with grotesque, rubbery expressions that made him look like a monster. To give his ricocheting mental aberrations a little religious zing, he'd mouth half of what he'd say in cryptic parables—philosophical mumbo-jumbo intended to elevate his wisdom in the listener's ears. It did nothing more than clog like wax. You had to already be susceptible to the sort of seeds he was planting in your head. You had to have shed who you were via tripping, or institutionalization, or some other source of personal misfortune. "Empty yourself," he'd say, so you could be filled with Charlie. And if you could be filled with Charlie, then you would do Charlie's bidding. That was the scam—that's how it worked.

If he couldn't be a star, then what he wanted, simply, was to be king of his own mountain, of his own stage, and to wreak small havoc—small like himself, but sufficient to set the world on its ear. For a man who'd been beaten, raped, tormented, twisted and abused most of his life, it was time to give them a little dose of their own medicine. There was nothing in "society" for Charlie. Like a dog that's whipped and chained and learned only the whip and the chain, there wasn't even a yearning to be free. There was only the whip and the chain.

Cut loose from prison—an alternative he dreaded and fought against—Charlie was dumped into society, a desperate, isolated vagabond waiting to be kicked around. All that he knew was pain and torment, and that's what he expected. Beneath the flowering facade of the new "counterculture" of hippies and light shows, Charlie found the unexpected. Unfazed by the rhetoric of freedom babbled by Timothy Leary and Ken Kesey and Allen Ginsberg and the clot of literary and scholarly has-beens looking for notoriety, Charlie saw with clear eyes, *new* eyes, accustomed to a wall, a basin, a cot and someone with a stick.

"It was nothing but a joke," Charlie would say later. "These people on the street were like me—thrown out of life, like your paper coffee cups and hamburger sacks and rags and stinking Kotex pads and old rubbers. They were garbage, floating around garbage and shit and stuff that sticks to the sides of your toilet. That's what they were doing as hippies—floating-around like orange peelings, sinking to the bottom like rotten garbage. Food for the fucking sharks and barracudas.

"I can use garbage," Charlie told me, "I can use your old tires and tin cans, and I can go out in your deserts and make use of all the junkyard, and so I took these people that were garbage, that'd been thrown away by society to all stick together like scum, and I put them to use—

237

I made them put water in cans and make things work in order to keep living on the outside . . . The biggest joke is I never wanted to be on the outside. You put me on the outside, and whatever's gone down is what you created—that is *your* reality."

He later put together a book in prison—supposedly in his own words, though written by another inmate—in which he portrays himself as killing a black man. "Charlie was all mouth," said one of the Family members closest to Manson. "He never killed anybody. When it came down to letting blood, the most he could do was cut off your ear or your hand. He couldn't cut off a head anymore than he could pull a trigger and point-blank lay you out . . .

"But he *knew*, man, he knew who *could* do it—he could smell it in you, like you had a disease and it was sticking on you. He knew even though you didn't know what you were capable of doing yourself. He put the guns and the knives and rope in our hands and said, 'Over there, you go over there and do it,' and we all went over there and did it. He didn't even watch it, but stayed home rockin' and day dreamin' like some old Aunt Jemima, or someone's grandma waiting for the chil'run to come on home and wash up for supper . . .'"

He wanted to kill the hot-shots. He wanted to *hurt* people who had fame and fortune and what the rest of the world imagined as the good life—the life of which Charlie had always been deprived, before he even knew there was a life beyond the chains and the rapings and the beatings. "He picked out certain people to be put to death like you'd figure out a Christmas list," the Family member said. "He picked people everyone sees as heroes—Steve McQueen, and Frank Sinatra—Tom *Jones,* for God's sake, and Elizabeth Taylor, and broads like that, that everybody adores. That's how you put the fear into people—you butcher what they dream of being. These are all the gilded replicas of fame and happiness, and when you smash them you can go right into the heart of the dark . . ."

McQueen claimed he started carrying a gun when he got word of Manson's hit list, but he'd been toting the weapon long before Manson launched his attack against society. Divorced from his first wife, Neile—though continuing to see her on the sly—he married his second wife, actress Ali McGraw. He'd said, "She thinks I'm cheese on the mountain, and I am." But by then he was heavily into dope and becoming increasingly paranoid, suffering desperate frustrations over failing to "break through the gilded image" into the realm of authentic and lasting achievement. He believed that he'd become nothing but a shell.

Twice I saw Ali McGraw with McQueen, and she seemed subdued, almost shriveled in his presence, the kind of wife who takes a quiet, daily battering. I felt she was hiding an essential part of herself. She couldn't be who she was. She had to be some decor to drape over the shell of McQueen, like you'd dress a dummy in a window. There was no room for individuality. You took your beating and licked your wounds on your own time, not on Steve's.

The second time I saw McGraw with McQueen was at a party. She was laughing, faking hilarity with glassed-over eyes. Again, McQueen's furtive glance sought me out and held me for a few seconds—not so much riveting as sneaky, as though he was a crook and I was some cop on his tail. He knew I had something on him—something worse than murder—and the hatred cooking just beneath his gaze was apparent.

I'd never see him without that same look on his face, as when his drunken mother was falling down in Louis' bar, grabbing at the legs of some guy while Steve ran away—a face full of dread, as if his guts were dropping out.

I felt sorry for Ali McGraw, prisoner for whatever reason to Steve, a fixture on his quivering one-man bandwagon. The hold was there, as it had been with Neile, and with Gena. He wouldn't let them go, and none of them would be free until he was dead.

So he started carrying the gun. He'd flash it around to impress the women, but knew it wasn't really for protection, or for firing at anyone, other than himself. When the time came around, he'd be prepared. He liked to threaten others, point the gun at them, but for McQueen death was already on its way, whether or not he was ready for it, and no matter how much dope he sucked in to kill the pain.

Neither was there any limit to the dope consumed by Dennis Hopper following his debut as director. The picture they called *Easy Rider* was released and making money, and now Dennis could reach for the ultimate high. He could max out selling his share of the movie— go for broke. Like Janis, realizing that the high was king, more important than career or commitment, Dennis wound up in Taos, New Mexico, pretending to be a kind of real-time extension of the *Easy Rider* movie. He bought the old house of Mable Luhan Dodge and threw open the door, creating his own free-for-all hippie gallery dope pad.

Over in Hollywood, a few were wondering about his dabbling with homosexuals while freely chasing the dope and booze. He'd make long distance calls to a scurrilous, gay Hollywood tabloid newsman who wrote about the sizes of the stars' cocks. Dennis would drone on about sex and Willy Nelson—playing Nelson's "Shotgun Willy" over and over, refusing to answer questions about my involvement in the movie he'd made. His marriage to Brooke had collapsed long ago, as had a second marriage, and all the roadside art and pop art he'd bought with Brooke's money was gone, as was the money he'd swilled away on dope and booze. Some estimates put the amount at a cool million— and all that he owed me was $750 for a story idea, and a credit.

During his intense chumminess with Taos gay blades, Dennis still wore the grungy costume he'd worn in the movie, and quickly—as when you boil a pig in scalding water—whatever bristle he'd had in the old days began to fall away. He'd roam about naked, lurking in hallways or passing out in the bushes. According to the Hollywood reporter, he'd been frightened of the impulses and actions he'd confided to the Hollywood scandal sheet and, by way of distraction, tried throwing himself into a variety of radical causes—anti-war happenings, Jane Fonda's get-togethers and gab-fests—but few were interested in Dennis's dope-spaced self-indulgences. One activist said, "He'd just show up and hang around and make stupid remarks. I believed his fucking mind was gone, if he ever had one to start with."

They thought he was an asshole, a stumbling stooge to some impotent, misguided romanticism. He clung to that as a kind of life line, unlike Nick Adams, another actor from *Rebel Without a Cause*, who'd coasted into television fame as Johnny Yuma on a show delib- erately called *The Rebel*. Sooner than later, Nick's failures got the best of him. Some attempts at self-mutilation and a rumored run at castra- tion, then he cashed it in with a bottle of pills.

But the compulsion for fame had Dennis by the gonads. His careen- ing through the crazies brought him to desperation: He'd outdo what was being done. He'd be on top again or he'd be "fucking dead."

Dead was a good place to go as long you went out with a bang, like Jimmy had done. No T.S. Eliot whimpers for Dennis. Rather than a clean suicide like Nick Adams, he'd blow himself sky high.

He quickly got the idea of exploding himself in a kind of dynamite chair. Happenings and performance art shows were everywhere the big thing, and Dennis was still determined not to be swept beneath the rug. He learned that dynamite blows outward, creating a vacuum like the eye of a hurricane. If one could place oneself somehow in that eye, the explosion—blasting outward—would leave him intact. That is, if everything went smoothly. Some small oversight or mishap and one *could* be blown to bits.

With his "Russian suicide chair," Dennis hung around auto races and speedways trying to gather a crowd to watch him blow himself up. He got some attention, some free dope on occasion, and got laid with a couple of girls hanging around the speedways. But he didn't blow himself up, as hard as he tried. Nor did anyone hire him to put him into a movie. He began to lose his mind.

Voices obsessed him. He heard them talking about torture and death. Alcoholism and drug abuse had taken their toll: Dennis the Menace was going crazy. After some time in and out of psychiatric wards, his juice gone but his brain cooling down, Dennis was pandering to Hollywood with hat in hand, promising to be good.

Afraid of going down like Barbara Payton, he'd give them the soul along with the body. Following *Blue Velvet*, he promised to behave— he'd wear suits, dress proper. He'd give interviews and eat salads and play golf, dovetailing his lobotomized Mr. Nice Guy behavior into a run of mediocre acting roles nobody would remember.

Dennis the Menace had died, shrieking somewhere down the corridor of some loony ward, shrugged off like a snake's skin to blow away in the wind. He wouldn't cause any more trouble, and the new Dennis wouldn't feel any more pain—it was simple logic.

Not so with another *Rebel Without a Cause* alumnus, Sal Mineo, who said memories of James Dean "keep coming as though they're really happening now, in the present, and this isn't going to settle until something drastic happens to me, or until I'm able to clear myself by setting something straight . . ." But he didn't know what it was, and he didn't know how he could do it. In the meantime, "boy wonder" Sal Mineo wasn't surviving but he wasn't going to "give up the ship or compromise."

I'd just written another quickie for another cheap producer about a detective who called himself "The Flea." The producer had Jayne Mansfield on tap, and we met her for lunch in a Beverly Hills deli. Mansfield was limping from some kind of fall, and seemed to be in pain. When the producer left the table to use the phone, Jayne said to me, "This is a terrible man. He's one of the worst people I've ever met . . . Not to mention he has terrible body odor."

"You want to *do* this picture?" I asked her.

"I need the work, she said. "What about you?"

"I need the money," I said.

"Is it possible to make something good out of this?"

"Oh, I don't know," I said. "That might be stretching it."

She said she had ideas for a "decent picture" that would take her off the road and put her back in the spotlight. She said, "I've talked them over with this character, and he's willing to give it a try." It was always a gamble, she said, but she feared that she didn't have anything to lose.

I felt sorry for Jayne. Despite her alleged high IQ, there was something so sorrowful about her, and so uninformed. She had a low-grade sense of humor; she laughed at outhouse jokes and thought she was really beautiful when there was something almost obscene and grotesque about her as time wore on. She was like a sad child walking on the edge of a steep wall in her mother's high heels.

I met two other business associates of Jayne's. One was drunk and the other was carrying two fifths of vodka in a briefcase. The one that was drunk was supposed to be a publicity agent. Jayne didn't cut the vodka—just floated a couple of ice cubes. We talked about *The Flea*, but whatever ideas Jayne had discussed with the producer seemed to get shuffled into the haze of drinking away the afternoons. After a couple of glasses, when she managed to spill a full drink down the front of her denim shirt, and she took it off to let it dry on the terrace of the office. She then continued talking while she sat in her wet brassiere with a bunch of paper towels wadded over her chest.

At one point, while I was sitting there staring at the mounds of white on her chest sticking out over the table, she said, "They've grown bigger. It has to do with physical improvement." We talked about the story for awhile, then she said, "But my hips are the same. I've gained a little in the waist, but not in the hips . . ."

She was dead that same year, killed in an auto wreck that decapitated her.

Though I'd been paid through a draft of *The Flea* script, and had been able to develop a kind of rapport with Jayne, the movie was dumped following her death. But I loaned Sal Mineo enough to pay his rent. He'd been getting evicted and was skipping out in the middle of the night. I said, "Man, I know that shot—my wife and I did it with the baby, snuck out of Frisco with two days of pancake batter in the baby's stomach."

What money Sal did earn on a bit part here or there was funneled into dope. Everything else was gone. He said he thought a lot about suicide, but was too "chicken to do it" himself. He said, "I'm looking for the fast combination, the one that'll do it for me."

He conveyed to me that it was vitally urgent that we be in "deep" communication, "an almost spiritual situation," and the talk we were to have had in New York so long ago unfolded over the next few weeks. He had landed the lead in *The Gene Krupa Story*, and Jean Seberg was up to co-star with Sal, but it turned out to be another picture she didn't do. Sal talked about Jean—how she'd been and what she'd become, how she seemed so sympathetic to the Black Panthers, giving them money, hanging around with some really dangerous characters. She'd become like Jane Fonda—only worse, Sal said. "Jane's a phony. It's all a stunt, it's all a front, but Jean's lost her friggin' mind, you know. She isn't the same person she was back then. She just doesn't have her wits anymore."

Sal's tailspin centered on drugs, the same as Janis, the same as Dennis. Sal didn't have that strange look he used to—like he'd been receiving electro-shock. When he came to borrow more money, he had on very low-waisted white pants, almost hip-huggers, and his shirt was open down the front. He'd shaved his body, like Dennis's agent Bob Raison used to do, and Sal and I came very close that afternoon to something happening between us. We spent a couple of hours at my place on Griffith Park, drinking and talking about his "vibrations" to do with Jimmy's spirit. At one point he had an erection showing through his tight pants, and he said, "You see, I can't talk about it without my body reacting on its own . . ." I had an impulse to reach across and touch his stomach, and he was waiting for that, but after a minute or so he started rubbing himself through his pants. He said he had to masturbate—he couldn't relax until he did. At that, he reached into his pants and brought out his cock. With his head back, he worked himself quickly, running his other hand over his bare stomach and chest. Then he pressed his cock hard against his belly, both hands covering it as he came onto himself.

I'd never thought about Sal sexually before that day, and never did again. He called my agent a few times and left messages, but we didn't connect. I had not expected him to return the money. Maybe if he got it together and made another picture . . . But as it was, it seemed as though I was paying a whore. Moreover, it seemed that he was getting pleasure or excitement from that feeling.

The "vibrations" were the unresolved conflicts he had about Jimmy and his own homosexuality. Sal had it in his mind that somehow, if we wrote something together about Jimmy—me helping him with the writing—"we" would bring these conflicts to a head. Then, he said, he could get over the "crash" of his life and move into "living it" on his own terms, instead of "playing it out over someone who's dead . . ." When he'd square himself—kick drugs and get a handle on life—he'd be able to fulfill the creative potential he believed he still possessed. One sad fact he overlooked: the potential was gone. Like Dennis, he'd drugged it into oblivion.

"Jimmy is dead and buried in the ground," Sal said to me. "I got to get him off my back because I don't want to join him down there."

Sal's ideas gave me the creeps. I wanted to help, but there was nothing I could do, and I didn't have any more money. In the long run, it wouldn't have made much difference. He was murdered in the garage of his apartment a block south of Sunset. People heard his scream as a hunting knife was plunged into his chest up to the hilt. "Some drug situation," I was told. "No real reason for the murder." A Strip hustler who knew Sal said, "They bagged his hands at the scene. I saw the plastic bags over his hands. His eyes were open, but he was dead."

An FBI agent who had worked close to J. Edgar Hoover during the last of the Vietnam War, while Jane Fonda was squeezing publicity from the situation, said, "Hoover said he was going to 'take care of those two bitches'—meaning Jane and Jean Seberg. But Hoover said it was Seberg who kept him awake at nights. He said Fonda was 'puff,' a nothing, publicity and money-hungry, and an opportunist—a true capitalist, Hoover said, playing pinko to keep her name in the news. He said, 'You watch the bitch get out in the clearing when nobody's looking to grab her, and you'll see the money-hungry capitalist cunt in full regalia . . .

"But the 'nigger-loving' Seberg presented the real threat to the American people, according to Hoover, who said she was giving money to 'radical niggers' and sleeping with them. As far as Hoover was concerned, there was nothing worse than a 'white woman giving her body to a nigger.' Yet it was not so much the idea of sex between the lily-white Seberg and the Black Panthers that distressed Hoover, but the fact that people could be sympathetic to her.

"With a smile, Hoover said he knew she was pregnant and the bureau was glad, because it offered the chance to spread the word to gossip columnists that a nigger Panther had impregnated Seberg, already married to a white man and a diplomat. 'She's willfully carrying this black baby . . .' Hoover made it very clear what he expected to be done about the gossip. He said, 'I want this finished.' I said, 'What do you mean finished, sir?' He said, 'You know fucking well what I mean finished, and when something is finished, then it's finished.'"

But when the gossip was spread, Jean tried to do the job herself, with an overdose of pills. The baby, born *white*, had to be taken two months early by Caesarean, and because of Jean's overdose, lived only two days. The father of the dead baby was French writer and diplomat Romain Gary, author of several successful novels and one of several men Jean married. Jean wanted to display the infant in a glass casket for the world to see that the child was white.

The frequency of Jean's breakdowns intensified, coming more quickly after the suicide attempt that killed the baby. Some of these collapses left her almost catatonic. In and out of French mental institutions, always just moments away from disaster and madness, Jean would finally manage to "finish" herself as per J. Edgar Hoover's wishes.

The agent said, "When we got word she was dead, I passed this on to Hoover, who was putting some kind of makeup on his face. It reminded me of what I'd heard about Goering—the Nazi transvestite and head of the Luftwaffe. All Hoover said was 'Good.'"

Jean used pills again, swallowing a bottle of them in the rear of her car. She'd maneuvered the vehicle into a parking space a short distance from the dingy Paris digs she shared with a young Arab. Her money exhausted, her talent gone along with her sanity, she rolled the car windows shut against the summer heat and, curling up in a blanket, finished her life huddled on the rear floor of the car. Ten days would pass before the car was located and her decomposing body found.

Another child, Jean's young son by Romain Gary, living with his father, was to receive her suicide note, asking the child's forgiveness. Then, some time after Jean's death, ex-husband Gary would abandon the young boy completely and wimp out of life by shooting himself in the head.

Back in Paris a few years later, I finally made it to Modigliani's grave. Then I visited Jean's grave. I was writing a feature script for

Orphée Arts, who'd had success with the soft-core classic *Emmanuelle*. The movie would have been a classic Jean Seberg vehicle, but so many confusing years had passed since the time Jean had been so pretty and incredibly pure. Blunders back then had set that fatal course in motion, as with Jimmy Dean. As Sal Mineo had put it before his own death, Jean was now a skeleton, down in the ground.

Her producer, Jean-Pierre Rassam, would say something that should have been written on Jean's grave: "She was her own Manson, her own Charles Manson."

From Pied Piper Smitty to the Bay Area's Zodiac killer, to Manson and Bobby Beausoleil—called "Bummer Bob" on Sunset Strip in the hippie days—the brutal torch was passed on. Beausoleil had committed the first of the "Manson murders," stabbing Hollywood musician and teacher Gary Hinman, then smothering him to death with a seat cushion. Beausoleil asked me several times to visit him on San Quentin's Death Row. My interest in him was not so much for his homicidal deeds as cohort to Manson, but for his extravagantly drugged-out live-in relationship with Kenneth Anger, *Hollywood Babylon* author and experimental filmmaker friend of Curtis Harrington. Anger featured Bobby as the Devil in his film *Lucifer Rising*, shot in the Haight in its hippie heyday. It was the LSD and the magical rites prompted by Anger, Bobby said, that took him over to "the other side," beyond good and evil. "Kenneth made me Lucifer—he constantly did evocations while I lay naked on black and red velvet, surrounded by skulls and witches ornaments and magical effigies. He convinced me that I was the Devil and that I would do the Devil's work . . ."

Janis was saying the hippies were dead. They'd been "swept under by a street cleaner," and what she had left to do was go back to who she believed she was at the start. She said she was sick and confused from making so many "moronic" blunders like Woodstock. I said that was a long time ago. It was yesterday, she said, as far as her career was concerned. We talked about doing a "Janis" documentary, which Robert Levy wanted to produce, and which she'd do for free as long as she'd be able to offer explanations for "rotten appearances . . ."

We had this talk while mixing tequila, gin, brandy and tonic water. She shook it until the tonic shot out, and then we drank most of what hadn't shot out with the tonic. When she came into San Francisco's Union Square hotel with me, she said, "This is the same place Michael's staying in." She meant Michael Pollard, who had stayed there at some earlier time—maybe even a couple of years earlier—but she had transposed it to the present. I'd notice a few of these little time warps, when the recent past became for her the present for a minute or so. Then she'd slip back into real time.

Her agent, Albert Grossman, was against the documentary Levy was talking about because, he said, Janis wanted to use it to retaliate against some rock critics—and anyone else who had said anything about her abilities having slipped. She wanted to tell her "side," like Smitty had wanted to tell his, why she'd had problems in Memphis and Woodstock and New York, and why she was pissed off at being on a talk show with Raquel Welch. "Being packaged," Janis said "like a box of dog food . . ."

The few bad performances—other time warps—seemed to sit on her head like a dunce cap. The general music world had long forgotten what she'd done or hadn't done, or it didn't care, but with Janis it was the *present* moment—faces leering at her, critics "throwing fucking tomatoes." She was tormented. She said to Levy, "I don't give a fuck whether they think I'm washed up or not. It's my life and career I'm talking about, so fuck my agent's concerns, because I'm the one payin' *him!*"

She was wearing patchouli oil and something she'd mixed with it, a strong gardenia smell. The scents didn't blend, but stayed separate, so that as I became desensitized to one, the other would kick in, and together they were almost overpowering. She'd brought me some beads she said she'd strung—but they weren't really beads, more like monkey bones or some other animal with little bones. She put them over my head and kept her hands on my neck. She kissed me, putting her tongue in my mouth, and it was a strange moment, as though she'd put a lei around my neck with a kiss, welcoming me to her island. She became someone else, some other sort of person—all woman, all female. She took me into a soft, deep place with some sort of a curving upward motion that shook through each of us. I could feel her heart beating in her ribs. I was penetrating through her, coming out the other side of her body. Her thighs moved like arms, and she made sounds—strange, foreign sounds that had nothing to do with who we were or where we were. Some desperate connection was being forged. We weren't the same people we'd been just moments before. Something was happening, but even as it erupted there was that edge, that impasse that let you know it would never happen again. It was only circumstance—like a murder. I pressed my mouth deeply to her, to take her into myself. Then, when it was finished, when we'd caught our breath, she said, "I need a *drink!*"

That's also when she said, "Shit, there's just enough in each jug to get a good mix." When we mixed the booze, we began our taped interview for the voice-over on the documentary. But halfway into it, she decided to hit a few spots since the juice was running thin. Another evening, night and morning were swallowed in a chaotic, kaleidoscopic binge. Somewhere in the middle of it, she seemed to discover that a thermos bottle—something out of a kid's lunch box—was missing. I couldn't remember her having brought a thermos, but she insisted that she had, and was frantic over losing it. We took cabs back and forth to bars we'd been to, looking for a thermos bottle. The cab fare was over fifty bucks.

At one place, she accused some people we'd been sitting with of swiping the thermos because she'd been crocked. She said one of them had taken advantage of that fact. She said she'd have the "fucking Hell's Angels" pay a call on the one who stole her thermos bottle. "They're my friends," she said, "and none of you fuckers are!"

On the way back she wanted to fuck in the taxi and climbed over my lap, facing me, her arms wrapped around my neck. It didn't work out too well, and she started singing "I Can't Get No Satisfaction" like Mick Jagger, letting her tongue wag out of her mouth. She made a squealing noise and said, "Look at me right in the eye. You don't want to ball right now because you think I'm ugly, right?" I said I couldn't do anything with the driver gawking through the mirror at Janis Joplin humping on the seat.

She whipped her head around and said to him, "What's your fuckin' *problem*, man?"

We were somewhere on Russian Hill, and she had to score some dope, and vanished into a building. The driver was staring at me and he said, "That's Janis Joplin, eh? The big rock and roll singer?" I said yeah, that's her. He said, "What's the matter with her—she some sort of crazy person?"

I didn't see her again until later in Hollywood. She'd taped a *Tom Jones Special* for television and was staying at the Landmark Hotel by the Hollywood Bowl, shooting smack night and day. We met with Levy at the Hungry Tiger restaurant on the boulevard, and Janis said she was ready to talk about the documentary. She gave us a list of top-ics she intended to cover, having printed them out very plainly. Everything had to do with the so-called "facts" of her failing career—Woodstock having been the most regrettable, according to Janis. Levy was intrigued, but confused and disturbed by her apologies for "short-comings" no one else seemed to recognize or be concerned about.

"No, no," Janis said, "the fucking writing's on the wall by *them*, you know, to bring me *down!*" She seemed to suggest that some conspiracy was in the works, with her "old band" playing a part in it. She wanted an agreement that time would be allotted for her to address these issues, explaining why she'd failed to achieve what she'd intended. The "record has to be set straight," she said.

Levy tried to tell her he thought the Woodstock performance and the others she'd complained about were "absolutely terrific." He found no fault—though he admitted he was hardly a music critic. It wasn't the critics that made a star, he said, but Janis—the artist. She'd struck chords in everyone who listened to her. He said it didn't seem "completely" reasonable for her go on record, setting herself up as having *failed,* when no one seemed aware of it. But she wasn't listening to what he was saying. She reached across the table and took his hand, squeezing it gently, and said, "You're an honorable man, Robert. You're a fuckin' honorable guy."

The next time I saw Janis was in San Rafael, where she did a bene-fit with Big Brother for a Hell's Angels convention. It was a raucous melee, a sort of surrealist nightmare, and Janis was so stoned she screeched and lurched, arms flailing, half-falling. She passed out and was carried off into the wings. I saw her outside the auditorium for just a moment. Michael Pollard was there, almost as sapped as Janis, his face red and puffy. I put my hand on his arm and said, "You okay?" His eyes were staring blankly, as though through a fog.

A few months later Janis was dead. She'd returned to Hollywood to cut another album. I tried to see her, but we kept missing. On the phone she told me she was marrying some guy from New York, some one not in the music business. A square. I asked her what she was going to do with a square? She said she was maybe going to get the fuck out of the rat race—the music business. I said she couldn't do that, that it wouldn't work for her. She said, "He's moving to the West Coast to marry me, and right now it's not such a bad idea—can you believe some people are saying I'm a dyke! Can you beat that?"

She didn't finish the album. She was found dead in her room at the Landmark, only in panties, her body wedged between the bed and night stand where she'd fallen on her face. One of the band members snatched the dope from the room to protect her, but when the cops began questioning them, the dope turned up in the waste basket. A balloon of smack so sweet it packed maybe ten times the hit of normal-cut street shit, forty-five to fifty percent pure. None of the stuff Janis shot had been cut. She couldn't have known that, or she'd never have shot it. Even so, she'd been tough enough to go to the front desk in the lobby, get change and smokes, and make it back to her room before the shit hit home.

She'd stipulated in a will that twenty-five-hundred bucks be blown on a party when she bit the dust. In some way she knew she was going to die—something she couldn't get a grip on had just kept spinning around her. Several hundred people showed up for the party, boozed-it up, got loaded and danced until the juice and dope were gone. The next morning Janis's corpse was cremated and her ashes thrown into the ocean.

Al Wilson, a musician I knew from the Canned Heat group, said it was hard to imagine Janis dead—and harder to picture her smoldering down to a pile of ashes no bigger than a quart of beer. Wilson said, "She was the best there is. She had the fame you dream about when you're busting your ass to make it. The kind of fame no one forgets. You don't die—you go into history, man. She was what we dream of being . . ." Wilson shot up and died of an overdose a month after Janis was dead.

Jim Morrison's almanac would ring true: he'd be dead a long time before hitting thirty. Despite the empty music and the weightless poems, Morrison rode the snake, galloping down the death trip like Lancelot with a hard-on. He plunged in under some strange circumstances in Paris—no one really surviving with evidence of exactly how he died. His corpse was supposedly found in the bathtub with blood wadding up one nostril from a big hit of heroin.

I'd looked at the monkey bones Janis had given me. They still smelled of patchouli and whatever that gardenia stuff had been. I'd think about her tongue and that black paint on her toenails. I'd sucked her saliva into my mouth—drunk of her. I liked to think of her living in my blood. Maybe it was me that was the vampire.

Sometimes, at certain moments, little threads of acid sort of wiggle across some screen in my head like small strings of cells, a bunch of tiny glass compartments like the banded body of a dirt worm. There's a picture of the moon on the black ocean. There's another of a naked girl on the rocks. There's a quick picture of Jim Morrison's face—a mismatched mask sort of shifting for a place to settle, but it'll never settle. The eyes are black holes. He's the ghost of a time gone by, the true hero isolated and alone in this time capsule, like a shrunken head in a tube. Then the worm wiggles past and is gone.

Burn, Jim, burn.

One night boozing in the Palomino in North Hollywood, I was talking about Janis with Kris Kristofferson. "Frankly," he said, "she had a yearning to die. I want to see the sun come up tomorrow, and I want to get old and look out at the sky and look back on myself when I was young. Being young and beautiful and talented and dead, they don't get old, so we never get a picture of them being anything else but beautiful and talented and young . . .

"Janis only had the young part—like your pal James Dean, and like Hank Williams, man. There wasn't any old Janis on that menu of life."

For some reason I was thinking about Connie—the girl Jimmy and I had known. She'd gone back to Indiana when they buried him, and taken snapshots of the flowers at his funeral, and of some of the people in attendance. One was of her, dark eyes moist. They made me think of Jimmy's eyes after he'd been wandering around all night—looking, hunting. I remembered us walking towards Forty-Seventh Street and Eight Avenue in the rain, stopping to look in some store windows then walking on. It was light still, and I was wearing a leather jacket, and Jimmy had on an old green raincoat. By the time we got to Forty-seventh we were soaked. Rain kept pouring down over Jimmy's forehead and down the bridge of his nose, dropping off his nose and chin. He laughed at me at the corner of Forty-seventh, and I remember the way he looked at that moment—completely out of touch with his surroundings, yet at the same time such an integral part of them. His neck looked long, and his lion-colored hair stuck up wet in a bunch like a brush, and those mercurial eyes were screwed tight at the rain, as if they were saying things to it. What was he doing?

I felt a special closeness then, as though we were brothers; brothers living in a very fragile and delicate balance; brothers, I suppose, in pursuit of life.

Literally born and raised in Hollywood, **John Gilmore** has delved into the seamy underbelly of Fame in many guises: child actor, stage and screen player, screenwriter, low-budget film director, journalist, true-crime writer and novelist. Currently dividing his time between Los Angeles and New Mexico where he resides with his wife and son, Gilmore is at work on a novel and a second book of memoirs.